THE

SCIENCE

OF

A NEW LIFE

Eng.d by John C. McRae N.Y.

Sincerely Yours

John Cowan M.D.

What God, in the might of His wisdom and the greatness
of His love, has created, no man or woman need be
ashamed to read, talk of, learn and know;

THE SCIENCE OF

A NEW LIFE

For it cannot be that He has so ordered it that knowledge so essential to the well-being of mankind can
be destructive to moral purity.

THE

SCIENCE

OF

A NEW LIFE

By JOHN COWAN, M.D.

SOURCE BOOK PRESS

Library of Congress Catalogue Card No. 70-134183
ISBN 0-87681-071-7
SOURCE BOOK PRESS, a Division of Collectors Editions Ltd.,
185 Madison Avenue, New York, N.Y. 10016
Unabridged republication of the 1874 New York edition: First printing 1970
Manufactured in the United States of America

THE

SCIENCE

OF

A NEW LIFE

By JOHN COWAN, M.D.

"Knowledge must precede virtue, for no chance act can be a moral one. We must KNOW in order to DO."

NEW YORK
COWAN & COMPANY, PUBLISHERS
No. 139 EIGHTH STREET
1874

The reformation of the world can never be accomplished,—the millenium of purity, chastity and intense happiness can never reach this earth, except through cheerful obedience to pre-natal laws.—Page 137.

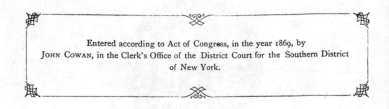

PREFACE.

INCE the creation of man, there has been no subject that so immediately concerns the life and happiness of the individual, the love and harmony of friends, and the stability and prosperity of states and kingdoms, as does that of the reproduction of the best, most beautiful and original forms of humanity for this world and the next. To this end have I recorded in these pages, in a plain, essentially practical, and thoroughly systematic way, my thoughts as to how this great *desideratum* can be reached by all classes—high and low, rich and poor.

Beginning with the requirements necessary to a perfect union of the man and woman; the importance involved in the right use of the social faculties; the glorious and perfect manhood that comes of a chaste and continent life; the positive and immense influence of the mother in the health, character, capabilities and beauty of the new life, and the preparations necessary to this end, a child is born—a child that, if originated under the conditions herein enjoined, must embody perfection of body, brightness of intellect, and purity of soul. In proportion as these principles are observed, just in that proportion will this earth be freed from sin, and unalloyed happiness secured; and in no other way, that I know of, can it be done so promptly and effectually.

In the last part will be found that which goes to make up the shadows of life, and the mode to be pursued to catch a glimpse of the bright side—the silver lining of the cloud.

And in the last chapter of all will be found hints and suggestions as how to bring within the bounds of love those who are "matched but not mated."

In the inscribing of the subject-matter in these pages, not a word has been employed that would offend the sense of the most pure in thought, let alone those who may possess the quality termed "mock" modesty.

Out of the fullness of an observing, earnest, truthful nature have come the words of instruction, of advice, and of warning that go to make up the pleasant and inviting pages of this book—words that apply to and concern every boy and girl, man and woman—married or single—who believes in a God and a life beyond the grave.

Without doubt, there are errors of omission and commission; yet I cannot believe that any person, who exercises the unselfish and impartial of his or her nature, can possibly read and reflect on its contents without being impressed, in a greater or smaller measure, with the requirements so necessary in all that goes to constitute life as God first planned it.

JOHN COWAN.

TABLE OF CONTENTS

PART FIRST

CHAPTER I.—MARRIAGE AND ITS ADVANTAGES.

CHAPTER II.—AGE AT WHICH TO MARRY.

CHAPTER III.—THE LAW OF CHOICE.

CHAPTER IV.—LOVE ANALYZED.

CHAPTER V.—Qualities the Man should Avoid in Choosing.

CHAPTER VI.—Qualities the Woman should Avoid in Choosing.

CHAPTER VII.—The Anatomy and Physiology of Generation in Woman.

CHAPTER VIII.—The Anatomy and Physiology of Generation in Man.

CHAPTER IX.—Amativeness—its Use and Abuse.

Part Second—The Consummation.

CHAPTER XIV.—The Conception of a New Life.

CHAPTER XV.—The Physiology of Intra-Uterine Growth.

CHAPTER XVI.—Period of Gestative Influence.

TABLE OF CONTENTS.

Part Third—Wrongs Righted.

CHAPTER XXII.—Fœticide.

CHAPTER XXIII.—Diseases Peculiar to Women—Their Cause,

CHAPTER XXIV.—Diseases Peculiar to Men—Their Cause,

CHAPTER XXV.—Masturbation.

CHAPTER XXVI.—Sterility and Impotence.

CHAPTER XXVII.—SUBJECTS OF WHICH MORE MIGHT BE SAID.

CHAPTER XXVIII.—A HAPPY MARRIED LIFE—HOW SECURED.

LIST OF ILLUSTRATIONS.

INTRODUCTION.

ARRIAGE, in the popular acceptation of the term, signifies the legal union of a man and woman for life —a contract, both civil and religious, by which the parties engage to live together in mutual affection and fidelity until death shall separate them.

The "legal union and contract, both civil and religious," is the rule generally observed in all civilized nations; the "mutual affection and fidelity until death shall separate them," the very rare exception, in both civilized and barbarous nations.

That there is, in our present age, and without any apparent drift toward a higher and better order of things, a large amount of sin and suffering, the result of mis-mating men and women, is a fact as sad as it is evident; and yet, when the various reasons, causes and objects are given as the desire for marrying and giving in marriage, the sorrow, in one of a pure mind, turns to disgust.

The girl growing into womanhood is taught and educated in the belief that the object and aim of her life is the securing of a husband; and, that failure may be impossible, a superficial education, deceit and lying, are ingrained in her very nature, the whole strategy of which is employed in compassing the body, if not the heart, of some "lord of creation," without any reflection as to whether the man is to make for her a pleasant or miserable married life; whether he is to cull for her the sweet-tasting blossoms of a joyous, happy, lovable life, or the sharply-pointed thorns of discontent, hate and misery.

From out of this wrongly educated life of the woman there is reflected, in the man, a sense of superiority that is physically wrong, and a sense of egotism that is morally wrong, the result being that he lives a life of constant advantage in all his relations with woman; and, until woman is educated up to a higher, a purer and nobler standard of life, and so reach her position as man's equal (which she is and should be in every relation of life), man will be the master—woman the slave, and love, perfect love, cannot be, and the present state of society, as exemplified in its social relations, will continue to the end of time.

The impartial observer and thinker will allow that two-thirds, if not three-fourths, of the misery of the world arises from the infelicity of the conjugal relations; and to no single country or nation is it confined, but it pervades all society the world over.

"For a result, then, so universal there must be a cause or causes as universal, not depending on any particular customs, manners or religion or political institutions. And what are these causes? Many things do puzzle me in this strange world of ours—many things in which the new world and the old world are equally incomprehensible. I cannot understand why an evil everywhere acknowledged and felt is not remedied somewhere, or discussed by some one with a view to a remedy; but no—it is like putting one's hand into the fire only to touch upon it; it is the universal bruise, the putrefying sore, on which you must not lay a finger, or your patient (that is, society) cries out and resists, and, like a sick baby, scratches and kicks its physician."

That marriage, consummated under right conditions, for right purposes, bears intimately on the prosperity and welfare of communities and states, and is the source of all industry, subordination and government among men, the author firmly believes. He, therefore, who shall succeed in rendering marriage a matter of serious consideration, and not blind experiment, will deserve well of society, and cannot offend against delicacy or religious feeling.

Closely allied to a true and perfect marriage is the command to increase and multiply—a command that, among the better and higher classes of society, is in danger of being sadly neglected. Its importance in the solution of life's problems—the hopes and fears, pleasures and pains, health and sickness, prosperity and adversity—is not lightly to be estimated. In the propagating of the species knowingly and understandingly, the father and mother can do more toward a true solution of the questions of the age, than can all the temperance societies, religious denominations, and reform institutions in the world. Parents, exercising a lovable and true use of this life-giving power—the power of creating man in God's own image—can, it they earnestly will and work for it, re-create and people the world with mortals just, pure, loving and Christ-like. A great and arduous responsibility rests on every father and mother who entertain the desire of bringing into life a new being, but it is a responsibility which, if exercised as unperverted nature intended it to be, brings with it naught but ineffable pleasure, holy joy, and unalloyed happiness.

But this heaven-ordained law to increase and multiply and replenish the earth is being, in this our age and continent, greatly perverted, avoided, broken, and by ways and means that not only prevent the carrying out of the spirit of the command, but, with a just judgment, bring the perpetrators thereof to a life of bodily sickness, mental suffering, and, in thousands of cases, are the direct and controlling means of shortening life. The one great cause of this wide-spread sin is the universal ignorance of the masses in this "Science of a New Life." Sexual physiology and its outlying branches are frowned down, hid away in dark corners, or talked of in whispers, as knowledge that is contaminating, and therefore dangerous, and to be avoided ; and, when carefully inquired into, it will almost invariably be found that the men and women who most decry this species of knowledge are the ones who, through wrong and perverted natures, have committed sexual sins, and for the right guidance of whom to a strong and perfect manhood, and pure and lovable womanhood, just such knowledge is required.

Springing out of the disobeying of the laws that govern the sexual system are diseases innumerable ; but, primarily, the nervous system is so influenced and disorganized as to lay the sub-structure for all the positively nervous, and nearly all the inflammatory and chronic diseases that afflict mankind, and especially womankind. If there was one proof more than another required to show the prevailing ignorance on sexual subjects, the one of universal nervousness (which implies want of nerves, or absence of nerve-power) abroad among all man and womankind would of itself suffice.

To live a true, pure and successful life—socially, morally and spiritually—should be the object and aim of all ; and, as one of the steps toward this end, is advised the reading and digesting of this "Science of a New Life."

PART FIRST.

THE PREPARATION.

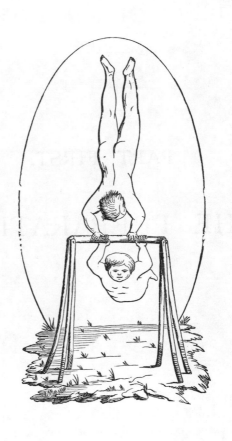

THE
SCIENCE OF A NEW LIFE.

CHAPTER I.

MARRIAGE AND ITS ADVANTAGES—OBJECTS IN MARRYING.

THE growing tendency of the age inclines toward celibacy in man, and, as a result, maidenhood in woman, and the reasons advanced for declining to enter into matrimony are many and unsound.

One of the prime and most universal reasons is the want of money to support the wife in the position in which she has hitherto moved. A young man with a stated salary, or commencing business, dreads the responsibility of a wife and the subsequent family. This fails in being a good reason, for it proceeds as much from selfishness as from dread of poverty. A man who advances this as a cause for remaining single, will be found, on examination, to spend more money on his own person and friends than would easily support a woman having his interests, welfare and happiness at heart. Especially is this so if he be of the kind termed "fast," for such men, as well as all who associate with such, exercise assiduously the animal part of their natures, and in the sowing of their "wild oats" their feet tread dangerously near the paths that lead to destruction; and the money required to pay their way would, if they married a true woman and lived a pure life, give them glimpses of heaven they never would know of in their degrading, doubtful single blessedness.

Others dread the care, trouble and doubts that are usually associated with married life. For such it is better that they remain single; for, wanting the strength that comes of just endeavor, and the requisites that lead to perfect manhood, their progeny is not desirable.

Others, again, decline marrying through fear of being united to a woman who, not suited to their temperament, will make their life anything but a pleasant one; and yet others, who have the desire to marry, but, judging from the accounts of the family quarrels, divorces and separations that are continually coming to the surface in the daily and weekly records of our time, have a dread of the very word marriage. In the light of a new method of choosing a wife, to be hereafter herein recorded, these doubts and dangers can be avoided, and success, or comparative success, be secured, and all risk as to unhappy marriages evaded.

That marriage is a natural condition of adult life, and a requisite to every man and woman's perfect happiness and success in this world, requires no argument, or needs none of the many divine and human authorities to attest the fact; and no man who fails to enter this condition at the proper period can be considered as compassing all the relations for which his Creator designed him—in other words, he is not a complete man. This also applies to woman.

The great desire and aim of life is *happiness*, and a first requisite to an attainment of this end, in a man or woman, is matrimony. In the shadows of the present records of separations and general unhappiness in married life this may be doubted; yet, these things being due to avoidable causes, it does not in the least alter the fact.

Another requisite in the acquirement of happiness is *health*. The single state being an abnormal and unnatural condition, it is, as a rule, unfavorable to health and longevity. That this is true of length of life is demonstrated by the fact that, in the list of individuals who have lived to a great age, there are no unmarried persons.

It is almost a universal belief that the accumulation of property and the possession of wealth are requisite to happiness. This is open to doubt; but, allowing it to be so, in no other way is success so certain and easy of attainment as in marrying. (In all these allusions to marrying, it is to be understood that the parties united are suited to each other, mentally and physically.) In the getting of riches, the selfish propensities are brought powerfully into play, and of these acquisitiveness takes the lead. In marrying, this saving and acquiring faculty is greatly increased, and in years is doubled and quadrupled. Young men, as a rule, before becoming husbands and fathers, are as wasteful of their time as they are prodigal of their money; and should it be their desire to reform and become prosperous and wealthy, the best known recipe is to marry, not a rich, but a frugal companion.

A meal eaten alone may gratify the appetite; yet even the pleasures of the palate are greatly increased by the exquisite satisfaction derived from eating at our own table, surrounded by our family and friends.

What is true of acquisitiveness and alimentiveness is equally so of all other faculties, the combining of which, individually and collectively, with each and all other faculties, augments their power of exciting to the highest pitch of pleasurable or painful action, according as they are properly or improperly directed.

Nothing has been said as to reproduction, in which happiness is most highly symbolized, as it will be written of elsewhere.

Matrimony gives the opportunity and occasion to improve all the domestic, social and higher faculties of the mind, and of guiding the man and woman to a higher and holier standard of life.

OBJECTS IN MARRYING.—The motives which influence the majority of men and women in contracting matrimonial unions are generally false, selfish, and most detrimental to the happiness of the individuals, and to the procreation of sound and vigorous offspring—such as ambition, wealth, rank, title, interest, a love of independence, of an establishment, a desire to escape parental restraint, anger, a determination to disinherit relations, disdain for a faithless lover or mistress, necessity, obligation, passion, imitation, and very rarely the only proper motive—pure and virtuous affection. It is also generally admitted that parental authority cannot reasonably or morally compel alliances, when the inclination of the individual most concerned is opposed; although we see too many forced and unhappy marriages which are to be ascribed to this cause.

There is no other business in life undertaken with such false objects in view as the business of choosing a wife or husband. Men, at the commencement of an undertaking largely involving their reputation and interests, carefully canvass every possible shade of profit and loss, risk or gain; but in the choice of a wife, in the absence of a systematized mode of choosing, they undertake it blindly, if not ignorantly. The admiration of some single quality in a woman results in many marriages. A person, sinking the imaginative of his nature into the practical, well knows that a small, soft hand, or a beautiful face, or a small waist, or graceful carriage, or good talking, will not, in themselves, indicate the true character of their possessors, and yet how many unions are formed through some one or other fancy, the result almost invariably being a sudden waking up to a realization of the fact that it takes other qualities than a beautiful hand or face to constitute a happy married existence.

Another reason for marrying, though one not generally observed, is the marrying of those afflicted with peculiar diseases, it being popularly supposed that, in some mysterious way, marriage will assist a recovery, if not effect a cure. No more dangerous doctrine ever was promulgated, for the effect on the sick individual after marriage is constantly, and often rapidly, toward an increase of the sickness and a shortening of life; and even if this could be doubted, and possibly were not so, the joining of a sick man to a healthy woman, or the reverse, is, to use a mild phrase, barbarous; but the entailing of disease on the offspring is worse than barbarous—it is sinful. Let no man or woman marry with any such object in view. If through sin you suffer, bear the whole burden on your own shoulders; and, if otherwise unavoidable, die with it; but do not saddle posterity with it.

The true object of marriage, and the only one that should be entertained, is the perfection of existence that comes of a physiological union, and the propagation of offspring that go to make such a union complete, and it is the combining of all which perfects love, intensifies happiness, and makes life worth living for.

CHAPTER II.

AGE AT WHICH TO MARRY.

HE proper age for marriage, as fixed by law in all countries, conflicts with the physiological law that guides the growth of the body. The capabilities to reproduce, as indicated by the arrival of puberty, is the time usually fixed as the marriageable age. In countries having climates of moderate temperatures, this takes place, in girls, at from thirteen to sixteen years of age; in boys, at from fifteen to eighteen years of age, depending greatly on the temperament and mode of life. Very rich and nutritious food, spices, tea, coffee, alcoholic liquors, tobacco, life in large cities, and moral influences, greatly and unnaturally accelerate this very important period.

As heat increases the vital energy in all organized bodies, and renders their growth more rapid, it must necessarily hasten the period of puberty; and, as a result, in all tropical climates puberty in women commences much earlier—generally from nine to ten years of age.

This early development of the reproductive organs and functions is by no means advantageous, for individuals reaching maturity early are generally short-lived; beauty early departs, and old age comes on rapidly. On the contrary, the slow arrival at maturity insures the retaining to an advanced age of strength, beauty, and reproductive power.

The great error in fixing the present age for marriage arises from taking the arrival of puberty as the proper time, it being popularly supposed that when this is present the woman is capable of reproduction and ready for marriage. This is a fallacy, for marriage should be consummated only between a physiologically perfect man and woman. Physical perfection implies ripeness, indicated by the full growth of every organ in the human organization. Now, when puberty first shows itself, the osseous part of the system is not fully grown, which implies—seeing that the osseous frame is the structure which supports the muscular, nervous, arterial, digestive and other parts of the body—that the reproductive element is not full-grown; but its appearance only indicates its continuance to perfect growth, in harmony with all the other organized parts of the body.

There are many bones of the body that are not completely ossified or full-grown until the twenty-fifth year of age. The clavicle, or collar-bone—appearing before any other bone in the body—does not attain its full growth until the eighteenth year. The scapula, or shoulder-blade, is not completely formed until the twenty-fifth year; as also the bones of the pelvis and leg. Now, this being so, is it not reasonable to argue that the appearance of puberty at fourteen to eighteen years of age is *not* an indication of ripeness of body. Careful investigation shows that the women of temperate climates do not get their growth until the twenty-fourth year. They may get their height at, perhaps, sixteen or eighteen; but until twenty-four, if a right mode of life is allowed them, they grow broader, more solid and robust.

In man, the period of perfect growth does not arrive until the twenty-eighth or thirtieth year. Through the early excesses of men, or rather boys—for they are usually enacted before the thirtieth year—nature is thwarted in her endeavors to build up a perfect manhood, the life-power is directed into wrong channels, and a weak, inferior, unhealthy organization is the result.

In woman, child-bearing—omitting to mention the results of excesses—before the age of twenty-four, are much more noticeable; for the life-power, changed from the building up to perfect growth of the body, is directed to the nourishment of the embryonic life, the result being the birth of an unripe child from an unripe mother.

The children born of early marriages are feeble, liable to disease, and generally die young; and, though they have an appearance of perfect health and robustness, they seldom reach the age of manhood, and old age is out of the question.

The growth of the mother is arrested and diminished, delicate and bad health follows, with all its attendant miseries, and old age rapidly comes on; for it may be stated, and it can be affirmed from personal observation by any person anxious to test the assertion, that for every year inside of twenty a woman marries, she takes on three years of premature age.

The man who marries before twenty-eight or thirty, or who commits sexual excesses, or lives other than a life of strict continence, arrests the growth of his body, weakens his entire system, his muscles become pale and flabby, nerves weak, brain forever oppressed and clogged, and he is no more capable, in his work in life's vineyard, to make a name for himself among the earth's great ones, than the veriest born fool. Disease, premature age and early death make his life a sad failure.

Writing on the subject of early marriages, the author of a valuable work entitled "Marriage" says:

"Very early marriages are, in our opinion, a serious evil. Acting under the impulse of headstrong passions, or caprice, or dissatisfaction, young persons too often prematurely rush, thoughtlessly and blindly, into engagements which, in after life, become matters of deep and painful regret. The fancy visions of love's paradise now vanish, and the sober realities of life, its cares, its difficulties, and its positive evils, soon lead to discontent, and, worse than all, to a growing mutual indifference. Would that such cases were only rare, or only speculative; but the fact is otherwise. We every day see boys and girls at the head of families who want discretion to direct themselves. No wonder that families are ill-governed, children ill-managed, and their affairs ill-directed, when the helm is intrusted to unskillful and inexperienced hands. Is it possible, we would ask, that wives of sixteen or eighteen years of age should possess that discretion, prudence and wisdom so essential to enable them to govern households, rear children, and form their tempers and their principles?"

The ancient Germans did not marry until the twenty-fifth year, previous to which they observed the most rigid chastity, and in consequence of which their offspring acquired a size and strength that excited the astonishment of Europe. Common sense should indicate that a giddy youth, at the age of puberty, with the down on his chin, can not communicate a perfect vitality; or that a girl, at puberty, with the disorders of pregnancy, and the fatigue of labor and suckling, cannot develop other than sickly, puny offspring.

No man or woman should perform the act of marriage until the body has acquired all the development necessary to its full growth. Nature always tends to perfection in all her operations, and assuredly a feeble being, and one imperfectly grown, can not be the source of a sound and vigorous generation; at the same time, the premature exercise of certain functions, essentially debilitating even to individuals fully developed, cannot but remarkably retard the growth and vigor of persons under the adult age.

All unions between persons of disproportionate ages, on account of pecuniary or other worldly considerations, should be avoided, for they are usually followed by much misery. The power of fecundity ceasing with one party is the cause of great immorality, leading the husband to debauchery, and the wife to all the excesses of jealousy. Offspring, the result of such ill-assorted marriages, are always delicate, and physically and mentally worthless.

This especially applies to old or elderly men, for such unions, being entirely contrary to all physiological law, entail naught but suffering on the perpetrators; yet, if there be such men, who are tired of health and life, there is no more certain method of acquiring disease, and reaching a rapid end, than by this way.

Says Parise: "There are great risks run; for in the extreme disparity of age, and ofttimes condition—as when the man is rich and the girl is young—Nature avenges herself by spreading scandals, doubts about paternity, and domestic troubles; everything is at variance—age, disposition, character, tastes and amusements. 'What shall I do with him, and what will he do with me?' said a clever young girl of eighteen, whose parents wished her to marry an old gentleman. With regard to health and vital force, it is easy to foresee what will become of them in these unequal marriages, where a young and fresh girl is 'flesh of the flesh' of a man used up from age, and perhaps from excesses. Evidently she commits a suicidal act, more or less certain or rapid. On the other hand, experience shows that the elderly man, who thus risks his repose and his existence, speedily finds his health grievously affected."

The time required for the full growth of the body, owing to climate, temperament, and other influences, differs in almost all individuals—the difference not amounting to any great degree, yet sufficient to fix an age for marrying that would be equally applicable to all. Nevertheless, it is safe to say that no man, having a just desire for the acquiring and retaining of health and happiness, should marry under twenty-five years of age, and it would be better that he wait until the thirtieth year before marrying.

Woman, with greater risks and more arduous duties to undergo, and who for these reasons require the full amount of health and strength that comes of perfect growth, should under no consideration marry before twenty-one years of age, and it would be much toward her after welfare if she did not marry until she arrived at the age of twenty-four.

The wife, owing to her unphysiological mode of life, to child-bearing, and the licentiousness that belongs to the majority of husbands, takes on premature age much sooner than does the husband, and, for these and other reasons, the husband in all cases should be from three to six years older than his wife.

A man, having arrived at thirty years, full grown, perfectly developed, and desirous of marrying, should choose a woman who is not below twenty-four years of age; and a woman, at twenty-four, perfectly developed, ripe and lovable, should choose—or perhaps I should say accept—for a helpmate a man not less than thirty.

The union of a man and woman at these ages, under right conditions, constitutes the first step toward a perfect marriage.

CHAPTER III.

THE LAW OF CHOICE.

T having been decided that it is not good for man to be alone, one of the most important questions that arises in the seeker for a mate for life is : How am I to choose a wife ?—how a husband ? Which of the scores of women in the circle of my acquaintance will make me the best better-half ? What mode should I employ to determine which of all or any of the women will suit my temperament ? What of love in the choice ? Is there a positive method of choosing the right one, and so avoid after mis-mated consequences ? Or am I to attempt it ignorantly and blindly ?

These and many other questions of a like nature only sometimes trouble thoughtful persons in their reflections on the subject ; the majority of mankind, in their love for wealth, station and pleasure—especially the pleasure that comes of overgrown amativeness—are generally satisfied to attempt it blindly.

This should not and need not be. There must be a law as applicable to the choosing of a life-companion as there are laws governing every other relation in matter that goes to show God's greatness in the ruling of a world. But man, living a wrong life in thought, word and deed, has, in his desire for the unattainable, so blotted and blurred the pure and spiritual that is within him, as to constantly break this law, as he has done all other laws intended for his welfare and happiness.

A brief glance at the mode of forming matrimonial alliances among the people of different nations will show some striking peculiarities.

The ancient Assyrians once a year assembled at a great fair all the marriageable girls of a province, when the public crier put them up for sale at auction. First were put up the most beautiful, for whom the rich strove against each other, until the competition carried up the price to the highest point. When one beautiful woman had thus been disposed of, one less favored by Nature was put up; and here the auction was reversed. The question was not how much will any one give, but how little will any one take; and he who bid her off at the lowest dowry took her for his wife, so that the price paid for the beautiful went to give dowries to the ugly, an advantage the Assyrian ladies had over their modern sisters, inasmuch as none were without husbands.

A Chinaman may, and often does, sell his daughter in marriage, with as much unconcern as he does his other merchantable property.

The Moors betroth their children in infancy. The girl may dislike or despise the man chosen for her; but, if his character is good and he can pay the purchase money, the hatred is regarded as a " womanly freak," and all her entreaties are of no avail.

In Sumatra men purchase their wives, and, if they find they have been duped, they gamble them away, or sell them for a mere pittance.

The Turks are allowed four wives; but the wife or husband has no choice, for they never meet until the marriage day.

In Western Tartary women cost from twenty to five hundred roubles, though among the pastoral tribes, where they are cheaper, a very pretty girl can be bought for two or three roubles.

The marriage of the Soongas, a Tartar tribe, consists of a race on horseback. The female is mounted on a fleet horse, and, if she permits her lover to overtake her, he conducts her to his tent, and she becomes his wife, with no other ceremony than a marriage feast.

In Siberia, after the marriage feast, the wife pulls off her husband's boots, as a sign of her subserviency. In another part of this province, the bride's father presents the bridegroom with a whip, with which he disciplines his wife as often as he thinks proper.

It is noticeable, in examining the records of these and all other barbarous and semi-barbarous nations, that they, in common with modern civilization—modern, *progressive* civilization—regarded women in the light of slaves, in the widest, broadest sense of this term.

The custom of purchasing wives appears to have generally prevailed as soon as the rights of property began to be respected. From the moment that the rights of property were recognized, everything was considered as such, even to a man's wife and children, and the idea of property in wives and children has never been lost, and is fully recognized by our common law.

How of modern marriages ? To what purpose do they tend ? In what do they differ from the marriages of those outside the circle of civilization ? The difference, when carefully compared and analyzed, is not much. "A man wants a cook, washerwoman, housekeeper ; he wants a woman to contribute to his happiness, and to satisfy the demands of his perverted nature. He wants a wife because Nature designed the union of the sexes. But, instead of learning the divinity of *soul*-marriage, he has only been taught the marriage recognized by law and theology—material unions, for fame, home-comforts, position, etc.

"And how does he choose a wife? He looks about among the girls in his own sphere, and selects the one best suited to his interests. In his best attire he goes wooing the fair maiden. Like persons in a masquerade, they flirt and say soft and sentimental things, without knowing anything about the brain behind the mask. After a few flirtations, the wife-seeker proposes himself in marriage, and the woman, often by virtue of necessity, accepts the offer. The two go to a minister or magistrate, when the man promises support, and the woman obedience."

The results of such marriages are every day demonstrable. Before the honeymoon has well reached its full, indications—at first slight—commence to crop out that life has in it some gall, and as the cloyed sweetness of the animal pleasures wears off, and life in its practical, every-day aspect appears, the gall and wormwood is tasted in all its positive bitterness, and matched but not mated life is but a series of petty troubles, disappointments, doubts, despairs and miseries, splendid in the gilt and glitter of its setting, or hideous in all the wretchedness of its rags.

And why should this not be so? Why should there be so very few really happy married lives in this nineteenth century of ours? To every man and woman who will consult their own inner lives as to why and wherefore they married, the answer will be apparent. For every reason and under every condition but the right one did they marry. This step of choosing a husband or wife has more to do with the happiness and success of the individual than has any other attainable desire in this world, and deserves all the thought, plan and argument that can be brought to bear on its enlightenment.

When a man is desirous of purchasing a farm, he carefully examines the nature of the land, and its bearing and supporting qualities, by rules and laws as affirmed by chemistry, and in no wise need he err in a choice that will repay him ample interest on his investment.

If, after purchasing, he desires to stock it, he need make no mistake in his choice of animals. His horses and cattle, judged from well understood anatomical rules and peculiarities, and from desirable qualities imparted to them by their parents, are just such as suit his requirements.

But in the choice of a wife, the same man, if he be a bachelor, inquires for no laws, seeks for no peculiarities, and has no rules to observe in his choice. Some habit in the woman is plainly observable—she is strong, or perchance fine-looking, or is a good housekeeper; and, without other thought, he imagines that she will make him a wife good and true, and he may have secured such; but the probabilities are greatly in favor of the reverse.

This comparing the choice of a wife with that of a farm, horse or cow, may be thought inappropriate; yet the illustration is perfectly applicable. A man need no more err in choosing a wife than he would in choosing a farm, if done knowingly. The difference arises in its importance. Most men give exceedingly more care, inquiry, and investigation to the choice of a horse, property, or any business venture or speculation, than they do to the choice of a wife. This may have an appearance of exaggeration, yet it cannot well be disputed.

The first and greatest error that occurs in the popular mode of choosing a mate is in doing it through the propensities or feelings, rather than through the intellectual or observing, comparing and reflective faculties, guided by the moral sentiments. More unions are formed through the abnormal workings of amativeness and acquisitiveness than through any other aim or object. For a man or woman having matrimony in view, and possessing no broader or higher aim than the securing of a home, wealth, position, or the opportunity of exercising the impure that is within them, it is next to needless to write of higher hopes, purer aspirations, and the rational object and mode of soul-union.

But there is a rapidly growing class of mankind who,

though sorely encumbered with society's many-corded trammels, yet have that within them that longs for, desires and hopes for a plainer way, a purer life, and a more successful existence.

This should be a law with all seekers for a wife or husband, that in their choice they must keep dormant that part of their natures broadly termed the feelings, and exercise *only* the intellectual. This will be more fully understood and appreciated when we come to what constitutes the requirements for a perfect union, and the true definition of sexual love.

It may be premised that love, in the popular acceptation of the term, as existing between lovers and the newly married, is a misnomer, as is also love at first sight. Why this is so will presently appear.

It is necessary to a *perfect* union—a requisite to happiness and a higher and more æsthetic culture—that the man and woman to be married have no positive traits of character that differ in the least from one another. A husband, having abnormally developed amativeness, married to a woman in whom it is well balanced, is sure to breed discord. A husband, having a deficiency in the moral sentiments, joined to a woman who aspires after goodness, virtue and purity, will assuredly make married life other than a success. And so in all that goes to make up character a similarity is necessary, to insure a close joining of soul to soul.

If the man have the social faculties fully developed, so should his wife. If the man have a large moral and religious nature, so should the wife. If the man possess well-developed perceptive, reasoning and reflective power, so should the wife ; and so, in the selfish sentiments and propensities, it is necessary to a perfect union that the man and wife be equally developed, or as nearly so as possible.

There may be one or two exceptions to this rule—as in the money-getting faculty. A man having the ability to make money, but lacking the ability to hold it, could, by the possession of an economical and saving wife, get rich ; yet as wealth is but a minor requisite to happiness, it may be doubted if such a disresemblance is requisite.

The question is suggested while reading : Would it be right to join a man having very large amativeness to a woman with it equally developed ?   Decidedly so ; for if the man is married to a woman having it small, the result is disgust—ending in separation or divorce ; whereas, if both husband and wife are equally developed, and especially equally uneducated in its legitimate use, they together acquire ill health, and together prematurely leave this world, and so allow room for others whose objects in life are higher.

Would it be right that a man having large destructiveness, secretiveness and cautiousness, and deficient in the moral sentiments (the requisite faculties for an essentially bad character—a thief or murderer), to marry a woman having similar developments ?   In the first place, a man possessing such qualities of character should not be allowed to marry ; yet, if allowed, the woman should be none other than one having the like mental similarity, if a perfect union was looked for. But you say, if a woman of higher developments was united to this man, it would have a tendency to lead him to her standard of life.   Such results seldom or never occur; it runs contra to the philosophy of things.   The tendency on her part would be downward, making her life a failure and his miserable.

And so, in all the greater or smaller shades and shadows of mental development, the resemblance should be complete, or nearly so.   The man having well-developed amativeness, a large love of offspring, a greater love for home and home associations than he has for outside friendship and pleasure, versatility of thought and feeling, a strong attachment for one, and *one only*, of the opposite sex—all these things should the wife of his choice be in possession of.

The man having combativeness enough to resist imposition and ignorance, a full requisite of acquisitiveness, a good and hearty appetite for plain food and drink, a fair desire to acquire property, candid, open-hearted, truthful; large prudence and forethought, moderately ambitious, high-minded, independent and self-confident; a just amount of stability and firmness of character; in all these things should the wife of his choice be his counterpart.

The man having a sense for the beautiful and pure, an appreciation of the sublime and magnificent in nature and art, a bright, sunny, laughing nature; the perceptive faculties fully developed; a philosophizing, investigating, original cast of mind; governed by the highest order of moral principles; sanguine and enterprising; large spirituality—reverence for religion and things sacred; a heart overflowing with kindness and sympathy for humanity; in all these traits should the wife chosen resemble the man.

In no way can this unity of thought, feeling and action be so well secured as through Phrenology—a science that is to do more for the welfare of the human race than any heretofore or hereafter to be discovered. Through the right application of this wonderful science, no mistake need be made in wife or husband-choosing, no risks need be run and no doubts need be entertained, but all is made clear as the truths of which it is the exponent. Masks avail nothing—deception, hypocrisy and untruth avail nothing—under the searching analysis of the brain's soul-chambers.

" But I don't believe in Phrenology !"

Then you have my sympathy; and my advice to you, and all who think alike, is to study and cultivate the higher orders of your nature, and grow into the belief of this science of the mind, and so claim brotherhood with the progressive army of noble workers, whose motto is "Onward and upward."

George Stearns, in a little work on "How to Marry," gives the following rules as a guide to conjugal harmony:

" Marry your conjugal mate—your personal duplicate—your approximate equal in development, and your like—

" 1. *In Age.* The old and young are as non-intermarriageable as black and white.

" 2. *In Temper.* They who love spiritually should not marry such as love carnally. Between Platonic and Epicurean lovers no fellowship is possible.

" 3. *In Intelligence.* A simpleton is a poor associate for a sage, as well as a clown for a scholar.

" 4. *In Sentiment.* Let not progressives consort with conservatives. A liberal soul cannot be harmoniously married to a bigot.

" 5. *In Devotion.* A husband and wife should have but one sanctuary, whether it be under a steeple, or be roofed only by the broad canopy of heaven.

" 6. *In Taste.* A tidy woman cannot admire a sloven; and every man who has an eye to port abhors a slattern.

" 7. *In Habitudes.* A vegetarian, at the table of a pork-eater, remembers the fox that dined with a stork. Mr. and Mrs. Will-ey don't sleep together, because he eschews feathers and she can't endure straw.

" 8. *As to the Goal of Life.* They who are always aiming at *what is in a name*, should not be sought in marriage by such as care only for *what is in Nature*. One who lives for *aught* in any calling will be more successful, and therefore happier, without a colleague, than with such a pretender as really lives for *nought*."

It having been assumed that unity of mind is the principle which lies at the base of a perfect marriage, and that the science of Phrenology is the lens through which we approximate this unity, one of the mists of the ages, in the right choice of a mate, is cleared up, and bright and clear as noonday appears the Law of Choice.

CHAPTER IV.

LOVE ANALYZED.

F this mode of mate-choosing is physiologically and psychologically right, as all clear-minded and right-thinking persons will allow, then it must, as a result, dispense with the attribute of love as a preliminary requirement. And so it does. Love, in the popular sense of the term, as applied to the union of the sexes, is a fallacy, and is not only not required, but is an impossibility in the initial requisites to the choice of a wife or husband. This may be regarded as absurd, for the reason that we never hear of a marriage (rare cases excepted) but that love is not only believed to be present, but the universal use of the word is supposed to indicate that people cannot well live without it. And this is so, in a measure, but can be explained by its correct analysis.

Poets, from the laureates to the village aspirants, have given, in good and bad verse, in every manner and all measures, words concerning love; novelists have written of it, and readers, on and off the stage, have acted it; and yet ask any of these readers or actors what they understand by the word love, and they are, with the poets, hopelessly adrift at sea. Verse piled on verse, and line upon line, enough to easily fill a score of books of this size, might here be quoted, and an inquirer might patiently and carefully wade through all of it, and not succeed in getting enlightened on the subject.

The great mistake in the use of the word, in relation to the union of the sexes, is, first, in its *part application ;* and, second, the supposition that mock love—a species of Mesmerism—is true love. Perfect sexual love comes only of a perfect union—a union of resemblance in mind, soul and body, and this is one reason for my so earnestly advising the employment of the reason in selection ; for in and through the intellect you only can choose one who approximates to your standard of character in all its details. The union being consummated, perfect love results as naturally and harmoniously as do all the workings of all other of Nature's laws, and this love, guided by the moral sentiments, through the similarity of its component halves, grows strong, more lasting, pure and holy through the days and months of life's pilgrimage, and in years its purity and strength meet and affiliate with the spirit of the great I AM, whose presence and power are only exercised through love.

Filial love is only found in those children who were knowingly, earnestly and lovingly desired, by the parents, and such children, having transmitted them the counterparts of their originators' mental and moral organization, will, cannot help, being largely filled with love of parents—sweet, earnest, pure and perfect filial love. In the increase of a family under like conditions, the children will love each other, constituting perfect brotherly and sisterly love.

Love of God, in its perfect manifestation, is an impossibility—at least in this present age of the world. It is approached in its exercise only by those who earnestly strive after and continually endeavor to so regulate their every-day thoughts, words and actions as to avoid all that is wrong, and to grow into all that is right. In the doing of this, the mental, moral and spiritual nature of the individual takes on, in a measure, perfection, establishing reciprocity of soul-thought with that of Christ, and so constituting love of God.

And this love of God can only be experienced in this way; for sudden conversion to a love of God, like sudden love between man and woman, is a misnomer, and is contrary to the law that governs the birth, growth, and perfection of all matter.

Love, as applied to the present mode of courtship and marriage, is, as already stated, used but in part. A woman marries a man because, as she says (and perhaps believes), she loves him. How? Because her self-esteem prompts her to avoid being an " old maid," and inhabitiveness or *love* of home, and acquisitiveness or *love* of money, prompts her to marry the man of her choice. It matters not what may be the man's acquirements as compared with hers, *provided* he possess money and a home for her. This woman marries through love; but it is a selfish, animal love, and is widely different from the pure and holy love that comes of a perfect union of soul with soul.

A man marries a woman because, as he says (and probably believes), he loves her. How? Because, through his ideality or *love* for the beautiful, and through his perverted amativeness or *love* for the gross and sensual, ambition prompts him, and perhaps opposition determines him, to marry her. This man marries for love; but it is a love that is as evanescent as the wind, and a miserable help to happiness.

Again, there are thousands of women, and tens of thousands of men, who imagine they marry through love, when it is only a counterfeit—mock love, a species of magnetism or Mesmerism which one party, knowingly or unknowingly, brings to bear upon the other. A few days of wedded experience sadly dispels the illusion. When you hear of a man, a perfect stranger, passing through a country district, and in the space of say a month, being married to half a dozen women, and perhaps engaged to a dozen, these marriages and engagements were affairs, not of love, but of magnetism or love in part. When you hear of a seduction, mock love

is involved—*never true love.*   When you know of a moping,
haggard wretch, who looks as if he were going to hang himself, because Mary Jane does not " care a straw for him," it
is a plain case of mock love.   When you hear of a woman
having committed suicide because of unrequited "love," you
can be assured that there was no true love involved in the
matter—nothing more or less than mock love.   True love
NEVER acts in any of these directions, or under any of these
conditions.

These cases will illustrate what is meant by marrying
through *love in part.*   Instead, when being mated, all of
the domestic and selfish propensities, intellectual, and especially the moral sentiments being alike, or nearly so, in both
man and woman, so constituting a basis for the birth and
growth of *perfect sexual love,* modern love is expressed only
in part through some one or more of the propensities or sentiments, making the most desirable of all earthly requisites
—perfect love—utterly impossible.

Another assertion may be recorded as a support to this required similarity in the mental organs, constituting perfect
love—namely, *that there can be no true love where there is no
reciprocity.*   The man having large benevolence, it is necessary to reciprocity of feeling that the woman should be
possessed of a like quantity, else disagreements and no love.
The woman having ideality largely developed, it is necessary
to perfect reciprocity of feeling that the man have it developed in like manner, else disagreements and a bar to love.
In like manner, through all that goes to make character, a
similarity must exist to allow a reciprocity of thought, feeling and action, and the growth of love.

The disregard of this Law of Choice lies at the foundation of the bulk of the misery associated with married life,
and in no other way than by obedience to this law can a
happy union be secured.

Judged by this law of required similarity, love at first sight
is but a phase of fiction ; for it, in accord with all other of

Nature's laws, is of slow growth; and, where it is asserted to exist, it is but the exercise of some single faculty of the mind.

People vary so much in what constitutes character, that it may be doubted if a man and woman could be found of perfectly similar organization. This may be so; but it is not absolutely required that they be similar, yet *it is necessary that they as nearly as possible approximate in the greater shades of character*. The nearer the similarity is secured, the nearer is the approach to a perfect union, and a secure basis for the birth and growth of love. When such a union is consummated—and especially if guided by religious aspirations, in the exercise and friction that comes of united endeavor—all the minor shades and shadows of difference in mind and soul are softened and harmonized; and, as the months wear on, the similarity increases; and, as the years wear on, the similarity is complete and love is perfected.

In this growth to perfect love, there are other things required beside the similarity of mind. It needs that the united man and woman have all the physical functions in vigorous and normal exercise—good health, with positive freedom from pain and disease, for it is only through a sound and vigorous health that the mind is enlarged and love grows. Sickness and its attendant miseries are in contravention of Nature's laws, and in opposition to the harmony and unison necessary to love. A man using tobacco or alcoholic liquors, and living on gross food, is no more capable of growing into perfect love and its enjoyments than he is capable of appreciating what constitutes perfect health. Perfect love is of and from God—pure in its exercise, holy in its aspirations, and *how can* such a man, possessing as he does a body and soul foul with the disgusting emanations of tobacco, whisky and wine, find a pure thought within for its lodgement. The conception is not only absurd—it is sacrilegious.

Therefore, in addition to the required similarity of the mental and moral natures, it is required that a sound, healthy, ciean and sweet body is essentially requisite to the perfecting of this soul-union.

> " Time, Force and Death,
> Do to this body what extremes you can ;
> But the strong base and building of my Love
> Is as the very centre of the Earth,
> Drawing all things to it."—SHAKESPEARE

CHAPTER V.

QUALITIES THE MAN SHOULD AVOID IN CHOOSING.

O a man earnestly desirous of being lovingly mated, no other rules than this Law of Choice, and its resulting Law of Love, would be necessary; but to the heedless and doubting, whose natures lack the intelligence and culture to appreciate the benefits resulting from such a union, there are general rules, easy of application, which, if observed, will help palliate, if not altogether prevent, much after misery in married lives.

Taking it for granted that the man has arrived at a marriageable age—twenty-eight or thirty—and that he be of sound mind and perfect health, and desirous of marrying, he should avoid, in his choice, any woman having ill health, and especially if she be of a family having consumption or scrofula in its organization. There is no more important peculiarity to avoid than this one of inherent or transmitted sickness. Scrofulous or consumptive women, with colorless faces, flabby muscles, and waxy skins—even if they have the appearance of being tolerably strong themselves—cannot possibly have other than sickly and short-lived children.

Avoid marrying, if possible, a woman of an *hysterical* temperament. A few tears may be very interesting during that treacle period called the honeymoon; but, in after life, there is no misery for a man greater than to be united to a woman of delicate fibre and weak digestion, who upon all and no occasions throws herself into that incurable and misery-causing malady—a fit of hysterics." A sound mind in a sound body lies at the foundation of all that goes to make life a success.

An outward indication of an abnormal, unhealthy and unphysiological life is a small waist, whether abnormally natural, or caused by the wearing of corsets ; avoid them as you would the plagues of Egypt, for they encompass sickness, premature decay and death. Such women are not capable of pure love, or right judgment, or, what is so essentially important, giving birth to healthy, vigorous offspring. Their very souls are malformed in harmony with their bodies. Some men admire small waists, but they are men who possess but a modicum of brains—or, if otherwise, they may admire, but they carefully guard against ever marrying them. If it is your desire to secure a wife that will be free from eternal nervousness, headache, pains, ill temper, and especially if you aim to have children that will not be sickly and short-lived, I pray you avoid marrying a woman with a small waist. I consider this matter of *large* waists such a necessity, in a woman who aspires to be a wife and mother, that, to impress it more positively on the minds of all men in search of wives, I will again repeat, in large letters, SHUN SMALL WAISTS, and act on the rule of " NATURAL WAISTS, or *no wives*."

If you be a man of full or large stature, avoid marrying a small woman; for large men, in some way, have a partiality for small women. This should not be, for many self-sufficient reasons, the principal one of which is, the difference in physical qualities entails intense suffering on the part of the woman, and intense disappointment on the part of the husband ; and, should the wife bear him a child, great danger of life attaches to the mother, while the premature death of the child, in innumerable cases, results. A full sized, or large

and well-developed woman, is at all times the most desirable
wife for a large or small man.

In your search for the attainable, avoid the ignorant and
wrongly educated.   There is current a dread of the learned,
otherwise called " strong-minded" women, and broad doubts
of their making desirable wives.   Let this not trouble you ;
given all the required conditions for a perfect union, your
wife cannot possibly be too learned.

When I allude to educated women, it must not be understood as including the so-called "modern accomplishments."
It is best to be shy of women possessing such, unless you
may want a singing or dancing wife, or one possessing enough
of the modern languages to show her ignorance of them.
For the acquirement of these and other similar "accomplishments," girls will study for years ; eventually they marry, and the honeymoon has not well waned ere these superficial modern accomplishments are forgotten, and the learning of the practical, every-day duties, so entirely misplaced
and neglected during girlhood, begins, under disadvantages
great and many.   See to it that the woman of your choice
be educated in the practical details of every household duty;
that she be as capable of cooking a relishable meal as she is
of playing a gem from the last new opera on the piano ; that
she is as competent to mend her stockings as to dance the
quadrilles ; that she is as qualified to make a bed, a shirt, or
dress, as she is to speak the French, German or Italian languages ; not of a necessity that she be required on marrying to cook, mend, make beds or dresses, but that she possess such a knowledge of the details of all household matters that she can, with just judgment, direct their doing.
What would a merchant, possessing a ship and valuable car-
go, want with a captain who did not know the practical use
and application of every rope and yard in a vessel ?   No
more, then, should a husband with a wife who is not educated in household details ; and this knowledge, as with the
captain, is used only in directing and ordering, unless when a

stress of weather or poverty comes; then shine out bright and clear the benefits accruing from a personal, practical knowledge of details.

Especially should you avoid being lured to an engagement through a superficially beautiful face—a face that may hide much other than the requisites for a true wife. Deceit and hypocrisy are so universal in our day that, by other than a scientific analysis of the brain and face, surface indications and manners go for little. Beauty—unless it is the outgrowth of the soul's goodness and purity, reflecting in well-cut features and rounded outlines the joyous, happy and bright light from within—is but an evanescent affair. A man soon gets tired of the doll-beauty of his wife, which, in a very few years begins to fade, while the beauty of a strong, pure and educated woman grows, increases and ripens with age, a joy for ever.

Avoid being misled through extravagance of ornament. Women who are overloaded with outre-shaped ear-rings, bracelets, finger-rings, and other cheap, gilt trinkets, approach, in their want of taste, simplicity and common sense, the Indian in his paint and feathers—growing away from the true line of a simple, chaste and pure life, and relapsing into barbarism. No woman should wear other ornament than the rich and unfading one of a meek, pure and lovable spirit, save and except the circlet of gold that is the emblem of her union with a kindred spirit.

As in ornament, so in dress—false hair, false "forms," etc., on any woman is deception personified, and her inward life may be justly inferred from her outward form.

Extravagance in dress is to be shunned; for, apart from the costliness of such a quality, it may be set down as a rule, that the handsomest, most sensible and desirable girls and women are those who dress plainest; for such women, especially if they be beautiful, do not require the extra adornments of dress and jewelry. Whenever, therefore, you see one of the gaudily arrayed creatures of fashion, you can arrive at a just conclusion that she is not naturally beautiful, in either body or mind.

And yet another woman to avoid is one who is indolent and constitutionally lazy. A young man may well think twice before committing his fortunes and future prospects into the hands of such a wife. Though the man's income be never so great, it will all be necessary to support the waste and extravagance of a lazy wife. An indolent girl or woman is almost sure to be a peevish, fretful one; she has nothing to do but brood over her cares and worries until they become mountains. They are not desirable either as companions or wives.

"Would it be right for me to marry a woman who is a near relation—say a cousin?" This question is being continually asked, and deserves a careful inquiry. If judged by the statistics of charitable institutions, the reply would be in the negative; for these figures (which are supposed to be incapable of lying) show that a majority of the deaf, dumb and blind, a limited number of lunatics, and a much larger number of feeble-minded or idiotic children, are the offspring of the marriage of cousins. Carpenter, in his "Principles of Human Physiology," says: "Out of three hundred and fifty-nine idiots, the condition of whose progenitors could be ascertained, seventeen were known to have been the children of parents nearly related by blood; and this relationship was suspected to have existed in several other cases, in which positive information could not be obtained. On examining into the history of the seventeen families to which these individuals belonged, it was found that they had consisted in all of ninety-five children; that of these no fewer than forty-four were idiotic, twelve others were scrofulous and puny, one was deaf, and one was a dwarf. In some of these families, all the children were either idiotic, or very scrofulous and puny; in one family of eight children, five were idiotic." There is, judged by statistical tables, just cause to avoid intermarriage of relations; yet these statistics are almost valueless, as they give no idea of the hereditary antecedents or physical condition of the parties.

I opine that this fearful array of idiocy and feeble mediocrity should be ascribed to other causes than the one of intermarriage. Ill health, abused amativeness, wrong living, disproportionate ages, a low organic quality of the brain, all would tend to propagate the low and idiotic. If a robust, handsome and healthy young man marry his own cousin, who is equally healthy and beautiful—all other conditions being in accordance with the Law of Choice—and should they propagate offspring under conditions recorded further on in these pages, their children could not possibly be other than strong, beautiful, talented and long-lived. If consanguinous marriages result injuriously, it is because the hereditary imperfections, like factors when multiplied into themselves, produce their squares.

There is a family of Jews at Amsterdam who have intermarried for centuries, and yet their physique is superb.

To elucidate the truth of the general thesis, that consanguinous marriages produce disease and idiocy in the offspring, M. Voisin, of France, has made some very minute researches in the commune of Batz, a little place at the mouth of the Loire, which contains a population of three thousand three hundred people, exclusively occupied in the cultivation of salt marshes. Hardly any outsiders are ever drawn to this place, and the marriages take place, by special dispensation, even within the degrees of consanguinity forbidden by the Church. M. Voisin minutely investigated the circumstances of forty families resulting from such marriages, and has prepared tables to show that neither vices of conformation, insanity, idiocy, cretinism, deaf-muteness, epilepsy or albinism existed among any of these families, but that otherwise the stock had remained very handsome and very pure.

A remarkable story, verifying the old adage that "truth is stranger than fiction," was lately told of a woman in one of the Western States, who married her second husband, which marriage was an intensely happy one. Through a chain of circumstances not necessary here to mention, the husband and wife found out that they were brother and sister !—both being ignorant of the fact that they possessed a living relation. Two children were born of this union, who were bright, beautiful and healthy.

And yet I do not advise the intermarriage of relations. If there were a scarcity of women to choose from, the marrying of cousins might be allowed ; but facts show the reverse—there being two and, in many places, three marriageable women to one marriageable man. Again, although it may, in exceptional cases, appear that such consanguinous unions are free from other than perfect results, it does not follow that the conditions exist for its practical, every-day demonstration. Far from it. Men and women will have to live a more correct, pure, abstemious and holy life, before they can attain to a standard of health and strength that will enable them to marry cousins with impunity. As long as mankind continue in this wrong course of life, and marry and intermarry under these false conditions, so long will we have among us the blind, the deaf, the dumb, the lame, the deformed, feeble-minded, idiotic, lunatic, etc.

Therefore, I counsel you not to marry your cousin, or any other woman closely or distantly related to you, unless there happens to be not one other marriageable woman within one thousand miles of you, and even then I would not advise you other than to remain single until the arrival of some emigrant train, when a choice could be secured. The adoption of this plan will insure you against all doubts of consanguinous results and their attendant miseries.

Much importance is attached by some physiologists to the temperamental conditions of those who marry ; for, say they, if, when both parties to a marriage are temperamentally the same, there will probably be no children ; or, if they have children, they will either be still-born, or die at the end of two or three years. If the temperaments of parties differ only in part, or are physiologically incompatible, they will have children who will eventually die of consumption, etc. This I consider open to much doubt. If the causes of sterility, blindness, deafness, monstrosities, consumption, imbecility, etc., usually ascribed to mis-mated temperaments, could be thoroughly investigated, it would be found that the causes lay entirely outside of the temperamental conditions, and would be found in the wrong habits of life observed by the husband and wife. If the parties married are of a suitable age, perfectly healthy, joined under conditions that look to similarity of character, and adopt chaste, continent and hygienic habits of life, the results will be all that are most desirable. If others think that a judicious crossing of temperaments, without reference to aught else, embodies a perfect union, why, let them think so.

It is best to avoid marrying widows, who may have had one or more men as husbands, whose premature deaths were caused by other than accident, or other plainly unavoidable cause; for, as will be explained further on, they are likely to possess qualities inherent in them, that in their exercise use up the husband's stock of vitality, rapidly weakening the system, and so causing premature death. It is best, with Samivel Weller, to " beware of vidders."

For reasons good and evident, but hardly necessary here to record, it is advisable to avoid marrying a divorced woman, or even the daughter of such, or a woman of a widely different religious faith.

Especially avoid all women who in any way show disrespect for their parents, or who dislike children, or who lightly talk of religion or kindred subjects, or who have a greater fondness for balls, parties, gossip, than for home associations; for it is a requisite in all women who aspire to be wives and mothers, that they be possessed of large parental love, and a deep and broad sense and feeling of things moral and religious. No conditions so favor a more perfect union, and a pure and holy love, than does the marriage of an eminently Christian woman with an eminently Christian man.

There are other qualities to be thought of in the choice of a wife—as money, station in life, etc., which the good sense of the individual will appreciate at their just value.

These objections having been considered and established, the man's next move is to put these Laws of Choice into practice, and much might be said of the proper use of the observing powers in this direction. A prime requisite in visiting ladies for this object, is to try and see the woman in her every-day life, before awakening in her mind any suspicion that you may possibly be her lover. If attainable, become a member of the family of which she is a member, by boarding or otherwise. In doing this, show yourself in *your* every-day attire and your every-day temper. Hypocrisy should be shunned, for it is dangerous both to yourself and to her to pass yourself off for what you are not. Let the rough points in your character stand out in all their natural ruggedness. If it shock her to come in contact with them, the sooner the better. If she turn you off upon the discovery of them, so much the more fortunate for her, at least, if not for you.

But there is a more satisfactory and more positive mode of choosing—one in which hypocrisy and deceit avail nothing, and one which every man and woman is earnestly enjoined to adopt. It is by and through Phrenology. Go to a good phrenologist and obtain a written analysis of your character, with a fully marked chart, which retain for comparison. When you, in your search for a wife, come across a woman who you think has an appearance of approximating your standard of character, have her secure a chart (if she already does not possess one) and show it to you, when, having all her perfections and defects in print, you can compare it with yours. In doing this, do it fully above board, giving the fact expression that you are in search of a wife, and believe in this mode of choosing and in no other. On comparing her chart with yours, if the comparison results unfavorably, plainly tell her so, and, if necessary, give her the reason. If the comparison is favorable to a perfect union, then an engagement may be formed, *and until this precise point is arrived at, love, impulse and the feelings should not be exercised, but kept perfectly dormant.* Now, if the man believes not only in the Law of Choice, as recorded herein, but also in the Law of Continence, etc., so positively urged, he should immediately after his engagement purchase for, or loan, a copy of this " Science of a New Life" to the woman of his choice for her perusal and enlightenment. The Author laments the fictitious modesty that prevents such matters being talked of and canvassed at any and all times between those immediately interested, and longs for a brighter day, when these vital subjects may be conversed of as freely, between the engaged man and woman and parents, as would be the bridal outfit.

Chosen in this way, it is impossible to err—impossible to secure other than a union that will result in unapproachable happiness, unalloyed bliss, and is worth all the endeavor of a score of years.

Perhaps it would be well to re-assert that this perfect choice cannot be secured if the feelings are in any way engaged. Reason, observation, and judgment should and must only be employed; for if you sink your judgment, and allow your feelings and impulses to run rampant, instead of choosing and marrying a woman suited to your characteristics, you will probably choose and marry a ringlet, a dimple, a set of white teeth, a silky eyelash, a peach-blossom cheek; a lithe and willowy waist, a glimpse of a pretty ankle, a chance touch of tender taper fingers, the lingering echo of a winsome laugh—either of these, or any of numberless beautiful things, none of which are, in themselves, necessarily required in a choice.

Cultivate the philosophic in your nature, and observe, judge and choose with your eyes wide open.

Just here a new difficulty may arise. You have canvassed the qualities of every lady within the circle of your acquaintance, and even have solicited introductions to numberless women, and yet you have failed in finding one that will, as you think, approximate your character ; and the next question that naturally arises is : "What am I to do ?"

Do not regard it as absurd and wrong if I advise you to do precisely as a farmer would, who, desiring to purchase a farm, and having examined all within his county that are for sale, and finding none that will suit him—*he* advertises. Comparisons are, as a rule, allowed to be odious. Comparison, in this connection, I allow to be just and applicable. The world, in its progressive, onward march, with its thorough intermixture of race and quality, offers a broader and wider field for the selection of a rightly constituted mate, than does the narrow field of a village or city ward, and the people of this wide-world area can in no better way be reached than through the advertising columns of the newspaper.

You draw up an advertisement, stating in as few words as possible your idiosyncrasies, and inviting replies from only those who imagine they approach your standard of character. You insert it in one or more papers of large circulation, and it is read by thousands of marriageable women, and among them, it is possible, the one who would make you an unapproachable mate, and who, of course, could not possibly have ever heard of you other than in this way. A correspondence is commenced with a score or more of those having an appearance of suiting ; a phrenological analysis of the character of each is requested by you, and which, being received, is compared and returned ; presently the right one is discovered, and an engagement follows.

There is much that could be said in favor of this mode of selection, the best of which is that it prevents the feelings being engaged in the choice, which of itself is an eloquent and convincing argument in its favor. It allows an im-

mensely wide field for a right selection, and in a dispassion-
ate and philosophical manner, each correspondent acting on
the Law of Choice, and in writing unfolding each other's char-
acteristic traits ; or, what is more preferable, more desirable,
and requiring a much shorter correspondence, temporarily
exchanging and comparing phrenological charts of character.
They encompass ends that in no other way could be approached.

And something might be said against this mode.   Characters of impure formation might adopt,—probably have
adopted this way of securing a victim to their lustful
natures.   This is allowed ; but this rule is applicable, in a
hundred times its intensity, to the usual mode of choice ; and
no such wrong results need occur, if care is only observed.
An undesirable termination is less likely to occur in this way
than in any other, if a few plain rules are observed.   In this
direction, as in all other directions socially, woman is generally the wronged party and man the wrong-doer, and, I presume, will continue to be, until women are educated to a
higher and purer standard of life.   The exercise of common sense—a sense termed common, yet so very, *very*
rare—and the observance of the ordinary rules of right and
wrong, will be a sufficient guard against all undesirable results.

Therefore, I record and advise that, if you desire
a woman as a wife who approaches or duplicates your
physical and mental characteristics, and cannot find such
in the circle of your acquaintance, that you *advertise*—
advertise thoroughly and continuously, and in papers of all
shades of opinion.

It needs no argument to show that there is something radically wrong in the present mode of mate-choosing.   The
every-day records of family quarrels, scandals, separations
and divorces, too sadly prove the fact that the present method of forming matrimonial alliances must in some measure
be changed, if a happy and enjoyable married existence is

desired. That the adoption of Phrenology and advertising can make matters worse is simply absurd, as all right-thinking persons must allow; and so I repeat the assertion, that to secure a perfect love-union the parties should use Phrenology as a guide, and—failing to secure a choice in the circle of their acquaintances—that they use the advertising columns of a widely circulated newspaper.

CHAPTER VI.

QUALITIES THE WOMAN SHOULD AVOID IN CHOOSING.

S there are qualities in women which men in their choice should be careful to avoid, so there are qualities, positive and lasting in their effects, which women who desire a happy married existence should be especially careful to avoid in men.

Women do not as yet possess the privilege of making marriage proposals, but they do in the very broadest sense of the word choose the one whom they prefer, and this choice, affecting so vitally their welfare, should be positive in its enlightened exercise. Though marriage and parentage are the purposed intention of woman's existence, yet they should not allow the anxiety of a feverish and misdirected desire to constantly obtrude itself at all times on all observers; for until the age of twenty-one or, better, twenty-four is reached, woman should do naught but grow in body and mind, cultivating—in the quiet walks of life, in the busy marts of trade, or in the sphere of the professions, as her lot may be cast—those positive traits of character and finer qualities of soul which spring out of a life well and perfectly grown—a ripe woman, truly capable of working, thinking, loving, and especially of taking on the tender duties and arduous responsibilities of a mother.

A girl does not reach perfect womanhood until she is twenty-four years of age, and until she arrives at this age the thought of marrying and marriage should be to her a very minor consideration. But if she has arrived at twenty-two or twenty-four years of age, fully grown in mind and body, free from disease, well versed in all the requirements necessary to the working and governing of a house and family, she should avoid, in her choice of a husband, a man who has not perfect health. Ill health, whether inherited or acquired, is not to be desired in either the father of a family or the provider of a family, and all women who think more of health than sickness, or pleasure than misery should unhesitatingly reject such.

Closely allied to ill health—it may be the underlying cause of it—are habits essentially bad, foul and filthy—namely, the use of tobacco and alcoholic liquors; and the victims of these two habits, O woman trusting and pure, I warn you to shun! I warn you, as you hope for a clean, healthy and enjoyable married existence, to avoid marrying a man who comes to you—exuding from his breath, his clothes, his body, his very soul, the dirty effluvia of tobacco, the excreted essence of his selfish, unnatural, perverted desires—with the intention of marriage, with a hope of uniting his foul body to your pure existence. Reject, promptly and positively, his acquaintance, as promptly and positively as you would a chew of his fine-cut tobacco or a puff from his cigar.

It has been to me one of the unsolved mysteries, how a woman with fine instincts, clear intuition, pure mind and clean body, could accept the company of—much less live in union with—such a man. There are thousands, aye, millions of women who do it, and *how* do they do it? Will some such woman inform me? It can be accounted for only by the supposition that such women take after, and are the daughters of fathers whose existence was tinctured with tobacco, and who therefore get, not to like it, but simply to endure it. In no other way can it be explained; for—and the question again asserts itself—how can a healthy, pure woman, born of healthy, pure parents, affiliate with a man impure, unclean, unhealthy from the use of tobacco ? Girls, women and mothers, think of these things, and reflect and act on them.

A lady friend of the author declined three different offers of marriage, and all of them from men of influence and position, simply because they used tobacco, and she remained single until the opportunity presented itself of a union with a man who had never known its use, and she now enjoys a happy, pleasurable married life. Women, one and all, I urge on you the rule of *freedom from tobacco, or no husbands.*

An adjunct and accessory in those who use tobacco are divers other bad habits. A man who uses tobacco will generally be found an intensely lustful man, and for this reason especially to be avoided by all right-thinking women; but pre-eminently is the tobacco-user an imbiber of strong liquors. Tobacco and alcoholic liquors are as closely and harmoniously connected as are day and night. The exceptions to this rule are so rare that it may be considered a law, that no man chewing, smoking or snuffing tobacco, but publicly or privately uses alcoholic liquor, in some one or other of its poisonous formulas. This being so, the reasons for women avoiding all tobacco-users increase in an intensely vital ratio.

That alcohol and alcoholic liquors—whisky, rum, brandy, champagne, wine, beer, ale, cider, etc.—are detrimental to the welfare and happiness of the individual, no right-thinking person will deny. That they in themselves are the cause of wide-spread sickness, sin, suffering and misery, all observing natures will affirm. A man whose finer senses have grown blurred, whose inner conscience is paralyzed, whose soul is deformed with *moderate* drinking of strong drinks, is not the man to look to for high hopes, pleasurable expectations, or holy aspirations, and is to be carefully shunned as a choice for a husband, or even as a companion. It does not require that a man be seen on the streets drunk to affirm his character as a lover of or victim to spirituous liquors; for a man may use liquor a life-time and never be drunk, and yet his body, soul and mind may be so befogged, blurred and grimed with moderate drinking as essentially to place him below the level of some of the higher order of inferior animals. If a man is the son of a parent or parents who have been moderate or immoderate users of liquors and tobacco, you can with a certainty decide that the son, if not already, will soon be a follower in their footsteps. Poverty, sickness, rags, misery, premature death, follow closely on the wake of users of tobacco, and moderate or immoderate users of alcoholic liquors; and therefore, O woman, be guided by these facts—etchings from the records of ages—and shun the users of tobacco and wine, and let your decision be, FREEDOM FROM TOBACCO AND ALCOHOLIC LIQUORS, OR NO HUSBANDS.

As already mentioned, there is allied to and ingrained with liquor and tobacco an overgrown, perverted amativeness, exercised not in the bright light of day, or in the pure social companionship of sister, mother, or a " nearer and dearer" one; but in the dark ruts of disease and pollution, and with those "whose feet take hold on hell." Why should a man live a life of social sin, breaking every week of his single existence the seventh commandment, and yet be looked upon by society with favor? Why is it, that if a woman makes one mis-step in the obeying of this same commandment, society points its finger in scorn at her, tramples and crushes her to the earth? Can you tell me why this is so, and with whom the solution rests? Who is it that looks with such favor on the acknowledged " fast man" or " rake," who is thought so much more of because he is sowing, or has sowed, his " wild oats?" Woman! Who is it that so unpitifully and unmercifully tramples under foot the woman on whom the wiles and deceits of, perchance, this same "fast" man has doomed to but one breaking of this same seventh commandment? Man? O no; woman! Is this just? Is this righteous? If woman desires to elevate her own sex, to rise out of the position of slave to her right one of equal, she must disown and refuse to acknowledge any acquaintance with a man who has a reputation for licentiousness, and instead of putting to shame a fallen sister, take her by the hand and help her to a higher standard of life, and instead of courting the acquaintance of her traducer, trample *his* reputation in the mud, and shut him out from the circle of all pure society. Believe me, dear women, if you adopt this correct and only just mode of procedure, you will do much toward the right adjustment of one of the great wrongs of our social life.

Therefore, as you value a pure married existence, a happy, enjoyable love-union, avoid marrying a man whose reputation is tarnished with either tobacco, wine or women.

Avoid accepting an effeminate man, for he, lacking the requisites that go to make a perfect man, and lacking the formation for a perfect woman, approach the mediocre, and is as small and effeminate in soul and mind as in body. A full or large and well-built man approaches to the noble, generous and perfect in mankind, and is always the most desirable for a husband.

But if the woman is of small build, she must avoid marrying one of these large men, and accept one nearer her own height; and she can do this and yet avoid the effeminate man, who is essentially neither tall nor short, but an almost distinct genus, and almost impossible to confound with any other type of the race.

In this connection, it might be attempted to demonstrate that the effeminacy of the majority of men can be established by the nature of their occupation. Witness any of our dry-goods establishments, and the men therein, who sell you a spool of thread or a yard of tape, monopolizing a branch of trade that is essentially woman's. Think you, dear woman, that a man possessed of the innate qualities of a *true* man—largeness of soul, strength of character, clearness of mind, and freedom of spirit—would be confined in a close atmosphere of slavery, from early morn to late night, doling out threads, tapes, cottons? No; he would accept, as more supremely honorable, manly and ennobling, the position of a hewer of wood and drawer of water. With the untilled lands of half a continent waiting for the turning up, and into, wealth, health and happiness, what business has this class of men, with their legion of effeminate co-workers, in our cities and towns? Do not marry, or recognize as a companion, a man whose soul is not educated to compass more than a yard of tape, or the contemplation of a row of pins.

Especially avoid a man who has got no visible means of support, for the suspicion of a misused life is always to be attached to such.

The argument against the man's marrying his blood-relations applies with equal force to woman. She should not marry her cousin, nor any man nearly or distantly related.

So also of widowers, or men who have had one or more wives, whose premature deaths—as is the result in nearly all such cases—have been caused by a hugely overgrown, misdirected, abnormal amativeness, causing, in the minds and bodies of his so-called wives, intense misery, bitter disgust, sickness, and altogether a wretched existence, cut short by premature death. It is not necessary to here say more of such men, for every town, village and hamlet has its living prototype. No woman having fine and clear intuitions, and a lover of the pure and right, need be warned against the marrying of such licentious Bluebeards.

In the same category, and next in number and nature, are divorced men. Do not marry a divorced man.

Nor a man of irreligious and profane shade of mind.

Nor a man who is known to frequent gambling tables, and places of like character.

Nor a man who has an established reputation as a mean, sordid, close-fisted man.

Nor a man who has the out-croppings of a lazy, inert, shiftless character, for such carry in their wake a world of untold misery.

Nor a man who treats his sister or mother unkindly or indifferently. Such treatment is a sure indication of meanness and wickedness.

Nor a sloven, for a man who is negligent of his person or dress is filthy in his habits, and his external appearance is a sure index of his soul.

Never marry a stranger, or one whose character is not known or tested. *Some women jump right into the fire with their eyes wide open*

And finally, never marry simply for money or a home. These things are requisite accessories to a marriage; yet no woman having a just respect for her independence of body and soul, should so far degrade her higher nature as to marry for other reasons than the full acquirement of perfect happiness, that comes of a union in harmony with the Law of Choice.

These objections being considered and noted, the question occurs: How is the woman to put them into practice? She being an entirely passive party in the required approach to a choice, not much is required, other than that she shun hypocrisy and deceit, showing herself in her every-day character, and in her every-day thoughts and habits of action; and that the man or men who visit her have none other than reputations that approximate a high standard, and characters that do not in a large measure conflict with hers. This knowledge can be acquired by well-directed observation and inquiry; but, better still, a talking of, followed by suggesting and asking his or their phrenological analysis of character. On its receipt and perusal she can tell if he possess such traits of character as are desirable in an acquaintance or companion; or, if she possess a chart of her own, she can by comparison tell whether he approximates her level of character, and by spoken words, or plainly expressed likes or dislikes, can so impress her male friend as to give him to understand her thoughts on the situation, and in this way reach the desired end.

Not succeeding in this mode of finding a desirable mate, the thought occurs : " Am I, too, privileged to advertise ?" Though I have warmly urged men to advertise for wives, I am in doubt as to the desirability of extending the privilege to woman. Not but that she is equally entitled to this privilege ; but society's " prudish prudes" would put wrong constructions on it, and more especially because the world is cursed with a class of men who, wherever woman is implicated and the chance offers, exercise the low and filthy of their natures. Yet these vampires may be thwarted ; and should the woman possess that requisite of character that can laugh at society's sneers, she may and can advertise as does the man. If she possess a father, brother, or male friend, who, when replies come to such an advertisement, would open and read them, and so sift the chaff from the wheat, all danger and impropriety could be avoided.

Should these two modes of securing a husband, in accordance with the Law of Choice, be without success, what then ?

Wait patiently and hopefully, doing the work accorded you in life's vineyard—not with mute repining or grievous complaining, but smilingly, trustingly, nobly, making your existence one of practical usefulness, reflecting in your face a life well lived, radiating from your contented soul joy, happiness, and peace to your fellow-workers.

This feverish desire of girls to get married before they have reached woman's estate, is in itself an evidence of things wanting—of a body undergrown, and a mind narrow and perverted—of a growth and cultivation at variance with Nature's just laws. These wrongs are largely—if not altogether—to be ascribed to the mother, who, before the girl is well out of pinafores, instills in her mind the absurdity that her aim in life is to get married, and, to reach this end, no opportunity must be shunned to secure its attainment. Of the results of this education, in its practical application, there is no need to write of, for are not the highways and byways of life crowded with heart-sore devotees of early marriages, whose unhappiness, if not suffering and misery, should determine all rightly educated girls and women to patiently wait and knowingly choose?

"But I dread the name and life of an ' old maid !'"

This, again, proceeds from your wrong growth and education. The term " old maid" is used in derision only by those whose natures are of a low order, and whose opinions, therefore, are of very small moment. "Some of the nearest approaches to the perfection of a woman's nature have been made by maiden women, and they reach this high eminence without brushing off the bloom of their modesty by ostentatious displays of their self-sufficiencies. They pursue their high calling without noise, almost without being aware that they are moving in an exalted sphere. Their thought is not of spectators. They ask not the acclamation of the world. Their eye is not upon their reward. In their work they find their motives and their wages. They live in their sympathies, and walk in the sunshine of their own broadly-diffused love."

I record it as an indisputable assertion, that, unless a woman is united to a man according to the Law of Choice so clearly enunciated herein, that she had better, if her desire in living is as it ought to be—happiness and a pure and perfect growth in body and soul—remain single—live single, die single; and if you are inclined to doubt this assertion, observe and inquire for yourself into married life as it is, and any doubts you may have will be speedily dissipated.

Girls! entertain no thoughts of marriage until you be full-grown—until you have arrived at the time termed womanhood. Women! choose and accept only such offers of marriage as will tend to make your united existence a perfect unity, as is required for the birth and growth of love and its attendant pleasures. Failing this, *remain single*, doing your life-work with an earnest nobleness of purpose, growing in strength, beauty and purity of soul.

CHAPTER VII.

THE ANATOMY AND PHYSIOLOGY OF GENERATION IN WOMAN.

O far, our thoughts have been with the choice of a perfect union between the man and woman—a union from which the birth and growth of love so surely follows. Yet a something is necessary to the higher perfecting of this union, and the complete elevation and intense enjoyment of this love ; and this something is a baby—typical, in its beauty, and purity, and innocence, of the perfect joining together of the man and woman, and of an intensified peace, happiness and love that angels might envy, and that approaches in its exercise the very gates of Paradise.

To a right carrying out of this desire for a new existence, a knowledge of the anatomy and physiology of the reproductive system is essential ; and a thorough study of these branches, by all who think of entering the married state, should be held as indispensable as the rites which join the two in wedlock.

The reproductive elements in woman consist of the ovaries, or the germ-preparing organs ; the Fallopian tubes, which bring the germ from the ovary to the uterus ; the uterus, or receptacle of the germ, where it remains during gestation ; the vagina, or passage to the mouth of the womb; and the mammary glands.

Connecting the uterus with the *labia majora* and *labia minora* is the *vagina*, a membraneous canal, narrow and constricted at its commencement, dilated at its uterine extremity, and so attached to the uterus that the mouth of the womb projects a short distance into the vaginal canal.

At the lower part of the vagina is a thin fold of mucus membrane, extending across the orifice, of variable shape, called the *Hymen.* The presence of this membrane is popularly required as proof of virginity ; but this is fallacious, for through accident and disease it is often destroyed, and occasionally is absent altogether ; while in healthy women who are widows or long separated from their husbands, it will grow and reappear in some one of its many forms.

The *Uterus,* or womb, is the organ of gestation,

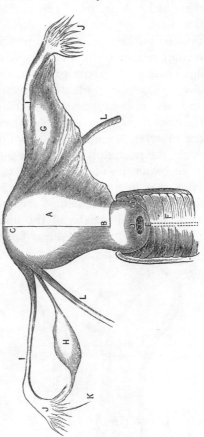

FIG. 1. THE UTERUS AND ITS APPENDAGES. ANTERIOR VIEW.

A, Body of Uterus ; B, Neck ; C, Fundus ; D, Vaginal Part, Anterior Lip ; E, Posterior Lip ; F, Interior of Vagina ; G, Broad Ligament ; H, Ovary ; II, Fallopian Tubes ; JJ, Fimbriated Extremities ; K, Bristle passed through Ostium Abdominale ; LL, Round Ligament which receives, retains, and supports the fecundated ovum during its development.

In its unfecundated, healthy state, it is pear-shaped, two to three inches long, one to two inches broad, about an inch in thickness, weighing from an ounce to an ounce and a half, and situated in the cavity of the pelvis, between the bladder and rectum, being retained in its position by the broad and round ligaments. Its upper or broad extremity is called the *fundus ;* the *body* gradually narrows from the fundus to the neck, its lower round and constricted portion, which is termed the *cervix.* At its vaginal extremity is an aperture called the *os uteri*, bounded by two lips, the anterior one being thick, the posterior one narrow and long.

To retain the uterus in its place are six ligaments—two in front, two behind, and two laterally. They are formed by folds of the peritoneum—the membrane that invests the whole external surface of the abdomen. The two *anterior ligaments* are the semi-lunar folds, which pass between the

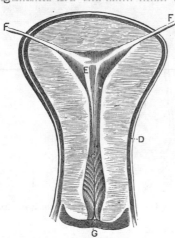

FIG. 2.   THE UTERUS,

Divided longitudinally, showing its interior cavity. G, Mouth; C, Passage from Cavity to the Mouth; E, Triangular-shaped Cavity; FF, Fallopian Tubes.

neck of the uterus and the posterior surface of the bladder. The *posterior ligaments* pass between the sides of the uterus and rectum. The two *lateral* or *broad ligaments* pass from the sides of the uterus to the lateral walls of the pelvis, forming a septum across the pelvis—which divides this cavity into an anterior part, containing the bladder, urethra and vagina, and a posterior part, containing the rectum.

The cavity of the uterus is small in comparison with the organ; the upper portion, corresponding to the body of the organ, is triangular; at each of the upper angles is a funnel-shaped cavity, from which spring the Fallopian tubes; at the lower angle is a small, constricted opening, the *internal orifice*, which leads into the cavity of the cervix; this cavity communicates be low with the vagina.

These two cavities not only differ in shape, but also in the structure of their mucus membrane—the mucus membrane of the body of the uterus being smooth and rosy in color, and closely adherent to the sub-adjacent muscular tissue. It consists of minute tubular follicles, ranged side by side, and opening by distinct orifices upon its free surface, the secretion of these follicles being destined for the nutrition of the embryo during the earlier periods of its formation.

The internal surface of the neck of the uterus (C), on the other hand, is raised in prominent ridges, having the appearance of arbor vitæ. The follicles of this part of the mucus membrane are of a globular and sac-like form, and secrete a very firm, adhesive, transparent mucus, the purpose of which is to block up the cavity of the cervix during gestation, and to guard against the accidental displacement of the egg.

The structure of the uterus is composed of three coats— an external, middle and interior coat. The external or *serous coat* is derived from the peritoneum, and invests nearly all of the uterus. The middle or *muscular coat* forms the chief bulk of the substance of the uterus. In the unimpregnated state, the muscular tissue becomes more prominently developed, and is disposed in three distinct layers. The internal or *mucus coat* is thin, smooth, and closely adherent to the sub-adjacent tissue. It is continuous, through the fimbriated extremity of the Fallopian tubes, with the peritoneum, and, through the os uteri, with the mucus lining of the vagina.

The *arteries* of the uterus are remarkable for their tortuous course in the substance of the organ, and for their fre-

quent anastomoses.   The *veins* are of large size, and correspond in arrangement with the arteries.   In the impregnated
state they are termed uterine sinuses or canals, in which the
highly vascular vili and tufts of the placenta are so closely
connected, and from which, through the umbilical cord, the
fœtus, is nourished during the middle and later period of its
intra-uterine existence.

During and after menstruation the uterus is enlarged and
more vascular.   During pregnancy it increases in weight
from one pound and a half to three pounds.   After parturition it nearly regains its usual size, weighing from two to
three ounces, but its cavity is larger than in the virgin state.
In old age, the uterus becomes atrophied, and paler and
denser in structure.

Branching off from each superior angle of the uterus, inclosed between two folds of the peritoneum, which constitute the broad ligaments are the *Fallopian tubes*.   (Fig. 1.)
They are about four inches in length, with an exceedingly
minute canal, widening gradually into a trumpet-shaped extremity, the margins of which are surrounded by a fringed-
like process termed *fimbria*, which process, during the required excitement, embraces the ovaries, and so conveys the
ova to the cavity of the uterus.

The *ovaries* are two oval-shaped bodies of an elongated
form, situated one on each side of the uterus, in the posterior part of the broad ligament, behind and below the Fallopian tubes.   They are of a whitish color, and present either
a smooth, or puckered, uneven surface.   In size they are
about one inch and a half in length, three-quarters of an
inch in width, about the third of an inch thick, and weigh
from one ounce to two drachms each.

The structure of the ovary is extremely dense and firm,
and incloses a peculiar, soft, fibrous tissue, or stroma, abun-
dantly supplied with blood-vessels.   Imbedded in the meshes of this tissue are numerous small, round, transparent vesicles, in various stages of development, called *Graafian fol-*

licles, which are lined with a layer of cells called the *membrana granulosa.* Each one of these Graafian follicles contains a single *ovum* or egg, which is a small, spherical body, situated, in the early periods of their growth, when the follicles are immature, near the centre; but in the mature ones, in which the follicles become enlarged by the accumulation of serous fluid in their cavity, near the free surface.

This will be more fully understood by referring to the annexed illustration (Fig. 3) of a Graafian follicle, full grown, and near the period of its rupture. First we have the tissue of the ovary, with its covering of peritoneum; next its albugineous tunic; next the membrane of the transparent sack or vesicle, with its thin layer of granular cells; the membrana granulosa, filled with a clear, colorless, albuminous fluid; and near its surface, surrounded by the membrana granulosa, is the egg, in which is seen the germinal vesicle, containing the germinal spot.

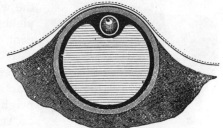

FIG. 3.   GRAAFIAN FOLLICLE, NEAR THE PERIOD OF RUPTURE.

The human egg is exceedingly minute, measuring from one two-hundred-and-fortieth to one-one-hundred-and-twentieth of an inch in diameter. It consists externally of a transparent envelope—the *zona pellucida,* or *vitelline membrane*—which is colorless and transparent. Within this, and in close contact with it, is the *yelk,* or *vitellus,* which consists of granules and globules of various sizes, imbedded in a more or less viscid fluid. Imbedded in the substance of the yelk is a small, vesicular body—the *germinal vesicle*—which is in size about one-seven-hundred-and-twentieth of an inch in diameter, and consists of a fine, transparent, structureless membrane, which contains the *germinal spot,* which is opaque, of a yellow color, finely granular in structure, and measuring from one-thirty-sixth-hundredth to one-twenty-four-hundredth of an inch.

When the time approaches for the egg to be discharged, the Graafian follicle, being gradually enlarged by the constant accumulation of fluid in its cavity, exerts such a steady and increasing pressure from within outward, that the albugineous tunic and the peritoneum successively yield before

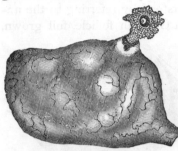

it, until the Graafian follicle protrudes from the ovary—the walls of the vesicle next yielding in its most prominent portion, and the egg with its contained fluid is driven out with a gush by the reaction and elasticity of the neighboring tissues.

FIG. 4. OVARY,

With Graafian Follicle Ruptured, showing Egg just discharged, with a portion of Membrana Granulosa.

At the moment of rupture, or immediately after it, an abundant hemorrhage takes place from the vesicles of the follicle, by which its cavity is filled with blood. The blood coagulates, and is retained in the interior of the Graafian follicle, for the opening by which the egg makes its escape being by a very minute, rounded perforation, prevents the escape of blood. This clot, which at first is large, soft and gelatinous, begins to contract by the separation of its serum, which is absorbed by the neighboring parts, and the clot grows every day smaller and denser than before, until after a time it becomes thickened, convoluted and solidified, when it receives the name of the *corpus luteum.* At the end of eight or nine weeks it is reduced to the condition of an insignificant, yellowish, cicatrix-like spot, and on cutting

FIG. 5. GRAAFIAN FOLLICLE,

Recently Ruptured during Menstruation, shown in longitudinal section.

open will have the appearance as in annexed engraving. After a period of seven or eight months it completely disappears.

There is a difference between the corpus luteum of menstruation and that of pregnancy, the latter taking much longer to disappear.

The formation, development and ripening of the Graafian vesicles continue uninterruptedly from infancy to the end of the fruitful period of woman's life. The ripening and discharge of the eggs is accompanied by a peculiar condition of the entire system, known usually as the " rutting" condition, or

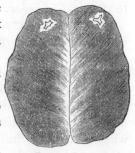

FIG. 6. OVARY,

Showing Corpeus Luteum nine weeks after Menstruation.

"œstruation," accompanied nearly always by a certain amount of congestion of the entire generative apparatus—Fallopian tubes, uterus, vagina, and external organs. It is only during or immediately after this season, in animals, that the female will allow the approach of the male—that is, just when the egg is recently discharged and ready for impregnation. At all other times the instinct of the animal leads her to avoid sexual intercourse.

MENSTRUATION.—The occurrence and ripening of an egg from the ovary, and its passage through the Fallopian tube to the uterus, and its discharge at intervals of four weeks, or successive lunar months, constitutes the phenomenon known as *menstruation.* The menses return with regularity from the time of their first appearance until about the age of forty-five years, during which period the female is capable of bearing children. After the forty-fifth year the periods become irregular, and then cease altogether, and their final disappearance is an indication that the woman is no longer fertile, and that pregnancy cannot take place.

If, during the child-bearing period, pregnancy occurs, the

menses are suspended during the continuance of gestation, and so continue after delivery, and as long as the mother nurses her child, after which they recommence and continue to reappear as before.

When the expected period is about to come on, the female is affected with a certain degree of discomfort and lassitude, a sense of weight in the pelvis, and more or less disinclination to society. These symptoms are in some instances slightly pronounced, in others more troublesome.

The menstrual discharge consists of an abundant secretion of mucus mingled with blood. This blood comes from the whole extent of the mucus membrane of the body of the uterus, and is discharged by a kind of capillary hemorrhage; but owing to its being gradually exuded from many minute points, and mingled with a large quantity of mucus, it does not form any visible clot.

The egg, when discharged from the ovary, enters the wide, fimbriated extremity of the Fallopian tube, and commences its passage toward the uterus. The Fallopian tube is lined with celiated epithelium, the movement of which is constantly directed from the ovary to the uterus, producing a kind of converging stream or vortex, by which the egg is drawn toward the cavity of the uterus.

It occasionally happens, through accidental causes, that the regular passage of the egg is thwarted. It may be arrested at the surface of the ovary, where, if impregnated, it gives rise to "ovarian pregnancy;" or it may escape from the fimbriated extremity into the peritoneum, causing "abdominal pregnancy;" or, finally, it may stop at any part of the Fallopian tube, and so give origin to "tubal pregnancy."

The egg, on its escape from the ovary and arrival in the uterus, is ready for impregnation; and if sexual intercourse takes place at this time, fecundation results, and if the egg remains after impregnation, and is attached to the walls of the uterus, conception is accomplished. If, on the other hand, coitus does not take place, the egg after a time loses its vitality, and is finally carried away along with the uterine secretions.

THE MAMMARY GLANDS.—The Mammæ, or breasts, are accessory glands of the generative system which secrete the milk that is to supply the offspring with food until the teeth are developed. They also exist in the male, but in a rudimentary form. They are situated in the pectoral region, corresponding to the interval between the third and sixth or seventh ribs, and extending from the sides of the sternum or breast-bone to the auxilla. Their weight and dimensions differ at different periods of life and in different individuals. They are small before puberty, increase during pregnancy, and especially after delivery, and in old age become atrophied.

The *Nipple*, situated on the surface and near the centre of the breast, is a conical eminence of a pink or brownish hue, its surface wrinkled and provided with papillæ, and its summit perforated by numerous orifices, the opening of the milk ducts. Glands at its base secrete a peculiar fatty substance, which serves as a protection to the integument of the nipple in the act of sucking.

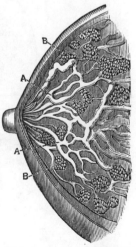

The mammary glands are conglomerate glands, consisting of numerous secreting sacs or follicles grouped together in lobules, each lobule being supplied with a common excretory duct, which joins those coming from the adjacent parts of the gland. In this way, by their successive union, they form larger branches and trunks, until they are reduced in number to some fifteen or twenty cylindrical ducts, which open finally, by as many

FIG. 7. SECTION OF MAMMARY GLAND.

AA, Galactophorous Duct; BB, Lobuli.

minute orifices, upon the extremity of the nipple, and which correspond with the number of globes composing the gland.

At the end of two or three days after delivery the secretion of milk is fairly established. The first fluid discharged from the nipple is of a yellowish, turbid mixture, which is called colestrum ; but at the end of two or three days this ceases to be discharged, and is replaced by the true milky secretion.

CHAPTER VIII.

THE ANATOMY AND PHYSIOLOGY OF GENERATION IN MAN.

HE male organs of generation are the Penis and Testes, with their appendages, the former of which serves conjointly as the organ for urination and copulation.

The *Prostate Gland* is a pale, firm, glandular body, which surrounds the neck of the bladder and commencement of the urethra. In shape and size it resembles a horse-chestnut. Its substance is of a pale, reddish, gray color, very friable, but of great density. Its secretion is a milky fluid, having an acid reaction, which presents, on microscopic examination, granular nuclei. The prostatic ducts open into the floor of the prostatic portion of the urethra.

The *Cowper Glands* are two small, rounded, and somewhat lobulated bodies, of a yellowish color, about the size of peas, placed beneath the fore part of the membraneous portion of the urethra. Each gland consists of several lobules, held together by fibrous investment. The excretory duct of each gland, nearly an inch in length, passes obliquely forward, and opens by a minute orifice on the floor of the bulbous portion of the urethra.   They gradually diminish in size as age advances.

The Testes are two small, glandular organs, of an oval form, from one and a half to two inches in length, and one inch in breadth, weighing from six to eight drachms, situated in the scrotum, being suspended by the spermatic cords. It is in these glands the semen is secreted.   Lying upon the outer edge of the testicle is a long, narrow, flattened body called the *Epididymis,* which consists of a central portion or

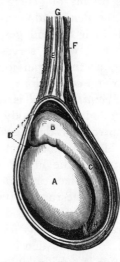

body; an upper, enlarged extremity, the globus major or head; and a lower, pointed extremity, the tail or globus minor.   The globus major is intimately connected with the upper end of the testicle by means of its efferent ducts, and the globus minor with its lower end by cellular tissue and a reflexion of the tunica vaginalis.   Attached to the upper end of the testis, or to the epididymis, is a small, pedunculated body, the use of which is unknown.

At an early period of foetal life the testes are contained in the abdominal cavity, behind the peritoneum.   Before birth they descend to the inguinal canal, along which they pass with the spermatic cord, and, emerging at the external abdominal ring, descend into the scrotum.   They are well protected from injury, having some six distinct

Fig. 8.   The Testis in Situ.

A, Testis; B, Head of Epididymis; C, Body of same; D, Tunica Vaginalis—Parietal Layer; E, Cremaster; F, Artery of Cord; G, Spermatic Cord; H, Tail of Epididymis.

coverings, the two outer ones, the skin and dartos muscle, forming the scrotum or bag.

The *Scrotum* is divided into two lateral halves, the left being somewhat longer than the right, and corresponding with the greater length of the spermatic cord on the left.   The external aspect of the scrotum varies under different circumstances; thus, under the influence of warmth, and in old persons, as well as in those who are sickly and debilitated, it becomes elongated and flaccid; but under the influence of cold, and in the young and robust, it is short, corrugated, and closely applied to the testes. One of the sure indications of a sound, healthy, unabused body is the close contraction of the scrotum. The man who has abused himself, either mentally or physically, and especially sexually, will have the scrotum elongated and flabby, indicating an extreme depression of the system.

The *Tunica Vaginalis* is the serous covering of the testes. It is a pouch of serous membrane, derived from the peritoneum during the descent of the testes, in the fœtus, from the abdomen into the scrotum.

The *Tunica Albuginea* is the fibrous covering of the testes. It is a dense, fibrous membrane, of a bluish-white color, composed of bundles of white, fibrous tissue, which interlace in every direction.

The *Tunica Vasculosa* is the vascular layer of the testis, consisting of a plexus of blood-vessels held together by delicate areolar tissue.

The *structure of the testis* consists of numerous lobules, estimated at from three hundred to four hundred, differing in size according to their position—those in the middle of the glands being larger and longer. Each lobule is conical in shape, the base being directed toward the circumstance of the organ, the apex toward the mediastinum. Each lobule consists of from one to three or more minute convoluted tubes, which tubes may be separately unraveled under water, and may be seen to commence either by free cæcal ends or by anastomotic loops. The total number of tubes is considered by Monroe to be about three hundred, and the length of each sixteen feet. In diameter they vary from one-two-hundredth to one one-hundred-and-fiftieth of an inch. They consist of a basement membrane lined by epithelium, consisting of nucleated, granular corpuscles, and are inclosed in a delicate plexus of capillary vessels. In the apices of the lobules the tubuli become less convoluted, assume a nearly straight course, and unite together to form from twenty to thirty large ducts of about one-fifteenth of an inch in diameter, and these, from their straight course, are called the vasa recta.

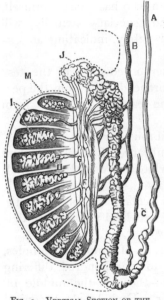

FIG. 9. VERTICAL SECTION OF THE TESTIS.

A, Vas Deferens; B, Spermatic Artery, C, Vas Aberrans; D, Body of Epididymis; E, Globus Minor; F, Rete Testis; G, Mediastinum; H, Vasa Recta; I, Tunica Vaginalis; K, Vasa Efferentia; L, Globus Major; M, Tunica Albuginea.

The *Vasa Recta* enter the fibrous tissue of the mediastinum, and pass upward and backward, forming in their ascent a close network of anastomosing tubes, which constitute the *rete testis*. At the upper end of the mediastinum, the vessels of the rete testis terminate in from twelve to fifteen or twenty ducts, the *Vasa Efferentia;* they perforate the tunica albuginea, and carry the seminal fluid from the testis to the epididymis.

The *Vas Deferens*, the excretory duct of the testis, is the continuation of the epididymus, commencing at the lower part of the globus minor; it extends along the posterior and inner side of the testis and epididymis, and along the back part of the spermatic cord, through the spermatic canal, to the internal abdominal ring. It is about two feet in length, and about a line and a quarter in diameter. Its walls are of extreme density and thickness, measuring one-third of a line, and its canal is extremely small, measuring about half a line.

The *Spermatic Cord*—composed of arteries, veins, lymphatics, nerves, and the excretory duct of the testicle, connected together by areolar tissue, and invested by its proper coverings—extends from the internal abdominal ring to the back part of the testicle.

The *Vesiculæ Seminales* are two lobulated, membraneous pouches, placed between the base of the bladder and rectum, serving as reservoirs for the semen, and secreting some fluid to be added to that of the testicles. They measure about two and a half inches in length, about five inches in breadth, and from two to three lines in thickness, varying much in size. Their upper surface is in contact with the base of the bladder, extending from near the termination of the ureters to the base of the prostate gland, and their under surface rests upon the rectum.

FIG. 10. BASE OF THE BLADDER, WITH THE VASA DEFERENTIA AND VESICULÆ SEMINALES.

A, Base of Bladder. B, Line of Reflection of Peritoneum. C, Triangular Space. D, Vas Deferens. E, Vas Deferens Dissected. F, Vesicula Seminalis Duct. GG, Ureters. H, Vesicula Seminalis, Unraveled Duct. I, Right Ejaculatory Duct. J, Prostate Gland. L, Urethra.

The *Ejaculatory Ducts*, two in number, one on each side, are formed by the junction of the duct of the vesiculæ seminales with the vas deferens.

The *Semen* is a thick, whitish fluid, having a peculiar odor. It consists of a fluid called the *liquor seminis*, which is transparent, colorless, and of an albuminous composition; and solid particles—namely, the seminal granules and spermatozoa.

The *Spermatozoa*, or animated filaments, are the essential

agents in producing fecundation. They are minute, elongated particles, about the one five-hundredth of
an inch in length, consisting of an oval extremity or body, and a long, slender caudal filament.
They are organic forms, of a homogeneous, firm,
albuminoid substance, and are produced in the
testicle, just as the eggs are produced in the ovaries. One of the peculiarities of these spermatozoa is their power of keeping in constant motion
—a motion analogous to that of a ciliated epithelium cell.

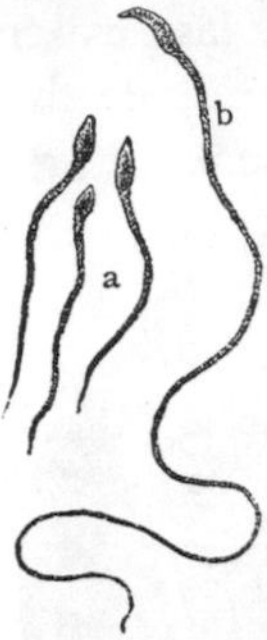

FIG. 11.
SPERMATOZOA.
a, Human; b,
of Rat.

By reference to the engravings (Figs. 9 and
10) this whole subject can perhaps be made
plainer. There is given off from the great artery
of the body—the aorta—a short distance below the renal
arteries, two small, slender arteries, called the *spermatic*.
These arteries, bringing the freshest and purest of blood,
carry it down to the testicles, where by many branches it is
carried to the several lobules of the vasa recta. Here, in
the glandular structure of the testis—the number and length
of which are wonderful—through some hidden and not yet
understood process, are slowly secreted cells. These cells,
developed in bundles of ten or twenty, being held together
by the thin, membraneous substance that surrounds them,
are afterward set free by the liquefaction of the vesicles, and
then filling the entire cavity of the semeniferous ducts, mingled with a minute quantity of transparent fluid, they slowly
enter the rete testis ; then into the vasa efferentia, which it
fills up and distends; and, consisting almost entirely of nucleated cells in an opaque, semi-fluid state, they enter the
single duct which leads to the globus minor and body of the
epididymis, following the long and tortuous course of this
tube—some twenty feet—until it reaches the vas deferens.

In the boy of sixteen or eighteen years of age, who has
lived and does live a pure life, whose sexual organism has
just awakened to life, when this secretion of minute cells

reaches the vasa deferentia, it is re-absorbed into the blood, directed into the nerve-channels of the system—and, as a result, his voice is altered, becoming more full and deep, hair begins to grow on his face, his figure is rounded out, his manner of thought and habit are altered, and he takes on a new life. In the mature man, who lives a life of comparative continence, the cells or semen is secreted very slowly, and on reaching the vas deferens is absorbed, and so endows him with a status of health, a clearness of brain, a strength of purpose and might of will that the poor miserable sensualist, in the wildest flight of his diseased imagination, knows not of.

Being further mixed with a glairy, mucus-like fluid, secreted by the walls of the epididymis and vas deferens, it enters the vesiculæ seminales, which serve as the reservoir for the semen, and in which the spermatozoa are evolved and elaborated from the cells. Here it is retained ready for use at a moment's requirement; and—as with the man who cannot get his morning dram or after-dinner smoke, who has a craving for unfilled desires, and who is miserable until obtained—so the man who has sexually abused himself, when the daily or weekly chance fails to offer, the vesiculæ seminales become so filled that they, by pressure on the delicate nerves, cause a feeling of fullness and oppression, until an early morning dreaming of past or desired pleasure relieves him by a night emission.

In the continent man the secretion takes place slowly, and is as slowly re-absorbed, making the strong man grow in strength, and day by day so renewing life that, if all other of Nature's laws are as faithfully obeyed, perfection of body and soul, as far as it is possible in this world, is realized.

When the evacuation of the sperm takes place, it is driven out from the seminal vesicles by the muscular contraction of the surrounding parts, and meets in the urethra with the secretions of the prostate gland, the gland of Cowper, and the mucus follicles opening into the urethral passages. All these organs are at that time excited to an unusual activity of secretion, and pour out their different fluids in great abundance.

The sperm, therefore, as it is discharged from the urethra, consists of the spermatozoa derived from the testicles, together with the secretion from the epididymis and vas deferens, the prostate and Cowper glands, and the mucus follicles of the urethra. Of all these ingredients, it is the spermatozoa which constitute the essential part of the seminal fluid. They are the true fecundating element of the sperm, while all others are secondary in importance, and perform only accessory functions.

THE LAW OF SEX.—That there must be a law that governs the development of sex, is as reasonable to suppose as that there is a law governing the tides and winds ; but what the nature of this law may be is more than modern physiologists have yet been able to fully comprehend.

It is asserted by some that the parent possessing the greatest amount of vital force will confer the sex of the offspring. This may be so in some instances, but as there are constant exceptions occurring, the principle does not seem to involve any law.

The strong and persistent exercise of the will power is also supposed to largely determine the result. The exercise of the will or soul power, in its intensity, would, I imagine, have some influence, as the same power when exercised in other directions—as in the recovery from, or avoidance of, disease —works effectively. Yet it is a question, whether under the conditions mankind are mated, the judicious exercise of the will power will ever be paramount to the blind exercise of lust.

Some believe that the relative ages of the parents influence the sex of the offspring. To some extent this may be so, and yet not serve as an index to the discovery of the law.

The next theory worth mentioning is that first given by a Professor, of the Academy of Geneva, M. Thury, and widely experimented on in the breeding of stock; namely, that "conception in the first half of the time between menstrual periods, produces female offspring and male in the latter." A physician who has observed the working of this theory writes, "Whenever intercourse has taken place in from two to six days after the cessation of the menses, girls have been produced; and whenever intercourse has taken place in from nine to twelve days after the cessation of the menses, boys have been produced. In every case I ascertained not only the date at which the mother placed conception, but also the time when the menses ceased, the date of the first and subsequent intercourse for a month or more after the cessation of the menses." The experiments of stock breeders, and the experience of observing physicians certainly appears to indicate that there must be some reliability, to be placed on this law—if it can be called a law.

The last theory that will bear analizing is that elaborated, if not originated by a German physician named Sixt. He believes that each testicle secretes its peculiar sperm, and each ovary contains its peculiar ovum—the right one being the male principle, and the left, the female, and that this sperm will fructify its peculiar ovum, and that only; that in coition the sperm is only injected from one testicle, which is drawn up in the scrotum before the orgasm.

His experiments on animals to prove this theory are said to have been very elaborate and successful in every instance. Whenever the left testicle was removed, the animal would beget males; and when the right one, only females—the same result being attained by extracting one or the other organ from the female.

Though the subject of the production of sexes at will, has been largely experimented on, it yet needs closer and more extended observation, to establish the true law.

TWINS, TRIPLETS, &c.—The rule is for woman to give birth to but one child at the time. When an exception occurs, it is usually owing to a transmitted peculiarity. This hereditary tendency to plurality of birth is often remarkable, and can be traced through successive generations, sometimes on the fathers side, and at other times on the mothers. The birth of twins and triplets are not desirable, because, as a rule, they are apt to be wanting in physical stamina and mental vigor, not to mention, bodily infirmities, imbicility, &c.

The fact that twins so closely resemble each other in looks, character, and talents, can be accounted for on the supposition, that they are the results of one conception—created at the same time.

CHAPTER IX.

AMATIVENESS—ITS USE AND ABUSE.

HE *cerebellum*, or little brain, is that portion of the encephalon which occupies the lower occipital fossa, or the whole cavity of the cranium beneath the tentorium cerebelli. It is the second ganglion of the encephalon in respect to size. It differs from the cerebrum, or large brain, in the form and disposition of its convolutions —they penetrating deeper, and being more complicated and numerous ; and though it is much smaller than the cereburm, it contains a much larger quantity of gray matter in proportion to its size. It also differs widely in size in different individuals, and in the same individual at different ages. The number of the convolutions, and the size, has much to do with the intelligence and strength of the individual. In the child it is comparatively undeveloped, and it is not until between the twenty-fifth and fortieth years that it reaches its maximum weight. It is relatively greater in the female than in the male.

The cerebellum possesses a two-fold nature—first, as being the seat of the domestic propensities ; and second, its power of associating or co-ordinating the different voluntary movements of the body. Flourens first described, and Dalton has affirmed by experiments on pigeons, that, if the cerebellum was extracted from the pigeon, the animal lost all power of harmonizing its muscular system, as shown in its peculiar uncertainty of gait, and in the movement of the wings. If the cerebellum was completely extracted, it lost altogether the power of flight, and could not walk, or even stand, only with great difficulty. The same experimenters, on extracting the cerebrum or large brain, found that the pigeon retained all of its muscular power, but plunged the animal into a state of profound stupor, in which it is almost entirely inattentive to surrounding objects.

That this harmonizing or associating power of the cerebellum is required in the ordinary positions of standing, sitting, walking, running, movements of the hands or fingers, or the still more delicate movements of the brain, cannot well be doubted ; for it is observable that a person with a large cerebellum, and, as a result, having large domestic propensities, invariably has a grace and charm of movement and action, and quick appreciation of men and things, widely different from the person whose possession of a small cerebellum is accompanied by an ungainly, ungraceful carriage, and slow physical and mental action. This cannot be explained other than by this supposable co-ordinating power of the cerebellum.

What concerns us more at this time is the fact that the cerebellum is the seat of the domestic propensities—and of these amativeness predominates. In the child or youth the organ of amativeness constitutes about one-twentieth of the whole brain ; while in those who have attained their full growth—twenty-fifth year—it constitutes fully one-seventh of the entire brain. This large size would lead one to think that it constitutes a very important organ in the government of the individual; and so it does. Yet, situated as it is on the lower story of the brain's workshop, it is included in the preservatives of life, rather than in the observing, reflecting and governing powers. It should be recorded here as a fact to be thought of and acted on, that *the higher the position of the organ in the brain, the greater the pleasure and happiness derived from its exercise.* This fact should be ingrained in the life-tissue of all mankind; for it is a widely spread opinion that, by and through the gratification of amativeness, the greatest enjoyment may be obtained. This error, in its every-day practice, has led to untold misery. The young man and young woman look forward to the time when the active exercise of amativeness can be indulged in, and frequently, impatient of the delay of growth of body, quaff riotously at the forbidden cup while yet they are boys and girls, and so bring sorrow on themselves, with its attendant pain, sickness, and premature death.

The early ripening of amativeness, especially if coupled with its early exercise, is an unmistakable sign of short life.

One of the products of the brain is a nervous fluid intended for the supply of the vital power inherent in the living body. When any special organ is greatly employed, this fluid is diverted from its ordinary channels to the organ exercised. If amativeness is greatly and constantly exercised, it can only be done at the expense of all the other organs. Cases have been known where men, in a supreme excess of licentiousness, have made such great and sudden draughts on the organ of amativeness as to cause death before reaction took place. Similar cases have been known in the sudden exercise of destructiveness—an organ much smaller than amativeness—when the draught on the vital fluid was so great as to prevent the formation of a fresh supply before death ensued, and the man literally died in a passion.

That the prevalence of sensuality is wide-spread, in this our day and generation, is a fact sadly evident. From the

7

lad at school, who, with his associates, in secret destroy themselves, all the way up to the full-grown and ripened man and woman, this curse of our age is practiced. In the matrimonial bonds and out of them, rich and poor, high and low, learned and unlearned, sexually thwart the chief end and aim of their existence. The abuse of amativeness is the great crying wrong of the age. The knowledge of its right use is the great requirement of the age, for it is only in and through the right application of this knowledge that mankind can hope for a purer life here and a higher life hereafter.

To make myself fully understood—by the " abuse of amativeness" I mean the practice of self-abuse in boys, girls and men ; but *especially* do I mean excessive cohabitation in man and woman—married or single.

The causes for this abnormal growth and exercise are as many as they are universal. Pre-eminently the first great cause stands out as being transmitted from parents to offspring. A wrong understanding of the laws of reproduction affects the unborn more in the direction of amativeness than any other single organ. This will be more fully explained and enlarged on in a future chapter. The man and woman whose parents have bequeathed them such an undesirable inheritance as abnormally-developed amativeness, have greater need of closely obeying all the laws that tend to continence, than those in whom it is acquired through ignorance of its results.

Next in the list of causes that conspire to a growth of licentiousness, is the perversion of the appetite by the food and drink used.

The large quantity of flesh meats, together with oysters, eggs, fish, salt, pepper, spices, gravies, beer, porter, cider, wine, and other alcoholic liquors, tobacco, tea, coffee, chocolate, salted meats, pies, bread made from fine white flour —all these things have a direct influence on the abnormal exercise of the sexual system. Tea, coffee, tobacco, alcoholic liquors, and animal food, are all *stimulating* or *narcotic* in their nature ; and whatever is taken into the body of a narcotic or stimulating nature irritates the nervous system, but especially the nerves of the sexual system, and through the reflex action on the base of the brain, amativeness is inflamed and excited, and in this way come lustful desires. Salt, pepper, mustard, salt food, and fine-flour bread, in their use, all tend to constipation, and, as a result, costiveness and hardened fœces, which irritate the nerves of, and press against, the vas deferens and vesiculæ seminales, and so produce morbid amative desires, which could not even remotely exist if the cause was removed. Costiveness, the result of concentrated food, is one of the many causes of self-abuse in boys and girls.

Let any man or woman who doubts these things live for a season on plain, nutritious, unstimulating food, and during the time lead a strictly continent life, and after getting their new mode of existence well established, let them take a cup of strong coffee or tea, and the desire for sexual congress appears at once ; or a couple of glasses of wine or ale, and amativeness promptly proclaims : " I am excited, and must be exercised ere I am appeased ;" or let them go to a hotel or boarding-house, and partake heartily of such conglomerate dinners as are served to the patrons of such establishments, and my life on it they cannot pass the night without licentious desires. I here lay it down as an undeniable law, that a man or woman, living as men and women usually live—eating what they eat, drinking what they drink, cannot live a pure life, cannot *possibly* live other than a life of debauchery and licentiousness.

The great provocative of amative desires in woman, next to a wrong quality and quantity of food, is dress. The constricting of the waist and abdomen by corsets, girdles and waistbands, prevents the return of the venous blood to the heart, and the consequent overloading of the sexual organs, and, as a result, the unnatural excitement of the sexual system. In the mode of wearing the hair, it is observable that the majority of women, adoring followers of the goddess Fashion, wear the hair in a large, heavy knot on the back part of the head, and when their own is insufficient to make a roll large enough, false hair is added. This great pressure of hair on the small brain produces great heat in the part, and causes an unusual flow of blood to amativeness, and, if persisted in, a chronic inflammation of the organ, and a chronic desire for its sexual exercise.

Closely allied to food and dress, in woman, as a producer of evil thoughts, is idleness and novel-reading. It is almost impossible for a woman to read the current " love-and-mur-der" literature of the day and have pure thoughts, and when the reading of such literature is associated with idleness—as it almost invariably is—a woman's thoughts and feelings *can-not be other than impure and sensual.*

" Something to do" is as great a necessity to womankind as it is to mankind, and yet in our towns and cities hundreds, aye thousands, of married men who, with their wives, live in hotels and boarding-houses, leave for business every morn-ing, not returning till perhaps late at night ; and the wives of these men, having absolutely nothing to do, perchance take a short walk, do some shopping, return, eat a stimula-ting dinner, read the last sensation novel—and can *anything* pure and good come out of such a life ? Or the novel-read-ing is followed by a confidential gossip with some man-boarder, married or single, who also has nothing to do, and the small size of whose soul is located in his amative pro-pensities; and the husband may not know what follows, but all acute observers within range do. " Nothing to do," as in times past, as now, and as it will continue, has done more to lower man and woman's nature—morally, mentally, so-cially, and physically—than the non-observance of any other requirement in living.

What are the results of this wide-spread, abnormal exer-cise of amativeness ? How does it affect the growing boy, the married man, the wife, and the unborn child?—the health and strength of mankind?—the happiness of the individual?—the welfare of the soul? These are important questions, and deserve careful and undeniably truthful answers; and, if such are granted them, the horrible enormity of this crying sin will stand out with fearful distinctness.

It may be well here to re-affirm the fact that in coition two important principles of the life-force are involved. First, the semen, which is elaborately secreted from the highest active principle of the blood of the man, and which is capable of giving life to a new being, and which, of a necessity, if re-absorbed into the blood of the individual, is capable, not of giving, but of renewing life. The second principle involved is that of the nervous system. In the exercise of coition through the abnormal development of amativeness, a great quantity of the nervous fluid of the brain is used up. This nervous fluid, when used in legitimate directions, is in a great measure supplied or vitalized by the re-absorbed semen, or rather the cells secreted from the testicle before the zoasperms are developed. This being so, the exercise of amativeness uses up the very life-power of the individual, and in doing this the life-force of the system is greatly lowered and weakened, laying the body open to all manner of diseases, contagious, inflammatory and chronic, insuring an existence weak and sickly, a life a great and miserable failure, and a death early and painful.

To prove these physiological facts, it is only necessary to record a few every-day illustrations of the abuse of amativeness.

The boy in school, or the young man out of school—impatient of slow growth and the legitimate exercise of amativeness, by example, or instinct bequeathed him by his parents—practices and delights in self-abuse; and, without knowing of the fearful penalty in store for him, he continues it, until, as in thousands of cases, idiocy, insanity, or death sets in, and his parents or friends account for his ill health and premature death as being caused by consumption, or some other disease of a like nature. These sad facts apply with equal force to the girls and young women, though perhaps not in the same ratio.

If self-abuse leads to such great and wretched results, no less does the promiscuous indulgence by the young or aged, married or unmarried. How sadly must the high and holier part of a man's nature be lowered who can, without the smallest whisperings of conscience, enter the den or palace of a professed prostitute, or the room of a " kept" mistress ! Where are the thoughts, the feelings, the souls of such men ? Have they mothers loving and true ?—sisters affectionate and pure ?—wives confiding and sincere ? Apart from the degradation of soul, do such men know the risks they run ? Do they know that every ninety-nine such women out of a hundred are more or less diseased ?—that over fifty per cent. of the women who ply the vocation that leads to destruction have syphilis ?—and that this dread disease, once in the system, *is there for ever*, and if they have offspring their children's children will have taints of it ? One of the saddest of sad cases to me was that of a boy five years of age— bright, intelligent and beautiful—a boy whom to see was to love. On his being requested to open his mouth, it was seen that nearly the whole of the upper part of the roof of his mouth had been eaten away by syphilis. Outside— clean, bright, beautiful; inside—decay, death; an unmerciful and yet a righteous judgment on the father for his licentious deeds. It is a fact to be noted, that on the first, and perchance the only, venture into the mire of prostitution, this disease may claim the victim for its own, and that nothing but a life of rigid continence, strict dieting, and right habits of thought and action will help palliate its destructive effects—for all the quacks in Christendom, and all the physicians, regular, irregular and eclectic, can do nothing for him.

This is no overdrawn picture—nothing but plain, indisputable facts. If any man who inclines to the licentious of his nature doubts these words, and is careless about adopting a true line of life, will come with me into any of our large city hospitals, he can be shown women in all stages of putrefaction—living deaths, the sight of which would make him vow, then and there, to shun the broad road that leads to destruction ; and, if this did not have its just effect, in another ward—in the men there exposed in all the hideousness of sores and ulcers—his own life and end would be foreshadowed.

It is a common belief that a man and woman, because they are legally united in marriage, are privileged to the unbridled exercise of amativeness. This is wrong. Nature, in the exercise of her just laws, recognizes no human enactments, and is as prompt to punish any infringement of her laws in those who are legally married as in those out of the bonds. Excessive indulgence between the married produces as great and lasting evil effects as in the single man or woman, and is nothing more or less than legalized prostitution.

A man with great vital force is united to a woman of evenly balanced organization. The husband, in the exercise of what he is pleased to term his "marital rights," places his wife, in a very short time, on the nervous, delicate, sickly list. In the blindness and ignorance of his animal nature he requires prompt obedience to his desires, and, ignorant of the law of right in this direction, thinking that it is her duty to accede to his wishes, though perhaps fulfilling them with a sore and troubled heart, allows him passively, *never lovingly*, to exercise daily and weekly, month in and month out, the low and beastly of his nature, and eventually, slowly but surely, to kill her. And this man, who has as surely committed murder as has the convicted assassin, lures to his net and takes unto him another wife, to repeat the same programme of legalized prostitution on his part, and sickness and premature death on her part.

There are women—strongly passionate and often diseased —who, like such men, are endowed with strong animal natures, who, when they marry, in the intense exercise of their lustful natures, soon reduce the husband to a standard that physically and mentally places him below the brute, and, long before the fulfillment of his just allotment of time on earth, he too dies. The number of such women is very much smaller than is the number of men with like tendencies; but when women are diseased in this direction, they go much further than is possible with men. It is for this reason I advised, in a former chapter, in the choice of a husband or wife, the avoidance of widows or widowers, the death of whose partners was caused by other than accident or well-understood disease; for when such cases, at the last day, come before the bar of judgment, it will be found that these premature deaths were murders, and that these sensualists were murderers.

The exercise of abnormal amativeness is known in all its positive intensity by those newly married. The honeymoon is one nightly repetition of legalized prostitution, sinking the pure, high and holy into the low, debasing and animal. Think you, oh! new-made husband and wife, that in this you do right?—that in this you elevate your better natures? —that in this you find peace, strength and happiness?— that in this you grow into that pure and holy passion akin to God in its exercise—the passion of love? Do not, I pray you, deceive yourselves; for in this exercise of the sexual part of your nature you lower your standard of body and soul; and, as for love, *no man or woman can possibly love or be loved who lives other than a life of strict continence.* This subject of newly-married excess is to be seriously thought of and carefully guarded against, for it is fraught with immense danger to the future peace, happiness, strength and love of the newly united. There cannot be a growth of love in such a union, for no man or woman ever practiced repeatedly the breaking of this Law of Continence, but that

a *mutual disgust was born of it*—a disgust that in time becomes chronic, and the source of all after mated misery. It
should be understood, by all married men and women, that
the result of marital excess is as disastrous to the body,
mind and soul of the individual as is unlegalized prostitution. It is necessary to a perfect sexual congress that the
wife have a natural desire for such, which natural desire occurs *only* immediately after her "monthly sickness." At
this time all healthy married women have such a desire; and
if she earnestly express a wish for congress, and the husband
accedes, a perfect union results. But if the husband *demands his rights* from the wife, who only accedes through
dread of consequences, the effect on the man's brain and
nervous system is very little different from that produced by
self-abuse.

To enter more into detail : the effects of excesses—and
whether they be produced by self, by legalized or unlegalized prostitution, the results are not greatly different—first
noticeable is shown in a general weakness of the nervous
system, and, through the medium of the great sympathetic
system of nerves, this want of nervous vital power is com-
municated to all the muscular departments of the body. The
stomach—the laboratory of the body—first feels the effects,
and shows its weakened power in its inability to promptly
digest ordinary food. After a time, should the excesses be
continued, dyspepsia takes place, which, in connection with
the failure of power in other parts of the body, is called general debility, which general debility is very soon followed by
consumption.

The fact that the small brain, in which amativeness is located, is also the co-ordinating or harmonizing power of the
muscular system, explains why sexual excesses are so soon
followed by a weakening of the joints, and especially the
joints of the knees, a softening of the muscles, a want of
strength, and a motion of an unsteady, dragging nature, differing so noticeably from the springing, strong, elastic carriage of the continent individual.

Noticeably in many ways do sexual excesses affect the brain. The faculty of memory is weakened and impaired, the person gradually lacking his usual power to remember men and things. The eyes are also affected; disordered vision is almost always a prompt indication of abused amativeness. The eyes are easily affected by night lights, and any ordinary effort strains and hurts them. The hearing is also in many cases impaired. Paralysis of the lower extremities occasionally results. Neuralgia, affecting any part of the system, is among the frequent consequences. More than half the cases of epilepsy are unmistakably owing either to sexual or self-abuse. Falling of the womb, barrenness, abortion, and cancer of the womb or breast, are directly or indirectly caused by excessive indulgence in married life. Fickleness of temper, irresolution, and premature old age, are penalties that attach themselves indiscriminately to all who violate the laws of their organization.

It is also noticeable that when any man or woman is affected with any of these maladies, their relatives, friends, and even physicians, ascribe the effect to an entirely different cause. This may not be done intentionally, for in a great measure it is the result of ignorance of the subject.

This list of diseases, the result of sexual abuse, is but a partial one; for in the abnormal exercise of amativeness, the great drain of the nervous fluid and the loss of semen—one ounce of which is equal to forty ounces of blood in any other part of the body—so lowers the life-force as to form the foundation for, and lay open the system to, all manner of contagious, acute and chronic diseases, and in this way— though sexual excesses may not be the immediate cause of sickness and premature death—it in thousands of cases is the remote cause.

Any reader who, with clear and impartial mind, will carefully read and consider these facts, will allow that, in and through the perverted use of amativeness, they depart from the true line of life's object—the securing of strength, peace and happiness, and the successful cultivation of the higher and more spiritual part of their natures. The thinking and reflecting man or woman who, through ignorance of organic laws, has done these things, and who, knowing that the time on earth allotted for the preparation for their appearance in the Great Beyond is so very short, will at once see the great need of adopting a purer line of life; for it is an unanswerable assertion, that in no other way can mankind so effectually fall from grace as through perverted animal desires. In no other way can mankind so soil, foul and debase the pure and spiritual that is within them as through the perverted use of amativeness.

These facts being established, the question naturally occurs: "What is right in the exercise of the sexual instincts? How often ?—for what object ?—and at what time should sexual congress be desirable ?" In the chapter on the Law of Continence will be found the only true solution of these questions.

CHAPTER X.

THE PREVENTION OF CONCEPTION.

NE of the sequences to licentiousness is a desire to prevent undesirable results in the wife or betrayed woman. By those married, the reasons given for the wish to avoid child-bearing are many, and a few of them may be entitled to some weight. Thus, a married woman having a small pelvis has a just dread of child-bearing. A mistake occurs in such a woman marrying at all, or at least to a man much larger in stature than herself. Again, through constitutional or local disease, she cannot become pregnant without endangering her life. Another of the reasons why conception should not take place, is through a desire to prevent the entailment of hereditary disease. People so situated, rather than seek means to prevent ill results, should be placed in such relations to life as would restore them to sound health.

The prime reason for the desire for knowledge on this subject is that licentiousness may have full play without restriction; and it will be found, in the great majority of married lives, that it is the wife who desires this knowledge, so as to guard her health, aye, her very life, against the unbridled passion of the husband. The pains, the troubles, the heart-burnings, the sickness, the danger of premature death, the woman has to experience through man's lust is beyond all comprehension, and if there is one direction more than another in which " Woman's Rights" should assert itself, it is in this one of choice of time for sexual congress.

To compass the end of prevention all manner of means are and have been used, but, as a rule, all tending more or less to the physical and spiritual harm of the individual.

The first mode to be noticed is that practiced, or said to be practiced by a community in the State of New York named " Perfectionists." It is briefly this : the enjoyment of amativeness, through sexual embrace, without a full orgasm —that is, stopping short of emission. It is requisite to this mode of prevention that the individual have a very strong will and a moderate development of amativeness. It is claimed for this method of sexual exercise that it will develop and augment more pleasure and happiness than could result from the complete fulfillment of the act. There are two de-cided objections to this mode of continence as practiced by the Oneida " Perfectionists." As mentioned in a former chapter, it is only through the exercise of the higher senti-ments and faculties that perfect pleasure and happiness can result. Now amativeness is located below the level of all the other organs of the brain, and in its exercise, as practiced by the " Perfectionists" and others, the resulting pleasure is of a low, animal nature, and cannot possibly be of a pure and spiritual nature. The second objection is that, in this part exercise, the zoosperms are developed from the sperm-cells located in the vas deferens and carried to the vesiculæ seminales, where, owing to the full condition of that recep-tacle, they must be thrown off in a night or morning emis-sion ; so that, though at the time the exercise stops short of emission, its only result is to delay it, and the effect on the man's health is the same as, perchance worse, than if he had had a full orgasm. These two reasons, coupled with the fact that not one man in a thousand possesses the health of body and power of will required to stop at the proper time, are sufficient, I think, for discarding this mode of intercourse.

Another method of prevention is in a measure similar to the above, and is widely circulated in many small and large books. It was practiced as far back as the days of Pharaoh, and can be found by referring to the ninth verse of the thirty-eighth chapter of Genesis. The least that can be said of this mode is that it is beastly, and not one iota different, in its effects on the mind and body of the man, from self-abuse.

The employment of coverings for the male organ, made of rubber or gold-beater's skin, is certainly effectual; but there is no pleasure, either animal or spiritual, derived from their use, and they so irritate the delicate, nervous mucus membrane of the vagina as to inflame and weaken it, and also produce ulceration of the womb, and altogether cause much after-trouble to the woman. A person once using these coverings never, as a rule, has a desire to repeat the experiment.

The use, by the woman, of sponge or rubber pads, placed against the mouth of the womb, to prevent the entrance of the sperm, are somewhat used, and widely advertised and sold under many different names by quacks. This, as with the rubber covering for males, prevents the very pleasure that is the object of licentious people; for it is the coming together of the extremely delicate and sensitive glands of the male organ with the highly nervous and sensitive lips of the mouth of the uterus that constitutes the highest pleasure of the sexual act, and sponge, rubber, or other substances, effectually prevent enjoyment. Owing to the very liable misplacement of the sponge, or other pad, by action, it is not in any sense a reliable method.

Another mode of prevention, and one widely advocated by latter-day physiologists, is that founded on the theory of the monthly arrival at and departure from the womb of the ovum. During each menstrual period an ovum ripens, is carried to the uterus, and in from eight to fourteen days is passed off. This allows about two weeks in which the uterus contains no germ-cell, and during which time, if sexual intercourse is had, no impregnation can follow. This, having a physiological basis, has an appearance of being free from dreaded results. But there are causes that would thwart this theory. It requires, for a perfect sexual congress, that the man and woman have each the feeling and desire for such—anything differing from this is, as already mentioned, as hurtful to the man as is self-abuse—and the woman, in her unfilled desire, must, as a natural sequence, get sexually excited. This excitement hastens the premature ripening and meeting of the germ-cell with the sperm-cell, and impregnation results, though intercourse does occur in the specified two-weeks' absence of the egg from the uterus. But if the woman—as nearly all women do who are used by their husbands simply as chattels—lie passive and motionless, the husband may have intercourse and no impregnation follow. As to the possible pleasure to him of such a union, he might as well practice solitary indulgence, for the one could not possibly do him more harm than the other.

During lactation, when the mother is nursing her babe, it is popularly supposed that sexual intercourse can be had with impunity. This is a great error, as many find to their surprise. Through the excitement of the act in the woman, the ovaries are affected, an egg is ripened and thrown off, and impregnation results. The nerve-force of the sexual organism being expended in the mammary glands, prevents the usual indications of menstruation, and renders it impossible to know when an egg has ripened.

Another method of prevention to be noticed is that by the use of the syringe, and the injection of cold water immediately after intercourse. This may or may not be successful, and there is really nothing reliable in it; beside, the injection of cold water into a cavity of such a high temperature as the vagina, carries with it much injury to the woman.

The same objections hold good when with the water is dissolved any of the many powders used for such purposes, with this addition—that it is much more damaging to the vitality of the part than when water is used alone.

Water—alone or with drugs—only has an effect upon the semen in the vagina; for if but one zoosperm enters the uterus, the injection of water fails.

There are other methods of prevention, and some of them more disastrous in their effects than any enumerated, the rationale of which it is needless to mention.

There is but one positively sure method of preventing conception—one within the reach of all, and which has no bad effects afterward, and that is *to refrain from the sexual act.*

And this is not at all difficult, if the parties but educate themselves to it. A man's morbid imagination, or morbid desires, have much more to do with his licentious acts than has the abnormal of his sexual nature; and if a man can so argue the subject in his own mind as to convince himself that a continent life is not only a true one, but that the effects of such a life, as affecting his growth toward strength and purity of mind, soul and body will be immense, he will grow out of his ever-present sexual thoughts, and so lose his unnatural desires, and, as a result, will be able without much trouble to accept and observe the law of abstinence as a preventive of conception.

Men and women in all ages have experimented on methods of prevention, and so far have been comparatively unsuccessful. When an exception does occur, it is always at the expense of the health of the individual. Than this fact, there is not a more convincing proof *that sexual connection was intended only for the propagation of the species;* for had God intended it otherwise, He would, in the greatness of His wisdom, have adapted some peculiarity of structure in the sexual organism that would have enabled mankind to exercise the lustful of their natures without the danger of impregnation following.

CHAPTER XI.

THE LAW OF CONTINENCE.

"So dear to Heaven is saintly Chastity,
That, when a soul is found sincerely so,
A thousand liveried angels lackey her."---MILTON.

HAT the mis-use of the reproductive element in man, is the underlying cause of much of the sickness, suffering, and premature death of mankind, is a fact that, standing out sharply as it does on the record of the world's progress, cannot well be controverted.

That this mis-use and its sad consequences are due to ignorance of the Law of Continence is equally beyond doubt; for, though there are multitudes that knowingly break the laws that govern their organization, yet the majority of mankind need but know these laws to follow them.

There is no other law connected with the directing and governing of the human body and soul that so affects the individual's welfare, happiness and success in life, as does the Law of Continence, and for this reason it deserves all the thought and argument that can be brought to bear on it.

By the use of the term continence is meant: "the voluntary and entire absence from sexual indulgence in any form, and the having complete control over the passions by one who knows their power, and who, but for his pure life and steady will, not only could, but would indulge them."

"Voluntary and entire absence" is not meant to exclude intercourse having reproduction as its object.

The foregoing definition, involving the principles of the Law of Continence, and especially the practice of it, will be regarded with much disfavor by a multitude of mankind, interfering as it so essentially does with the record of their past and present lives, for its popular definition is usually demonstrated in a ratio with the perverted amative power of the individual.

Ask a man of an overgrown and intensely perverted amativeness what he considers a right definition of continence, and he will tell you that having nightly intercourse with his wife is with him a law of necessity, and his definition of continence. And there are thousands of men and women—and especially those newly married—who by nightly debauchery record this as their solution of the Law of Continence; but it is a solution that involves in it immensely disastrous results to the individuals' present and future welfare of soul and body.

Ask another man, with more moderate desires, and he will tell you that thrice, twice, or perchance once a week, entitles him, as he considers it, to be classed as a continent man.

Ask yet another man, who, though possessing the full requirement of amative desires, yet has reflected and been somewhat enlightened on the subject, and he may tell you that, in his opinion, a man entitled to be classed among the continent men is one who, like himself, has intercourse monthly or semi-monthly.

This is about as high as you can get in the popular definition of this law.

What constitutes the basis for this wide difference in the popular definition of continence ?   Perverted amativeness, coupled with ignorance of the laws of life.   Just in proportion as a man is lustful is he continent ; just in proportion as a man has large perverted amativeness, and is ignorant of its true use, will he define and act out a continent life.   Therefore, this popular definition of continence, being based entirely on the individual's own selfish sexual nature, is worthless as a just law or true guide to the disciples of a chaste and pure life.

A true solution of this difficulty, and one having unperverted nature for its exponent, can be secured by establishing the periods at and between which woman should reproduce and bear offspring.

The highest enjoyable season at which a healthy woman desires sexual congress is immediately following the cessation of her monthly menses, and this is the season in which the reproductive element is most intensified, and when her whole organism is ready to take on the loving and holy duties of reproduction—the originating and developing of a new life.

The man and wife come together at this period with the desire for offspring ; impregnation and conception follow, and from that time until the mother has again menstruated —which occurs after the weaning of the child, and which in duration extends to about eighteen or twenty-one months— *sexual intercourse should not be had by either husband or wife.*

" Do you mean that the man should have no sexual intercourse for twenty-one months ?"

That is precisely what is meant—precisely what Nature intended.   *This is the only true solution of God's divine law in the government of the reproductive element in mankind,* and no man, since the time of Adam, has in the remotest manner broken this law, but has in some measure suffered the just penalty attached to it.

Though twenty-one months is the limit fixed for a life of purity and strict continence between the man and wife, I believe in a yet further extension of time. The twenty-one months of reproductive effort, on the part of the mother, necessarily in a measure lowers her vital powers, and therefore, after weaning, she should be allowed at least from one year to fifteen months to rest and recuperate. This may not be required in a perfectly healthy woman, but healthy women being an exception, the rule holds good. This would create an interval of nearly three years in which no intercourse should be had by the husband or wife, and in those who faithfully observe this rule is found the only strictly continent of mankind.

"What if the mother should either not want to, or not be able to nurse her child?"

The woman who lacks the desire to nurse her child has a something connected with the formation of her soul that is radically wrong or greatly deformed, and the woman who, through ill health or other cause, cannot nurse her child, should not be a wife, or at least not a mother.

A continent man, therefore, is one who possesses the power to reproduce his species, and who, through a true life and firm will, exercises his reproductive element only at the right seasons, and only for the purpose of reproduction.

I know that this rule is not the one generally advocated by medical or reform writers, and that it will have many opponents; yet there can not be produced in opposition to it an argument that can, in the remotest way, affect the truths of which it is the exponent.

What are some of the objections to a life of continence? Some writers would have us believe that because some ecclesiastic, monk or priest who has inhabited a monastery, and who, because having lascivious dreams, seeing voluptuous images, and having uncontrollable desires, with all the accompanying misery—a strictly continent life is to be avoided. A man having a large development of amativeness, shut up in the cell of a monastery, debarred from all healthy exercise of body and mind, could not well have other than abnormal sexual desires, and amounts to nothing as an argument.

Locke, Newton and Pitt, men of extraordinary power of will and great breadth of intellect, never married, and, it is well known, never in any way gratified the sexual desires.

Another objection occasionally advanced is that, through want of exercise, the male organ will decrease in size! When any such decrease in size does occur, it will be found to be caused by exactly the reverse—namely, excessive exercise by self-abuse.

Another objection that might be advanced is that, through a life of continence for two or three years, the ability to reproduce would be lost—lost, as in the above objection, through want of exercise. This is fallacious, never has occurred, and never possibly can occur in a healthy man.

What other objections are there to the adoption of a continent life? None, unless the blind assertions of over-developed amativeness be accepted as such; and these objections, having no reason or other foundation, will be adopted by the majority of mankind, who, through the intensely animal and selfish elements of their nature, desire to preach and practice a life of licentiousness in preference to a life of chastity. What are the elementary differences between a life of licentiousness and a life of strict continence?

The individual who leads a licentious life does, in part or in whole—

Weaken his nervous system, and through that the digestive system is disorganized, the stomach, liver, kidneys, etc., are diseased, and dyspepsia, rheumatism, apoplexy, paralysis, and a score of other diseases, assert their sway.

Weaken his lungs, and consumption appears.

Disable his special senses—his sight, hearing and taste are affected.

Disorganize his brain-tissue—memory is weakened, perceptive and reflective power is weakened, as seen in imbecility of plan and purpose, and indecision of thought and action; the moral sentiments are debased, the soul blighted, and love, religion and God cannot dwell within him.

Arrests his growth, and brings on premature old age.

Destroys his manhood, and the offspring propagated by him are sickly, scrofulous, deformed, and die prematurely.

And is, all in all, a blot and stain upon God's beautiful earth, a failure in this life and in the next a ——.

Note well the difference in the individual who leads a life of chastity—a strictly continent life:

The nervous system is invigorated and strengthened.

The special senses—the sight, hearing, etc.—are strong, delicate and acute.

The digestive system is kept normal, and the man knows not what a sick day is.

The growth of body is filled up and rounded out, and a full measure of years may come, but old age never; for the last days, in their pleasurable enjoyment of good health and a sound mind, are as were the days of his childhood.

The brain is enlarged and perfected, memory grows strong, the perceptive and reflective faculties increase in power, as shown in the ability to originate and execute, the calm, self-possessed strength to endure, and gentleness, courage, generosity and nobleness of character. The moral sentiments are elevated, love grows and ripens, and the soul, in its exercise, reaches up and commingles with the spirit of God.

The reproductive element is preserved, in all its life-renewing and life-giving power, until full ripeness of years.

This is, in part, the difference between a life of licentiousness, or semi-continence, and a life of strict continence. Which will ye choose?

That God intended the reproductive element in mankind to be used only as a means to propagate the species no clear-minded, right-thinking man can deny; and when used with any other object, it is a waste of one of the finest and most subtle essences of the soul's interior presence, and deserves—as it invariably receives—punishment prompt and lasting.

Knowing that a continent life is the true one, a difficulty arises, in the thoughts of those who have led a different life, as to how it is to be maintained.

Many who have been persuaded to attempt to live a continent life have failed, because they were lacking in strength of will, firmness of purpose and the knowledge of hygienic laws. A man who has been in the habit of using alcoholic liquors, on trying to abstain, will feel somewhat weak, irritable, and exceedingly nervous, and an almost intolerable desire to renew his drinking. It is precisely so with a man who has led a life of licentiousness, who, on being continent, will feel an irrepressible desire for sexual intercourse, and especially will this be so if he eat and drink as is usual with him. This is explained as follows: his licentiousness of a necessity caused a great drain on his vitality—such a drain as required the whole life-force of his system to supply; the nervous power that directs this supply to the testicles cannot stop as short as does the individual in adopting a continent life, and, as a result, the receptacle for the semen is crowded; this causes, by reflex action on the brain, an intense desire for intercourse. But if the individual has the strength of will to persist in his life of chastity, the system will be relieved by an emission. Now, if the man adopt the plan of life given hereafter, the sexual department of the system will gradually take on its normal action; but before this is accomplished there may be several emissions, and as long as seminal emissions occur it must be understood that the sexual organism has not regained its healthy action. It is a popular opinion that a healthy man who is continent should occasionally have seminal emissions, and, like many other popular opinions, is wrong. A perfectly healthy, continent man, living a right life socially, morally and physically, does not and cannot have seminal emissions. " Health does not absolutely require that there should ever be an emission of semen from puberty to death, though the individual live a hundred years, and the frequency of involuntary nocturnal emissions is an indubitable proof that the parts, at least, are suffering under a debility and morbid irritability utterly incompatible with the general welfare of the system, and the mental faculties are always debilitated and impaired by such indulgence."

A man who has grown with or established a continent life should be very careful at any time exercising his sexual organism, unless for reproduction; for "if any one wishes to undergo the acutest sexual suffering, he could adopt no more certain method than to be incontinent, with the intention of becoming continent again when he had 'sown his wild oats.' The agony of breaking off a habit which so rapidly entwines itself with every fibre of the human frame is such that it would not be too much to say to any young man commencing a career of vice : 'You are going a road on which you will *never* turn back. However much you may wish to, it will be too much for you. You had better stop now. It is your last chance !' "

There is a terrible significance in the words of Solomon : "*None* that go to her return again, neither take they hold on the paths of life."

In no way is the importance of a continent life so clearly shown as in the rules required for its attainment. It is required, in the individuals whose desire it is to join the noble army of the continent of mankind, that they relinquish many of their souls' idols. The object aimed at is a high one, and they will have many sore and bitter trials ; but the exercise of a firm will, the strength of a new manhood, and the courage of a positive soul will conquer, and so enable them to enjoy the glorious attribute of continence.

By the individual whose earnest desire is for a pure and healthy life, no suggestion or hint should be overlooked that will, in the remotest way, help to the desired end. An individual, be he never so incontinent or licentious, will, if he adopt this Plan of Life very speedily recover though it may cause him much mental and bodily misery. A sound faith, coupled with determined perseverance, will accomplish the desirable and happy end.

PLAN OF LIFE.

So closely is the nature of licentiousness interwoven with that of alcoholic liquors, opium and tobacco, that it is difficult to tell which depends upon the other for its stimulus; but be that as it may, it is required as an absolute necessity that the individual give up the use of tobacco in all its forms, and ale, wine, whisky, cider, and all other alcoholic liquors; for a man or woman cannot possibly live a chaste life, sexually or otherwise, who uses these soul-debasing articles; and if the individual cannot or will not give up these habits, it is almost useless for him to read further. No other two habits so blot, stain and deform the soul of man, made in God's own image, as do tobacco and alcohol, and it is useless for a man to try and live a healthy or continent life who, in the remotest way, continues in their use.

The next notable requirement in this Plan of Life is the being moderate in eating. An almost constantly-present result of licentiousness is gluttony; and when the first does not complete the work of destruction, the last invariably does. A licentious person is always a gluttonous person, unless when tobacco and alcoholic liquors are used, which in their effect take slowly away the appetite for plain and healthful food, and continue to do so gradually and more markedly until death asserts its presence. Therefore, ea only to live. All food of a sweet, greasy or stimulating nature should be avoided. Tea, coffee and chocolate should be dispensed with—especially should this rule be observed by women. No drink should be used but water, unless perhaps, if desired, a small quantity of pure milk. There ar three glands in the mouth whose office it is to secrete a wa

tery fluid intended for the moistening of the food during thorough mastication, evincing the fact that Nature requires the
food to be masticated and salivated, and not washed down in
lumps by tea, coffee or other drinks.   Pork and fat meats at
all times should be avoided, and when meat is used, it should
be but once a day, and consist of lean roast beef, beefsteak
or mutton.   All other kinds of animal food should be ignored, as should also eggs, lobsters, crabs, oysters, and fish
of all kinds, for these have a direct stimulating influence on
the sexual system, and therefore should carefully be avoided
by the continent man.

Bread made from fine white flour, owing to its very constipating effects and other causes, should never be used when
brown or Graham flour can be had.   Bread, being the acknowledged staff of life, is of more importance in the diet
of a continent person, than any other article of food.   The
true mode of making bread is first to have perfectly sound
winter wheat, free from smut, ground on rather sharp stones,
and *unbolted*, which with the only addition of pure water,
placed in pans about two inches square and three-fourths of
an inch deep, and baked in a *hot* oven ; this palatable and
delicious bread can be eaten while hot with impunity, and
altogether constitutes the true staff of life.

Salt, if used at all, should be used in very moderate quantities, and pepper, vinegar, mustard, and all other condiments should be eschewed.

The dress, adapted to the temperature, should be clean
and comfortable ; all constricting bands should be avoided,
and braces always used to support the pantaloons.

By women, corsets, garters, and all articles of clothing having a tendency to interfere with the full play of the internal
organs should positively be avoided.

Closely connected with food and raiment is exercise.   A
certain amount of physical and mental exercise and rational
amusement is required every day.   There is no more natural, healthy and invigorating exercise than that of walking—

and by walking I do not mean the mincing, affected, formal or fashionable style of walking; but the free, loose, natural swing of the arms and legs, and the harmonious action of the body in living, happy, exhilarating, electrical motion. Persons whose occupations are of a sedentary nature should on every day of their lives take a walk of from five to ten miles; and when the inner workings of a man's own brain are not sufficient to keep him from noticing the fatigue incident to the walk, he should have with him a companion —and perhaps it is always best to have such, and especially so if the companion be of a pleasant, social nature. A man or woman whose occupation is of a physical nature, needs, beside moderate walking, a daily exercise of the brain-power; and this is never to be accomplished by the reading of sensation novels, but rather by the study of some of the many arts or sciences. Cities in which horse-cars have been introduced do much toward creating a dislike for walking. Clerks and business men living in such cities would do much toward the acquirement of good health if they would at all seasons avoid cars, omnibuses and carriages, for no better exercise can be secured by such men than the morning and evening walk to and from their place of business—one, two, or five miles of a walk morning, and evening, should be hailed by such as a boon greatly to be desired and appreciated.

The bedroom should be large, light and well ventilated day and night. Feather beds and pillows should be avoided. The best bed is a mattress made from straw, corn husks, curled hair, or compressed sponge. No more bed-covering should be used than is absolutely required to keep the person comfortable; it is much more desirable to be a little cool or cold in bed than to be too warm No article of clothing should be worn at night that is worn during the day.

The individual should go to bed at a regular hour—say nine o'clock (eight o'clock would be better), and rise at five, six or seven o'clock, as is most desirable. The morning is an important period in the life of the incontinent individual, and the plan all such should adopt is to *leap out of bed as soon as they wake in the morning.* The close observance of this rule will enable the man to avoid many evil results. Thousands of men wake in the morning, having the rectum distended with hardened fœces, and pressing on the seminal receptacles behind, with the distended bladder pressing in front, and they think that the sexual part of their system is urgent for intercourse, when it is only their bowels and bladder that want evacuating. This should be well understood, for the habit of early morning licentiousness is wide-spread, and in many instances is caused in this way, and it can always be avoided by leaving the bed *immediately* on waking in the morning. If it is six, five, or even four o'clock, rise, bathe, dress, and go out for a good sharp walk before breakfast, and see how much better you will feel than if you had expended your vitality in sexual intercourse. Try it, practice it, and live up to it, for it will insure much toward a continent life.

A daily bath of the whole body is a necessity; but by this is not meant the immersing of the body in a large quantity of water, and the splashing about in it for half an hour or more, for this almost invariably has a debilitating effect. The principal and only object of bathing is for personal cleanliness. Now this can be done with a quart or half gallon of pure, fresh water in the smallest bedroom. Have a sponge, or small, rather coarse towel kept for the purpose; after wetting and rubbing a third of the body with another towel, dry rapidly, and so continue with the remaining two-thirds. This bath can be taken in ten minutes, and as thoroughly and effectually as if taken in the middle of Lake Ontario. This daily morning hand-bath should be taken by every man and woman, be their occupation whatever it may. If you are sick, avoid Turkish, Russian, Electric, and other baths of a like nature; but especially should you avoid them if you are comparatively well, and desire to lead a healthy,

continent life.   If you aspire to rival the Turk, in his effeminate, licentious life, take daily or weekly a Russian or Turkish bath, with or without its after-accompaniment of coffee
and tobacco.

Every-day employment should be as much of a necessity
to every man (and woman) as is eating.   A man who is constitutionally lazy and careless about working is nearly always
a licentious man.   An idle life and a chaste and continent
life cannot possibly be found in the same individual; therefore it is required in the man who desires to live a continent
life that he have constant employment, involving either the
healthy exercise of the brain or muscular system, or both
together.

The choice of companions is not lightly to be disregarded.
A young man, leaving the pure associations of a happy
home, and entering any of our large cities, can without much
trouble form the acquaintance of a class of associates that
will lead him very far from the pure, chaste, continent life he
hitherto has led, and in this way the ability and genius of
thousands of young men, who commence life with such bright
hopes and good prospects, are fouled, blighted, and eventually destroyed in the mire of tobacco, women and wine.
Choose for companions, my boy, only those who by precept
and example *will lead you up ;* shun as you would the Devil
personified those who by hint, innuendo, practice or precept,
will destroy your purity of soul and drag it into the filth.

Especially should the continent man exercise and train his
will-power, for the doing of this not only enables him to
lead a continent life, but it as surely guides to success in all
business undertakings.   Through the right exercise of the
will the body is strengthened, the soul enlarged, and right
habits of thought and action increase and grow; for every
victory over one's bad habits strengthens the victor.   The
first mis-step through want of will-power is but "the commencement of a long series of failures.   Every succeeding
conflict is harder, because the last has been lost.   Every

defeat lessens the last trembling remnants of self-reliance. And at last, with the bitterest pain of all—self-contempt—gnawing at his heart—with no strength to say, ' I will not'—under the tyrannous dominion of foul passions, which whatever of good is left in him abhors, the man slinks and stumbles toward his grave."

A young man, exercising a firm will and determined purpose, can surmount all obstacles that obstruct the path to a continent life. Says Acton :

" A striking example of what resolution can do was related to me lately by a patient. 'You may be somewhat surprised, Mr. Acton,' said he, ' by the statement I am about to make to you—that before my marriage I lived a perfectly continent life. During my university career my passions were very strong, sometimes almost uncontrollable, but I have the satisfaction of thinking that I mastered them ; it was, however, by great efforts. I obliged myself to take violent physical exercise ; I was the best oar of my year, and when I felt particularly strong sexual desires, I sallied out to take more exercise. I was victorious always ; and I never committed fornication. You see in what robust health I am; it was exercise that alone saved me.' I may mention that this gentleman took a most excellent degree, and has reached the highest point of his profession. Here is an instance of what energy of character, indomitable perseverance, and good health will effect."

To recapitulate, in as few words as possible, the following are to be strictly avoided by those whose desire it is to lead a pure, chaste and continent life:

Tobacco in all its forms.

All manner of alcoholic liquors.

Late suppers and over-eating.

Sweetmeats, candies, etc.

White bread, when it is possible to get the Graham.

Pork, and all fat and salt meats, sausages, pickles, oysters, lobsters, eels, etc.

Salt, except in moderate quantities, pepper, mustard, spices, vinegar, and other condiments.

Mince and other pies, and all manner of pastry.

Tea, coffee and chocolate.

All constriction of dress about the body.

Idleness and inaction of body and mind.

Feather beds and pillows, and heavy bed coverings.

Unventilated and unlighted bedrooms.

Remaining in bed in the morning after awaking.

Companions of doubtful or bad natures.

Irresolute will.

Uncleanliness of body.

Turkish and Russian baths.

Drugs and patent medicines.

Plantation and all other kinds of " *Bitters.*"

Quack doctors.

In the foregoing list there are many things that the majority of mankind will think twice about before relinquishing their use. Yet, to the individual whose desire is for a true life, all and each item of the list must be discarded. There is not an article of food, condiment, or so-called luxury, mentioned above, that is in the remotest way necessary to the growth and nourishment of a healthy body and soul. I assert, without the fear of successful contradiction, that any person disregarding, in whole or in part, the foregoing Plan of Life, cannot be healthy, chaste, continent, or even a Christian. A man cannot have a pure, clean, lovable soul in a foul, filthy body, and purity of soul is essentially requisite in a good Christian. Therefore, oh! man, young and hopeful —oh! woman, fair and trusting, see to it that you discard and avoid these abominations of modern civilization, and use, observe and enjoy only that required for your growth, purity and health of body and soul.

The things above enumerated you are commanded to discard, if you would avoid a sickly, irritable, fretful, licentious, and curtailed life. The things below enumerated you are requested to observe, use and enjoy, if you would live a healthy life, a continent life, a happy and a long life :

Moderate eating of food, and in as nearly as possible its natural condition.

Two meals a day—breakfast at seven or eight o'clock; dinner at two or three o'clock, P.M.

If more than two meals are taken, the supper to be not later than six o'clock, and very light—say, a piece of bread and a glass of water.

Regularity in eating.

Using as food—

Bread, mush or gruel made from unbolted wheat; mush or cakes made from oatmeal, cornmeal; hominy, samp, rice, etc.

Apples, pears, peaches, grapes, strawberries, blackberries, plums, melons, oranges, figs—not in the shape of jellies, preserves, etc., but in as nearly their natural state as possible during their season; out of their season, from the dried fruit, in the form of stews, etc.

Potatoes—common and sweet—green corn, tomatoes, green peas, squash, cabbage—cut up fine and eaten in its natural state without vinegar—shell and string beans, spinage, spring greens, etc.

Milk in moderate quantities, cream, butter and cheese in very small quantities, if perfectly sweet, fresh and new.

Lean mutton, lean beef, chicken ; as little animal food as possible ; best if altogether discarded.

Not a particle of food, candies, nuts, etc., to be eaten between meals.

The regular morning evacuation of the bowels. If possible, acquire the habit of evacuating them, at a regular hour, just before retiring to bed.

Bed and pillows made of corn husk, hair or sponge.

Rising with prompt and careful regularity immediately on waking in the morning, and going to bed at an early and regular hour.

Bedroom to be well lighted, and to be thoroughly ventilated at *night* as well as day.

A hand-bath to be taken every morning, thoroughly and quickly cleaning the surface of the body ; after drying, rapid friction with the palms of the hands (no Turkish or other coarse towels or brushes to be used for this purpose).   After friction, while in the nude state, slightly exercise the body by throwing the arms suddenly and forcibly in different directions ; and during all this time, if the sun be shining, allow its rays to fall directly on the body.   Between ten and twelve o'clock in the forenoon is the best time for this life-renewing bath and exercise ; but to those whose business will not permit this, the early morning hour after rising, or after the morning walk, will suffice.

During waking hours, excepting while at meals, the constant and active exercise of body and brain.

The daily walk of from five to ten miles morning or evening.

The cultivation of a firm and determined will.

The active morning and evening exercise of the religious sentiments.

In the right and faithful observance of these laws, man will find all the requirements necessary to the growth of perfect health, purity of body, nobleness of soul, and, above and over all, *continence*.   By the just observance of these laws, woman will acquire and retain beauty—beauty of face, form and character; and she will retain and gain strength—strength of body, mind and soul ; but, above and over all, will she be pure, lovable and chaste.

CHAPTER XII.

CHILDREN—THEIR DESIRABILITY.

"Give me children, or else I die."—BOOK OF GENESIS.

HE necessity for advocating the desirability of propagating and rearing children, most readers may think a superfluity; yet a few paragraphs on the subject are, nevertheless, required. It is absolutely essential to the perfect union of a man and woman that they be endowed with large parental love—the desire for and love of children; for if they possess not this requisite, it is next to needless for them to marry. The command to "increase and multiply" should be obeyed only in a pure and loving spirit. The originating of children in God's own image should be an intensely active, loving desire on the part of both man and wife. The non-observance of this requirement is the underlying cause of the dislike for offspring—a dislike that is observable among the higher and especially the wealthier classes. It is the underlying cause for the so-called trouble in rearing children; for when they are not propagated under right conditions, how can any sane parent imagine they can be reared under right conditions. Children can as easily be brought into the world with happy, sunny, laughing natures, as with cross, fretful, irritable natures.

It is a practice to be greatly deplored, this aversion on the part of intelligent, educated and wealthy people to having large families; for they could, if their thoughts and actions were rightly directed, do much toward peopling the earth with a better and nobler class of beings. As it is, what a pitiable sight! A husband and wife, educated and surrounded with all that wealth can command, with one or two pale, sickly children, the result of perhaps a ten or twenty years' union. And this dislike for rearing children is infecting the middle and lower classes, and the effects can be distinctly observed in many localities on this broad continent.

What is the cause for this growing antipathy to the generating of bright, sweet and beautiful children? There are many; but the great, prime cause is licentiousness. Abnormal amativeness may not—in fact, does not—often form a constituent part of the woman's organism; but abnormal amativeness in the man and husband is the answer that solves this riddle of non-desire for children. Next in the list of causes is the trouble mothers have to undergo in their rearing; and this, coupled with the sickness and danger, attendant on birth and gestation, comprises all the available reasons, on the part of the mother, that can be advanced, excepting those that are of a physical or constitutional nature.

There are some women born with very small parental love, who therefore do not wish nor care for children. Such women are to be pitied and shunned by all men desiring wives and mothers. This unnatural quality is as often— perhaps oftener—found in high life than in any other stratum of society.

Youth and beauty are both desired by mankind, but especially are they desired by womankind ; and married women need but understand this fact to appreciate it—that, in bearing children under *right* conditions, *beauty is retained, if not acquired, and old age is put off a very great way.*

A married life without children is an unlovable and unsatisfactory life.   It is incomplete.   It lacks the bands that make perfect the love-union between man and wife—the new birth, that makes the twain as one in flesh and spirit.   But this incompleteness continues, is widened and confirmed, when the new birth is undesired by either party.

Men and women do not reach their true status in this world—do not fulfill their mission to populate—do not attain the full royalty of their natures, until they originate and rear a child ; and in proportion to the number of children they rear is the royalty of their souls perfected,

Children !   Ah, yes ; it is a glorious privilege, an incomparable privilege—the privilege of rearing, under loving conditions, a family of strong, able, bright, intelligent boys, and healthy, beautiful and lovable girls.   Think of the pride and pleasure of Abdon, the Judge of Israel, whose forty sons and thirty grandchildren filed off before him, mounted on threescore and ten ass-colts.   How the old man's heart must have bounded with honest exultation when he beheld such a cavalcade of his own raising !

Children conceived under the laws laid down in these pages will be to their parents a well-spring of joy, desirable and enjoyable in their sweet innocence, their pleasant ways, their happy natures—emblems of a love-life here and a higher love-life hereafter.   In the ministering to the child's daily growth of body and expansion of intellect, the mother takes on a renewal of beauty, health and youth.   No pleasure so intense, no joy so unalloyed, as is the pleasure of a baby born under right conditions.   The pleasure, joy and happiness savor of heaven.

But the child born under undesirable conditions !   Ah, the sorrow, suffering and misery that attend its entrance into

and exit from this beautiful world cannot be here recorded.

A noticeable requirement, in those who endeavor to lead
a true and pure life, is that in their every-day expressions
and actions they be as little children ; and in no way can the
hard-worked man of business or labor so renew his purity of
life and freshness of youth as in the companionship of little
children—while with them to be as one of them, forgetting
all outside trouble, living only in the presence of happy,
smiling, talkative, lovable, innocent childhood.

> "Blessings on the blessing children, sweetest gifts of heaven to earth,
> Filling all the heart with gladness, filling all the house with mirth,
> Bringing with them native sweetness, pictures of the primal bloom,
> Which the bliss forever gladdens, of the region whence they came."

The advocating of increase in number of offspring, may
suggest to some minds the question of overcrowded populations, with its attendant starvation and misery. This probability has been a source of anxiety to writers on political
economy—one of them, a reverend philanthropic economist, having assumed that "population unrestrained will advance beyond subsistence"—"that population in most countries, at the present period, presses against the means of subsistence, and that it tends to do so in all countries." These
fears about overcrowding populations are groundless, for "it
is only necessary to remember that, notwithstanding the
immense power of reproduction possessed by the animal and
vegetable kingdoms, we do not find, after the lapse of many
thousand years since their creation, either the terrestrial or
celestial spheres insufficient to contain their inhabitants ; nor
has the incalculably large reproduction of fishes as yet filled
up the ocean ; nor is there, at this day, a civilized population in any country on the face of the globe without the
means of subsistence."

"If progress is the fundamental and all-pervading law of
the universe, and if the human race is no exception to that

law, there is and must be a self-adjusting principle to which mankind will eventually attain. Otherwise there can be no millennial period this side of the future state—no rational basis on which to predicate any great reform among men, or advancement of the whole human family in knowledge, virtue and happiness."

When mankind approach the standard of a true life, as they eventually must, the same area of country that now supports ten millions will then support a hundred millions. "The imagination of man cannot compass the magnificence of material wealth, beauty and happiness to which this planet is destined; or, what is the same thing, of which it is capable. It is not likely that God or man will stop short of working out all its capabilities."

CHAPTER XIII.

THE LAW OF GENIUS.

T O have children is a thing to be greatly desired; but to have children of well-balanced organizations, healthy, beautiful, and possessing the quality of genius in some one or other direction, is a thing every parent should long, strive and work for.

Why is it that there is so much of the plain and mediocre of mankind in the world? Why is it that, where there is one success in life's endeavors, there are thousands of failures? Why is it that there is so much sin, misery, suffering and premature death, and so little, so *very* little of genuine success and happiness? Why is there so much of the wrong in life, and so little of the right? These are important questions, and yet easy of solution; for when it comes to be understood that not more than one child in perhaps ten thousand is brought into the world with the consent and loving desire of the parents, and that the other nine thousand, nine hundred and ninety-nine children are en-

dowed with the accumulated sins of the parents, is it any
wonder that there is so much sin, sickness, drunkenness, suffering, licentiousness, murder, suicide and premature death,
and so little of purity, chastity, success, godliness, happiness
and long life in the world? The reformation of the world
can never be accomplished,—the millenium of purity, chastity and intense happiness can never reach this earth, except
through cheerful obedience to pre-natal laws.

All the educational institutions in the world—all the benevolent, industrial and reform societies—all the anti-tobacco
advocates—all the temperance societies and all the divines in
the world, combined and working harmoniously together,
cannot do as much in a life-time of effort, in the elevation of
mankind, as can a mother in nine months of pre-natal effort. This is an important assertion, and yet is one that has
law, right and God on its side.

It is a noticeable thing that, in the ruling and guiding of
this world, there is absolutely nothing done by chance, from
the growth of the smallest insect to that of the largest quad-
ruped; from the falling of a sparrow, to the death of a sin-
ner or a Christian; from the forming of the tiny crystal of
dew, to the laborings of the destructive hurricane. In all,
and through all, and over all, is the working of God's omnipotent presence—His unchangeable and undeviating laws.
In the production of offspring there too must be a law—a
law of right and wrong—and the non-observance of this law
entails on its violaters the penalty of a sickly, effeminate,
mediocre, short-lived progeny; while its close observance
brings with it an approach to perfection, in form, feature and
soul, of the new-born.

In the conception of a new soul, the mass of mankind observe no law, unless it be the law of chance. Out of the licentious or incontinent actions of a husband's nature, conception, after a time, is discovered to have taken place. No
preparation of body, mind or soul by either parent—simply
the accidental infusion of the man's hugely abnormal exist-

ence into the unimpregnated germ of the mother; and undesired by the father, as interfering with his incontinent nature, and dreaded and hated by the mother, a new soul is
born into the world—a soul having for its inheritance all the
essential qualities necessary for a puny, brief, and unsuccessful existence.

And such a formidable array of wrong does this chance
mode of creating new beings produce, that it might well
have caused angels to weep, and God to have sent His Son
as a living exponent of a right, holy and lovable birth, and
a pure, sinless and righteous life.   Witness the thousands of
the lame, the halt, the blind, the deaf and dumb, the deformed, the idiotic, the weak, the diseased, the drunkards,
the gluttons, the debased, that suffer the righteous penalty
of a broken sexual law, and that mar the fair surface of this
beautiful earth.

Next comes the great array of the mediocre of mankind,
who in conception may or may not have been desired, but
who, in the required abilities for the attainment of a high
standard of life, are sadly deficient; and it is with their abilities as with their sins—they are of the kind that may be
termed harmless.   They do not enjoy, for they cannot appreciate, the glorious privilege of a true existence.   It might
with truth be said of this large class: they do not live—they
only vegetate.

And next follows that class of mankind—few in number—
who, through accident, were generated under nearly right
conditions, and who, therefore, while on this earth, asserted
the strong individuality of their high natures, and who so
stamped the original of their souls on the world's highways
and byways, as to require no granite pile or marble monu-
ment to record the fact that they were born, lived and died.

And lastly we come to that class—fewest in number of
all—who, desired by both parents, were generated under
right, loving and holy conditions, and who in their life-pil-
grimage knew only of the bright side of life, and experi-

enced only the successes of life ; who, in their pre-natal formation, took on the joy, the glory and happiness that appertain to a soul in harmony with God's divine law of love, and who during life here maintained their supremacy of character and soul over their unfortunately conceived fellow-beings, and who during the life hereafter will increase and establish that supremacy.

The influence of a right birthright on the future welfare of mankind is immense. A statistician has estimated that every married couple producing offspring may calculate upon over four million of descendants in five hundred years. And then the influence of well-directed or mis-directed laws, in the conception of a new life, does not stop at its exit from this world. Oh ! no ; it extends into eternity. Give birth to a human being under conditions that will make it an imbecile or an idiot, and the parents or any sane person will not for a moment think that, after its death, it will in the next world bloom into a Shakespeare, a Milton, or Bacon. Endow a new life with a licentious, gluttonous, unclean and wicked nature, and no right-thinking observer will decide that, as soon as such a soul leaves this earth, it will take on the garments of purity, innocence, chastity and holiness. Therefore, it behooves all parents to see to it that they learn the law, understand and practice it.

The fundamental principles of genius in reproduction are that, through the rightly-directed efforts of the wills of the mother and father, preceding and during ante-natal life, the child's form of body, character of mind, and purity of soul, are formed and established. That in its plastic state, during ante-natal life, like clay in the hands of the potter, *it can be molded into absolutely any form of body and soul the parents may knowingly desire.*

And now for the unfolding of this law :

There are in this direction, as in many others, obstacles— some trifling, some apparently insurmountable. Let me notice some of them.

It is required, in the generation of healthy, intelligent and lovable children, primarily that the woman have perfect health—and this implies a rigid observance of the Plan of Life in a former chapter. Now some women are not healthy, and while there is the remotest indication of any mental or physical disease—nervous, inflammatory or chronic—they should not bear children until they regain their normal standard of life. Women who prevent the normal working of their life's internal economy by corsets, or strictures of any kind, should not bear children, for they cannot possibly rear healthy or desirable offspring. It is useless for this class of women to say that their corsets and bands are worn loose; for they must, if they desire the pleasures rather than the pains of maternity, discard them at once and for all time. If they assert that their smallness of waists are not made by corsets or tight dresses, but as Nature (!) made them, the reason is much more palpable that they bear no children until, through proper exercise and living, they assist Nature to give them a proper form.

Another class of women who should not bear offspring are those whose only aim and purpose in life is to observe, study and follow the empress Fashion. A woman—and there are many—having no higher aim or object in life than the desire to be in the latest fashion, cannot bring into life a being that will redound to her own honor and God's glory.

The requirements in the woman who aspires to be a mother, under the directions of this Law of Genius, are:

That she be perfectly healthy, having no acquired or hereditary disease.

That she be well formed, with a full-sized waist and broad pelvis.

That she be capable of nursing her children.

That she think more of the vital purposes of life than of the superficial follies and fashions of the day.

That she possess a religious nature.

The requirements in the man are:

That he be perfectly healthy, having no constitutional or hereditary taint of disease.

That he be well formed.

That he be free from the disgusting and degrading habits of using tobacco and alcoholic liquors.

That he be a continent man.

That he be a Christian man.

Finally,—what is most important of all,—let the husband and wife be one, or nearly one, in mind and soul, unselfishly and lovingly living together, and working together for the common object of success, and the pleasure that comes of success.

The perfectly healthy and loving union of the husband and wife being established, the next move leads us into the inquiry concerning the time or times of preparation for conceiving and establishing the character of the New Life.

The period of *transmitted influence* may be divided into three distinct divisions—the first, the one lunar month before the morning of impregnation, which four weeks may be called the *period of introductory preparation.* The next division—the nine months of intro-uterine life, or the *period of gestatory influence ;* and the last division—the twelve months of nursing, the *period of nursing influence.*

During, or rather at the end of the period of introductory preparation, the husband's impress of life and character is direct on the formation of the New Life. During the last two divisions his impress is only accessory—that is, only as he can influence and guide the soul of the mother.

During the different periods, the mother's influence is present and paramount, and on her, in the greatest measure, rests the high and holy destiny of the child.

When, in the woman, an egg leaves the ovaries, it is carried to the uterus, where it remains some days, and is finally cast off. The longer the egg remains in the uterus, the more it loses in firmness of texture, and this loss of firmness continues until it is thrown off. Therefore, the egg should be impregnated in its freshest and firmest state—and this is as soon after the cessation of the menses as is desirable. If then impregnated, you have a strong, firm, healthy organized child; whereas, if impregnated at or just before being cast off, the chances are a weak, puny child.

The period of introductory preparation, then, ante-dates four weeks from the time desired for sexual congress, which time is to follow the cessation of the menses.

Now, during this four weeks an egg is ripening in the ovary of the woman, and during this period the mother can exert a wonderful influence on the future life of the child.

In the husband, during this period of four weeks ante-dating sexual congress, will slowly be secreted—if he is as he ought to be, a continent man—sperm-cells. These sperm-cells, through his earnest desire for offspring, will slowly take on the nature of zoosperms, and as in proportion to the effort of his four-weeks' introductory preparation, and its impression on the zoosperms, so will his desires be incorporated in the life-tissue of the child.

It must be remembered that, in all these seasons of preparation, the husband and wife must have precisely similar objects in view. Their hopes and aims must be alike; their desires, thoughts and actions must be similar.

Though I have allotted but four weeks as the season of introductory preparation, yet, if either parent have bad habits they do not wish to transmit to their offspring, they should make this period much longer—say, four or six months, or, if required, twelve months. Some insects live from two to four years in preparation for the generative act, and then, so great is the drain on their life-force, that after it they live but an hour.

The man should—during this introductory period of four weeks, four or twelve months—

If he use tobacco, give up its use.

If he use alcoholic liquors, relinquish the habit.

If he be gluttonous, to "eat only to live."

If he have irregular habits, he should adopt order and method.

If he be of an untruthful nature, he should endeavor to be truth personified.

If he have profane tendencies, he should cultivate reverence for things sacred.

It must be understood that this four weeks of introductory preparation is only applicable to the man who approaches a high standard of life; four to twelve months being almost a necessity for the man whose habits of life are false, unnatural and undesirable.

The woman, during this four weeks, should—

If she dresses tightly, adopt a very loose and short dress, so arranged with braces that the weight of the clothes will rest on the shoulders.

If she be much in-doors, take a daily walk or pleasant out-door exercise.

If she be greatly troubled with company—friends or transient visitors—she should induce them to postpone their visits until a more convenient season.

If she have irregular habits of life, she should cultivate order in all the daily household requirements.

The husband and wife, during this period, should occupy separate beds, and altogether should follow, as nearly as possible the Plan of Life given in a preceding chapter.

The chief requisite in those who would transmit desirable qualities to the offspring is strength of will and firmness of purpose. The determined exercise of the will-power is an essential requisite, and one that all parents should assiduously cultivate. If a husband and wife say: " *We will* follow out the principles of this ' Science of a New Life'—*we will* do all these things," and constantly and persistently exercise the will-element in the required direction, they can, in the formation of the New Life, accomplish almost any idea of the human form desired.

If inquired into, it will be noticed that the majority of the parents of the world's acknowledged great and good men and women, were not in any way renowned for the gifts their sons and daughters so markedly displayed—that they in most cases are never mentioned, never even thought of. They simply, through the accidental observance of this Law of Genius, bequeathed to their children genius in full or great measure. This being so, it is not difficult to understand that the possession by both parents of an ordinary, or full and evenly developed organization, coupled at all times with the full exercise of the will-power, is all that is required, intellectually, to generate beautiful and talented children.

And this is so; although, where either parent has a combination of faculties that approximates in its exercise the quality of genius, by the assiduous cultivation of this quality during the periods of preparation, it can be greatly increased in quantity and quality in the offspring. Yet it is not absolutely required that the parents have other than an even and well-balanced mental and physical organization.

Perhaps, before going further, it would be well to define what is meant by genius. Webster defines it to be "the peculiar structure of mind which is given by Nature to an individual, or that disposition or bent of mind which qualifies him for a particular employment; a particular natural talent or aptitude of mind for a particular study or course of life; as a *genius* for history, for poetry, or painting."

It may be argued that, if this Law of Genius should be adopted by the majority of parents, the world would be overcrowded with geniuses. And this is just what is desired and hoped for by the author. Why is it that every trade and profession in life, from the boot-black to the teacher and minister, is so crowded with the mediocre, and therefore so unsuccessful? Simply from lack of genius. Why is it that so many fail in mercantile pursuits? Simply from lack of genius. Why is it that there are so few successful farmers?—so many inferior mechanics?—in short, so much misery ?   Simply and only because of lack of genius. It is required in a successful mechanic as much as in a successful statesman that he should possess genius.   It is required in a successful shoemaker as much as in a successful novelist that he should possess genius.   This being so, we cannot possibly over-people the earth with offspring having the divine quality of genius.

The demand for talent—which implies genius—in every department of life's efforts is great and constantly increasing.   Men (and women) of common-place abilities are super-abundant, whereas the men of energy, of ability and genius, are sadly few.   In this intensely progressive age, only those who are strong of body and brilliant of intellect are asked for and wanted.

Parents having a grown son, whose education is complete, a great trouble arises as to what particular department in the world's workshop he shall enter.   " Shall we make of him a minister or carpenter ?—an editor or peddler ?—a statesman or farmer ?"   And when eventually the choice is made, the chances are as one in a thousand that he has made a mistake—that the department chosen is not suited to his abilities.   Now, by the observance of this Law of Genius, this doubt of choice can be avoided ; *for it is required that the choice of trade or profession for the New Life be decided on before even its conception.*   The mother and father must decide, before the commencement of the four weeks of preparation, what character and occupation the coming child is to possess and follow, and by and through this decision the future success of the individual is not only settled but guaranteed.

Life being so short, and art so long, it is always desirable in the conception of a new being that but one trade or profession be fixed on, and but one branch of that trade or profession.   If, for instance, it is the desire of the parents to have the child an artist, it should be some one of the divisions of artist-life—either a painter of human heads, animals, or landscapes. If a farmer, that it should be a stock-raiser, a fruit-grower, a grain-grower, etc.—and so, in almost every department of labor, only one line or specialty should be adopted ; for the quality of genius, spread over many branches or departments of labor, is weakened; whereas, if embodied in one single quality or combination of qualities, it grows, increases and is strengthened by exercise, and is invariably more thoroughly effective in its action.

I think that there is no occupation so favorable and so desirable for the growth and welfare, prosperity and happiness of the individual as is farming. Farmers, under right conditions and habits of life, are, or should be, the blessed of mankind. From their loins should spring, in echo to the Law of Genius, the bright, the beautiful, the successful, the *geniuses* of the world. And yet this is lamentably not the case, and why ? Because they live under such wrong conditions of life, when it is within their reach to live as nearly within the line of Nature's laws as it is possible for mortals. Why is it that sons and daughters born on the farm possess such an eager, determined desire to leave it ? Because, through these same wrong conditions of life, the mother is worried, tired and sick of the drudgery of farm-life, and longs to be released from it. This desire by the mother is ingrained in the organization of the unborn, which is the reason so many young men leave the bright, beautiful country, and crowd into the dusty heated cities. Now there must be something radically wrong in the life of a farmer, else this could not be, and the cause of this particular evil happens to be the root of all evil—money. If I possessed the re-distributing of the land on this continent, I would apportion it thus : To all farmers, fifty acres each ; to suburban residents, five acres each ; and to residents of cities, one city lot each—with no privilege, at any or at all times, to increase these respective quantities. A farmer who does his work thoroughly and understandingly, can make more money (if this be his object in life) with less work and more pleasure and recreation, on a small farm of twenty-five or fifty acres, than he could by the possession of a farm of five hundred or a thousand acres only half tilled.

In England, many farmers support large families on the produce of six English acres of land, beside paying heavy taxes. Many in Germany do even better than this.

There are a few instances where men may occasionally succeed, but they are exceptions to the rule of large farming. The large farmer has to expend more than the small farmer in the way of teams, wagons, implements and machinery; hired help; heavy taxes on large tracts of land; stock and personal properties, which he necessarily has to accumulate; then there is the wear and tear of harness and tools; the continual expense of keeping up fences, buildings, etc. Last, and not least, there must needs be a great amount of capital invested in all this necessary outfit for a large farm.

The small farmer, on his fifty acres or less, with one good team, himself and a little hired help, or his own boys, if he has any, can perform the labor of improving his farm, cultivating and harvesting his crop, with a moderate expenditure; and when he foots up his accounts at the end of the year, will come out ahead of his large-farm neighbor. The secret of success in farming is manuring, deep plowing, and thorough tillage. This is more easily done on small tracts of land, and much more likely to be done, than on the large farm.

Small farming can be done more scientifically and systematically than it is generally practicable to have done on large farms; and the consequence is that more is produced to the acre than is the result of large farming.

The safe and sure guide for the farmer is to attempt the cultivation of no more acres than he can keep in perfect good heart, and every day's experience demonstrates the fact that, with occasional exceptions, a little farm well tilled is more profitable in the end than a large one indifferently cultivated. We once read a story of a Frenchman who had two daughters. One of them married, and received one-half of the paternal vineyard as her dowry. To the old man's surprise, the half he had reserved, receiving as much cultivation as he formerly bestowed upon the whole, yielded as much as the whole had. The second married, and he gave her one-half of what he had left, and still had as many grapes from his remaining fourth as he used to get from the whole. There is a whole volume of practical truth in this little anecdote. Its moral is: attempt the cultivation of no more land than you can cultivate well and thoroughly.

Another thing against the purity of a farmer's life, and especially so adverse to rearing of clean, healthy and beautiful children, is the unnecessary filth that usually attaches itself to the farms of those whose ideality is undeveloped. A pure, sweet, healthy child cannot be raised in the vicinity of a hog-pen, with its ever-present foul odors tainting God's pure atmosphere. But—to stop here at what farmers should not do—I will briefly mention what a farmer should do, whose desire is for the most legitimate, healthy, artistic and happy life on this earth.

He should possess a small farm of not more than fifty acres. He should adopt one—not more than two specialties—the raising of apples, peaches, small fruits, or grain ; horses, cattle and sheep, etc., to be decided on by the nature of his land, location, etc. It should be understood, in this age of rapid progress, that the man who adopts specialties is for many reasons most likely to succeed. He should employ, as fast as it is in his power to do so, all the modern implements of husbandry, and so allow him more time for exercise of brain and less labor of muscle. He should cultivate the beautiful on his person, family, in and around his house—and this does not imply a great outlay of money. Neatness and cleanliness of person, perfect order in all the household economy ; a vase of flowers here, and a house-plant there ; one or more steel engravings, lithographs, chromos or photographs adorning the walls ; a few books, and one or two weekly and monthly publications—all these are within the reach of the poorest, and should be adopted by all. A farmer's work should be so arranged as to allow him a certain portion of each day for instruction and recreation.

In nothing else are his mistakes so demonstrable as in the daily life of the women of his household; for if there be one position in life more than another in which the term "slave" is applicable, it is the position of wife and women-assistants to a farmer. A woman, in her health, youth and beauty, marries a farmer, and in a few, very few years she is woefully altered. The everlasting household drudgery of the farm-life dulls and lowers her fine organization, sinks all the spiritual into the animal of her nature, and unfits her to be a mother in Israel.

The principal cause of this overwork in the woman, next to the extra drudgery attendant on the possession of an over-sized and under-worked farm, is in the preparation of the meals for the family. It is popularly supposed that a farmer requires more nourishment than any other class of laborers. This is so only in a measure, and if farmers would adopt a vegetarian diet and the two-meals-a-day system, of breakfast at eight and dinner at two or three o'clock, they would do an immense deal toward helping their wives to a more enjoyable and natural mode of life; for it is noticeable that the breakfast is not well over before it is time to commence dinner, and dinner is not well cleared away before it is time for supper; especially is this so in the short days of winter. Now most of the overwork can be avoided by the two-meals vegetarian system. The adoption of this plan allows the woman time for recreation, reading, thought, observation; while the farm-laborers, husband and family will, after being acclimated to this new mode of life, be stronger, healthier, happier, more intelligent and wealthier. This system of vegetarianism and two meals a day is one among the great reforms of the age, and I earnestly advise, not alone farmers, but all other classes of society, to seriously think of it, to purchase works on the subject, to inquire into it, and especially to give it a long and thorough trial, and in no wise, without thought and reflection, set their faces against it. Next to licentiousness, gluttony is the great crying evil of the day, and in no way can it be so well avoided as by adopting the system of a vegetarian diet and two meals a day.

I do not intend, at this time, to enlarge on the benefits to be derived from vegetarianism and the two-meals system, but will here give an extract from Adam Smith's "Wealth of Nations," and hope it will tend to provoke inquiry, thought and action on the subject.

Adam Smith informs us that—

"The most beautiful women in the British dominions are said to be, the greater part of them, from the lower ranks of the people of Ireland, who are generally fed with potatoes. The peasantry of Lancashire and Cheshire, also, who live principally on potatoes and buttermilk, are celebrated as the handsomest race in England.

"The peasantry of Wales, Norway, Sweden, Russia, Denmark, Poland, Germany, Turkey, Greece, Switzerland, Spain, Portugal, and almost every country in Europe, from the most northern part of Russia to the Straits of Gibraltar, subsist principally, and most of them entirely, on vegetable food. The Persians, Hindoos, Burmese, Chinese, Japanese, the inhabitants of East India Archipelago, of the mountains of Himalayah, and, in fact, most of the Asiatics, live upon vegetable productions. The great body of the ancient Egyptians and Persians confined themselves to a vegetable diet; and the Egyptians of the present day, as well as the Negroes (whose great bodily powers are well known), live chiefly on vegetable substances. The brave Spartans, who, for muscular power, physical energy, and ability to endure hardships, perhaps stand unequalled in the history of nations, were vegetarians. The departure from their simple diet was soon followed by their decline. The armies of Greece and Rome, in the times of their unparalleled conquests, subsisted on vegetable productions. In the training for the public games in Greece, where muscular strength was to be exhibited in all its various forms, vegetable food was adhered to ; but when flesh-meat was adopted afterward, those hitherto athletic men became sluggish and stupid. From two-thirds to three-fourths of the whole human family, from the creation of the species to the present time, have subsisted entirely, or nearly so, on vegetable food; and always, when their alimentary supplies of this kind have been abundant and of good quality, and their habits have been in other respects correct, they have been well nourished and well sustained in all the physiological interests of their nature."

I earnestly enjoin not only parents who are farmers, but all other parents who purpose generating a new life, and desire to practice this Law of Genius, that they adopt the vegetarian mode of life, for it will tell wonderfully and powerfully on the beauty, health, strength, intelligence and ability of their offspring.

The cities would be no cities were it not for the country. The strength, the beauty, the ability, the bone and sinew of a nation's hopes and successes, lie dormant in the men and women of the country ; and for this reason have I said so much of farmers and farming—because of its very great importance.

The first thing the husband and wife should do, in the formation of the New Life, is to decide on the particular trade or profession, or particular department of that trade or profession, the unborn is to follow—a farmer, actor, watchmaker, tanner, singer, musician, orator, historian, landscape or portrait painter, milliner, merchant, soldier, shoemaker, manufacturer, sculptor, mechanic, lecturer, machinist, preacher, printer, phrenologist, gardener, inventor, florist, canvasser, engraver, chemist, contractor, author, baker, architect, dentist, physician, diplomatist, explorer, etc. Each of these trades or professions require different combinations of different faculties; and yet, as will be shown further on, it is not necessary that the parents have any previous knowledge of the practical workings of any of these trades or professions, to enable them to transmit the desired qualities to their offspring.

This having been done, the next move is a series of self-inquiries, by the parents, concerning different qualities, habits, or idiosyncrasies of character, that they do *not* desire to transmit to their offspring. Let me illustrate: if one or both parents are in the habit of using tobacco—this not being a desirable quality to transmit—it should, if only for a time, be rigidly kept out of the system; and so of alcoholic liquors. For be it understood, that a child born of parents who are perfect, pure, and clear from any taint of tobacco or alcohol, *will not, cannot*, during any time of its life on earth, be bribed or tempted to touch these abominations; whereas a child born of parents who use both will take as naturally to tobacco and whisky as does the father or mother. In this matter of transmitted vices, it is not necessary that both parents should practice them. The father alone doing so is sufficient. A husband using tobacco or alcoholic liquors, living in the same house, sleeping in the same bed with his wife, cannot do so without her organization absorbing from his, the debilitating essence of the excretory department of his body. This of itself is sufficient to transmit the habit, not to mention the husband's direct influence on the character of the unborn.

Again, if one or both of the parents lack system or order, they should, during the four weeks of preparation, as well as during the gestatory and nursing periods, cultivate assiduously the faculty of having a place for everything, and everything in its place. Order is the first great law of Nature. Order of thought of mind, of person, of surroundings, of action, is a fundamental necessity to success. Therefore, in all you do, from the least thing to the greatest, carefully observe order.

Again, if one or both parents lack truthfulness of character and action, they should strive, with the whole force of their better nature, not to lie in thought, word or action; for if there be one sin more wide-spread than another, in this our day and generation, it is that of lying

Again, if the parents lack reverence for God and things holy, they should cultivate the spiritual and devotional of their natures during this period.

Or if the parents have any other undesirable qualities of thought or action, great or small, which they do not desire to transmit, *they should persistently avoid them, and strenuously cultivate the opposite.*

So far, then, it is understood that the husband and wife are lovingly mated; that they are both in perfect health, free from all physical and mental incongruities; that they have lived strictly continent lives; that they have adopted the Plan of Life as their rule of life; that they have decided on the trade or profession desired in the offspring; that they have well-balanced organizations, and can generate offspring of happy, sunny, loving dispositions; having some one trait of character the exercise of which constitutes genius; and that, finally, they both knowingly, earnestly, and lovingly desire to produce a child.

Now we have arrived at the commencement of the period of Introductory Preparation—the four weeks preceding the time fixed for the generative act. This period should be characterized by its intensity of thought, feeling and action in the parents. They should work together lovingly, persistently, determinedly, in the direction for the formation of the character of the New Life. If they have bad habits of mind and body, they should, with the whole force of strong and determined wills, trample them under foot, annihilate them, forget them, and in their stead cultivate the right, the true, the pure and the beautiful.

This much determined on and acted on, brings us to the requisites necessary to establish, in the life-tissue of the unborn, the pursuit of life intended for its support and education, happiness and welfare, while in this world—a trade or profession—the faculty or combination of faculties required for such having in their origin and exercise the element of genius.

Just here a new difficulty may suggest itself. "What if we decide upon a trade or profession intended for an unborn boy, and a girl should present herself instead?" This can be avoided by attention to the paragraphs on the Theory of Sex in a former chapter. Yet, if these theories should fail in their application, no harm would be done—rather good. There should be no station in life in which man works that woman, under right conditions, should not be competent to fill. And she can and will fill it, in opposition to all opposers of "Woman's Rights," if from her birth she be endowed with the genius requisite for its demonstration. Endow the unborn woman with the genius for an inventor, lecturer, farmer, chemist, sculptor, editor, jeweler, navigator, soldier, etc., and she will, notwithstanding all opposition, assert her ability and individuality over her mediocre male competitors. Therefore, if, on closely following the Theory of Sex, it should fail in its hoped-for results, be not discouraged, *but carry out precisely the same line of preparation as would have been done if the birth had been of the male sex.*

I will, by way of illustrating the habits of thought and action the husband and wife should follow, give the details of preparation for one or more trades or professions :

Let us suppose that it is the desire of the parents to have a child who will be an inventor. In this case the parents should practically cultivate, by thought, word and action, the requirements for a genius for invention, and this choice of employment can be made through the attempt to discover a new motor power to the origination of some article or improvement that would apply to every-day household requirements, and that would be a necessity to the age. Make models of it, think of it, talk of it. They should subscribe to one or more scientific papers, should read the lives of eminent inventors, and especially study and interpret scientific works; the husband and wife to work together, think together, talk together, experiment together, with the enthusiasm of intensely interested souls.

Just here it would be well to observe that, previous to the commencement of any conformity to the Law of Genius, it is almost absolutely necessary that the parents should supply themselves with all the books and any papers that may be devoted to the specialty of the trade or profession they purpose endowing the New Life with.

This may entail some expense at the time, but nothing in comparison to what it would cost, in after years, to educate their children and train them for some special trade or profession, which they would probably have no taste for. And here it should be recorded that poets, novelists, inventors, etc., *are not made by education or training; they are and must be born with the quality of genius*, else all the teaching and training of a life-time will be of no avail. They will ever remain at or below the level of mediocrity; they never will, never possibly can, rise into the realms where genius predominates and directs.

There is no such thing as a "self-made man," concerning whom we hear and read so much of; for if a man has not transmitted to him by his parents the qualities necessary to great success, all the self-exertion of a life-time will not raise him above the line of mediocrity; whereas, if a child is endowed with genius—supposing he be suckled in poverty, reared in adversity, and attain his growth in rags—he will, despite his advent under such adverse circumstances, rise—slowly, it may be, but nevertheless surely—into the dignity of success, and the rank of that of a so-called "self-made man," which is but a name or indication of a worked-out and developed quality of transmitted genius.

In the expense for the education of a child, the debtor

side of the account should be opened before the child is generated—at least before the end of its pre-natal existence. This early opening of the account will do more toward the after-education of the child than all the schools, academies and colleges in Christendom.

If it is desired to make the New Life a fruit-grower (a more natural, pleasant, and happier life than which is not to be found), the parents should devote their whole attention to such. They should experiment with different varieties of fruits, should study the nature of fruit-sex, and the originating of new varieties, and they should together enthusiastically read, study and—eat fruit.

Or a geologist. They should together take long walks, into different parts of the country, and study the earth's nature or formation, and especially read, get interested in and admire books on the subject.

Or a working engineer. The wife, after discarding her fashionable, wide and long dress, and adopting a short, close, comfortable, and more natural costume, should have the privilege of assisting or working with her husband in a machine-shop or engine-room. They together, with their books on the subject, and papers with the latest mechanical discoveries, should get intensely interested in all the details of mechanical movements, power, velocity, etc.

Or a portrait painter. In the direction of artist-life, it is desirable that the wife have a slight taste for or knowledge of drawing. Yet, if the woman is anxious and earnest in the desire to have her child an artist, this may not be required. After reading books on the subject, the lives of eminent artists, and perhaps a few lessons (or lessons may be taken during the three periods of transmitted influence, though this would have a tendency to destroy originality), let the parents—but especially the wife—every day of this season of preparation practice drawing and painting. Let them encourage one another, help one another, and especially endeavor to excel each other. The same directions apply to landscape and animal painting, still life, etc.; only it must be remembered that in this department, as in all others, when they are capable of subdivision, *only one department or specialty must be adopted.* If it is the desire to have a child who will be a portrait painter—let it be *only* a portrait painter; if a painter of humorous scenes of life—let *only* the comic side of life be transferred to paper, and canvass.

Or, if a teacher, let the husband and wife take charge for a time of a small class of children—including their own, if they have any—on week-days, and a class on Sunday. Let them lovingly and knowingly educate these children, and in educating them let them apply the rudiments of phrenology and physiognomy in the character of the analysis of each pupil, and in their instruction and management let them be guided by this analysis. The position of teacher is one of the most important positions in this world, and I think no man or woman should be one unless they know how to apply the truths of phrenology. Beside this, the parents in turn should give the pupils short lectures or discourses on practical physiology, the right and wrong way of life, etc. The adoption of this pursuit for the unborn child, and its active and intense application by the parents insures to the New Life the genius for teaching, lecturing, and analyzing human character, thought and action. It is a splendid department in the world's workshop, this one of teacher and lecturer,—and one in which there is much mediocrity and very little genius.

Or, if a musician, let the parents learn, understand and practice music, and let it be but one of its many departments—sacred, operatic, social, martial, comic or national. Let them try to compose original pieces, and continue trying. A song-writer and music-composer combined in the same individual is rare, and yet it gives the composer a wonderful advantage to set music to his own words. The parents having the shadow of ability in this two-fold direction, should carry out and impress the desire on the soul of the unborn.

Or, if a short-hand reporter, let the parents obtain the books, learn the art, and together industriously practice it.

And so of any other trade or profession in life, from the smallest to the greatest, the positive, determined, and loving exercise of the faculties required in the knowledge of it will insure their great increase and improvement in the character of the New Life.

This Law of Genius can be followed by the poorest as well as richest, and is as much a requirement to the day-laborer as to the diplomatist. The quality of genius is as necessary to the making of a pair of boots as in the directing of an army ; as necessary in the hoeing of a hill of corn as in the construction of a steamship ; as necessary in the building of a stone fence as in the erection of a cathedral—and, for these reasons, this law should be observed by all mankind.

It must be understood that the parents, in the observance of this law during the period of transmitted influence, do not require to learn any trade or profession they fix on, so much as *to try* to learn it. *In this ten months of determined effort* lies concealed the influence that makes the child a genius. The active exercise of any organ or combination of organs, in the continued and persistent direction of any particular employment, causes a large flow of blood and increased nervous power in that organ, or combination of organs, which is reflected directly to the self-same organs of the child in utero, *which in their plastic state take on in size, quality and power, the elements which constitute genius.*

Therefore, parents will understand that in the exercise of the requirements essential to establish genius in their unborn child, it is not so necessary to acquire a full knowledge of the particular trade or profession as it is *to try, to experiment, to endeavor. Try hard, try persistently, try constantly, during the period of transmitted influence*, and my word on it—aye, my very life on it, the results will more than exceed your greatest hopes and most anxious desires.

Genius of itself, unless well directed, is not to be desired, and to this end there are what are called governing faculties, and faculties that assist and wait on the predominant power. The principal of these, and ones that should ever be present in the life-plans of the individual, are the moral sentiments. No child should be brought into the world without its having within it the essence of a religious nature, a Christian nature, a truthful nature, a hopeful nature, a benevolent, devotional, spiritual nature. Our existence on this earth being but transitory, and intended only as a preparation for a higher and holier life, the cultivation and transmission of the moral sentiments is a necessity to every man and woman born of the flesh.

And this being so, it is also a necessity to genius; for genius, guided by the religious element, is intensified and glorified; while, if directed by the propensities, it is apt to err, to trip and fall.

Therefore, when the parents have chosen the line of life for the unborn, in which they desire in full measure the quality of genius to be transmitted, they should exercise assiduously the religious of their natures. And this exercise does not imply only the attendance at church twice a week and an occasional prayer-meeting; for a man or woman may exercise the spiritual of their nature and never see the inside of a church. It is required that the parents live, in everyday thought, word and action, a religious life; for a religion that can be put on and taken off as a garment is not true religion—it is but a counterfeit. True religion implies that the parents daily and hourly should aspire after goodness, virtue and purity; that they knowingly do no wrong; that they look only on the bright side of life; that they have everpresent sympathy for the suffering, the wronged and oppressed, and do good without the hope of reward; that they possess faith, are spiritual-minded, and have a reverence for religion and things sacred. These attributes the parents should endeavor to cherish and intensify, and so incorporate them with the soul of the unborn. Every night and every morning, on bended knees, an earnest, whole-souled prayer should be sent heavenward, offering thanks for past successes, uttering hopes and desires for future plans. An intensely uttered earnest desire, repeated morning and evening, will originate the power to do, start the effort, and secure the end. In these morning and evening exercises, the husband and wife should alternately give voice to the expressions of thanksgiving and desire.

Closely allied to the power of genius and beauty of holiness is beauty of person. The fortunate possessor of beauty —a beauty that is the outgrowth of a strong and healthy body, lovable spirit, and educated intellect, has a magic talisman that wonderfully helps to success in all life's endeavors. It is wrong to discourage the culture of soul-beauty, for in all God's works there is an ever-present growth toward the beautiful. Parents can as easily have beautiful children as they can homely ones. It should be remembered, in this direction, that the highest type of beauty in the offspring is only attainable by those who live a pure, healthy, continent life, and who exercise the intellectual of their natures equally with the physical. The possession of surface, or doll-like beauty is not consonant with genius. To the end of attaining the beautiful in the child of genius, it is necessary for the parents to surround themselves with the beautiful in art and nature. Their living-room, which should be the largest, lightest and pleasantest room in the house, should have on its walls pictures that are gems of natural or idealized beauty. Plaster casts and bas-reliefs of face and form should fill convenient niches and corners, and if they live in or near a city, art and picture galleries should be frequented.

Now it might be that these requirements for the attainment of beauty in the offspring may not be within the reach of all parents; and this may be so and yet beautiful children may be generated. Let the parents get one picture—it may be an ideal face, or the face of a beautiful person—and let them get a picture of a perfect human form. The pictures may be lithographs, chromos, or photographs handsomely colored. Let the wife and husband impress the beautiful face of the one and the beautiful form of the other on their minds. Let them constantly admire them, and especially *earnestly* desire a child having a like resemblance, and they will without fail have embodied in their child's organization beauty of form and face.

" A gentleman had hanging in his room a beautiful portrait, of which a friend, as he once entered the room, when this gentleman's child was sitting in it, exclaimed : ' Why, what a fine likeness that is of your child !' 'No,' replied the gentleman, ' the child is the likeness of the picture.' ' How so ?' inquired his friend. It proved that the mother of his child had so intensely kept the image of this picture in her mind, and looked at it so much and so admiringly, during her pregnancy, that it reflected its beauties upon the young child's face ! It had daguerreotyped them there, both in color and in features."

As far back as the days of Jacob this law was understood and practiced, for in the Book of Genesis we are told that " Jacob took him rods of green poplar and of the hazel and chestnut tree, and pilled white streaks in them, and made the white appear which was in the rods. And he set the rods which he had pilled before the flocks in the gutters and in the watering-troughs when the flocks came to drink, that they should conceive when they came to drink. And the flocks conceived before the rods and brought forth cattle, ring-streaked, speckled and spotted. And it came to pass, whensoever the stronger cattle did conceive, that Jacob laid the rods before the eyes of the cattle in the gutters, that they might conceive among the rods. But when the cattle were feeble he put them not in ; so the feebler were Laban's and the stronger Jacob's."

Conceived under right conditions, a child may be made to take on any form of face and body—a beautiful face and perfect form, or a plain face and unsymmetrical form.   And this law, necessary to all parents and applicable to all natures, is as old as is God's conception of this beautiful world.

Next in importance to genius, holiness and beauty in the offspring, is a sunny, cheerful, laughing disposition.   One great cause of trouble in the rearing of a family—next to wrong habits of life—is the constantly fretful, irritable, peevish, cross, crying dispositions of the children, entailing on the parents a world of trouble in their care and management. Now it is just as easy for a mother to have a baby that will be of a cheerful, sunny nature, will be to her, in truth and in deed, "the sunshine of life," as it is to give birth to a child of a fretful and unhappy disposition, and be to her a source of life-long trouble.   To this end, during the period of transmitted influence, the parents *should not allow the shadow of a trouble to cross their paths*.   They should determine to make the best of everything.   If the house burn down, or they fail in business, or serious accidents occur, let them go uncomplainingly, joyously, even laughingly, and repair their losses.   As to the minor cares and troubles that infest life's pathway, let them persistently determine to laugh them out of countenance.   In all the greater troubles of life let them hopefully, lovingly and joyously look for and see only the bright side—the silver lining to the dark cloud ; if not at all times, at least during the season of transmitted influence.

Doing this faithfully and hopefully, you will have a child that, in its well directed genius, its perfect beauty, and happy, sunny, laughing nature, will be a joy, and glory, and happiness to you all the years of your life, and that will make you envied above all womankind.

A requisite to the acquirement of an intellectual, religious, beautiful and sunny nature in the life of the offspring, is a life of chastity—of strict continence.   I do earnestly advise that husbands and wives, in the practice of this Law of Genius, and during the period of transmitted influence, observe closely the Law of Continence, and refrain at all times and under all conditions from the sexual act, *save and only* as it is required to start the New Life on its voyage into life and eternity. Do you know why it is there is so much licentiousness in the world ? Do you know why a son, while yet a boy, practices self-abuse ? Do you know why a son, before even he has reached manhood, seeks through prostitution and seduction to foul, blot and weaken his soul and body ? Do you know why it is that a daughter allows her purity to be defiled, and takes so naturally, as many of them do, to a life of prostitution ? Would you, oh! parents, solve these questions ? You have but to ask yourselves : " did we obey this divine law of continence ? Did we, during the season of transmitted influence, refrain from all sexual sin ?" For if you have not done these things, and have exercised at any or all times the licentious that is within you, *you* have transmitted the qualities that went to make your boy an Onanist or a sensualist, and your daughter a prostitute, and *you* stand guilty before God for this great wrong done your children.

Much more might be said on the responsibility of parents in transmitting bad qualities of head and heart to their children, and the importance of the avoidance of these bad qualities by the parents during the period of transmitted influence; but as what I have already recorded will enable all parents desirous of propagating clean, pure, intelligent, truthful, religious, bright, happy, sunny, laughing offspring, it were needless to say more. Parents of advanced minds and ready convictions will need no further law or argument to decide them on following this only true mode of generating a new soul ; while of parents who are of slow, unconvinceable, mulish natures, all the laws and arguments of eighteen centuries compressed into a dozen pages would not persuade them to alter their mode of life. " No ; what was good enough for my parents and grandparents is good enough for me." In the rapid strides of social progress, this class of " doubting Thomases" must eventually see the folly of their *old* ways, and turn into the full light of this Science of a New Life, or else relapse into barbarism.

There is one more point to be touched on before ending this chapter, and that is the subject of money. The feverish pursuit of money is and will be a sad preventive to the general adoption of this Science of a New Life, for the hot haste for wealth leads mankind very far from the true line of life. The devotee of the god Mammon must, if he desires success, devote every hour of his life—apart from the few daily hours applied to eating and sleeping—in getting and keeping other men's earnings ; and in doing this, other men's wants and sufferings are ignored, and the human in his nature is blunted. He cannot enjoy the pleasures of life—not even the air he breathes, the food he eats, or the water he drinks. Wife and children are to him a very secondary consideration. Witness our friend Robinson ; " he has made one fortune, but did not consider it large enough, and is now busy in making another. He is off to the city at 8 A.M., never returning till 8 P.M., and then so worn out and jaded that he cares for nothing beyond his dinner and sleep. His beautiful house, his conservatories and pleasure-grounds delight not him ; he never enjoys—he only pays for them. He has a charming wife and a beautiful family, but he sees little of either—the latter, indeed, he never sees at all, except on Sundays. He comes home so tired that the children would only worry him. To them 'papa' is almost a stranger. They know him only as a periodical incumbrance on the household life, which generally makes it much less pleasant. And when they grow up it is to such a totally different existence from his, that they usually quietly ignore him. 'Oh, papa cares nothing about this ; no, no, we never think of telling papa anything'—until some day papa will die and leave them a quarter of a million. But how much better to leave them what no money can ever buy—the remembrance or a father ! A real father, whose guardianship made home safe—whose tenderness filled it with happiness—who was companion and friend, as well as ruler and guide—whose influence interpenetrated every day of their lives, every feeling of their hearts—who was not merely the author of their beings, but the originator and educator of everything good in them—the visible father on earth, who made them understand dimly ' our Father which is in heaven.' "

The feverish pursuit of wealth is to be deprecated and avoided by all men whose desire it is to " live while they live." Money, I grant you, is a requirement in life's travels; but in getting it make haste slowly—very slowly. Do not start in life with the intention of accumulating a fortune and then retiring to enjoy it. This retiring on the getting of a fortune is one of the great mistakes of life ; for no man or woman should think of retiring from life's work until they retire to their graves. The man who lives a true and pure life, works until he is forty, sixty, or ninety years of age— every day of his life, until the day comes when, tired of life's work, he desires and longs to leave this world; and he lies down to sleep, and in sleeping, without fear or pain, his soul escapes to higher realms.

Do not let the getting of money interfere with your endeavors for a true life. Get it by all legitimate means, but get only what is required for your present wants, and to guard against prospective accidents. In doing this you insure more practical enjoyment and happiness than ever was dreamed of by the man whose sole object in life is the getting of money.

This brings us once more to the commencement point in the period of transmitted influence—the four weeks of introductory preparation. The husband and wife, having decided on the right course to be adopted for influencing the character of the New Life, should with all the force of their wills and intensity of their natures practice, by thought, word and action, the desire for the implanting of a right life in the New Life. Especially should the husband, during this preliminary four weeks, exercise his department of thought and action, for it is his only chance to influence directly the character of the unborn. The following is an illustration from Darwin :

"A country gentleman, being much enamored of the daughter of a farmer on his estate, was unable to conquer her virtuous scruples; but her image being constantly present to his mind, his wife conceived and bore him a child whose features presented a perfect resemblance to the object of his affections."

It must not be forgotten that the husband and wife must have precisely the same objects in view, and that each parent, during this four weeks of introductory preparation, must, in thought, word and deed, act out this object, with all the vitalized intensity of will and desire their natures can bring to the effort.

PART SECOND.

THE CONSUMMATION

CHAPTER XIV.

THE CONCEPTION OF A NEW LIFE.

PROPER season for conception is an important consideration in the generating of a strong and healthy offspring.

The best month for this purpose is the month of August or September; this would bring the birth of the child in the month of May, when the New Life would commence its existence at the same time the old earth renews the youth of its years. The advantage in this choice of months, if any choice be necessary, is that the child can enjoy what it so much requires—out-door life. This, of course, applies only to the colder belts of the continent. Too much out-door light and exercise cannot possibly be furnished the young life, and at no season of the year is the earth so enjoyable to the old as well as young as in the spring, with its wealth of green verdure and its fragrant buds and blossoms, its warm atmosphere, clear sky and bright sun. Childhood revels in it—grows strong, healthy and bright in it. If a child of a score of weeks old, born in the genial spring-time, was gifted with language, its uttered reverie would run in this wise:

"Well, here I am—there is no doubt of that; but where I am is a question for early consideration. I have traveled, and know all about where I am. I have been into the garden and fields, and my private opinion to you is that this is a pretty world. When I was out I felt happy—very happy. I revelled on the green grass and among the beautiful flowers; I tried to catch the sun's rays, but could not. I could, I think, live here for ever, so bright and beautiful is this new existence. I have had a happy time; but I am very tired. I think, mother, your baby is going to sleep."

Children born in the fall and winter of a necessity have to be much in-doors, and this confinement in badly ventilated rooms greatly tends to fretting and sickness; whereas, if born in the spring, and having every day out-door exercise, their vital powers get so strengthened as to enable them to enjoy cold weather, and resist any bad effects arising from it.

As mentioned on a former page, conception should occur immediately following the cessation of the menses or monthly courses, because at this time the egg is in its firmest and freshest state, and, when impregnated, is more likely at this time than later to develop a strong and healthy organism.

Next in importance is the time of day that should be selected for sexual congress. As though there was something sinful and wrong in it, the hours of darkness are usually employed for this purpose. There is as little of reason used in this choice of hours, by the majority of mankind, as in the observance of any other department of the reproductive law. Now the best and only physiological time to generate a new life is in the broad light of a clear, bright day. Light implies health; darkness disease. Light is the source of life; darkness is the synonym of death. Let your New

Life be a child of light rather than of darkness. Not only should the hour of darkness be avoided, but also dark, cloudy and rainy days. *Only a clear, bright day, when the sun is shining, should be employed in which to generate the New Life.*

The hour of day most desirable for conception is next to be considered. The human body never has the same force of vital power throughout the twenty-four hours. Men and woman are never so strong at night as they are in the morning, and they are not so strong in the morning as they are in the middle of the day. After rising, the bodily powers increase until noon, after which they gradually decline until the setting of the sun. From nightfall until sunrise the strength of the body is at its lowest ebb—its weakest state. Therefore, the healthy husband and wife are in their perfection of physical and mental strength at between eleven and twelve o'clock in the forenoon, *and this is the only period in which a child of genius, beauty and strength should be generated.*

The sleeping-room should be one of the largest, pleasantest, best lighted and ventilated in the house. No blind or curtain should ever obstruct the sun's rays from entering therein ; and at night, as well as during the day, the pure air of heaven should be allowed to circulate freely.

To recapitulate : The husband and wife—lovingly united, in perfect health and strength—mutually desire to generate a pure, bright, happy, healthy love-child, having implanted in its organization the qualities of genius, chastity and holiness. They have fixed on the qualities to be transmitted, and the date for conception. They have assiduously, earnestly and lovingly observed the four weeks of preliminary preparation. They have slept during this time in different beds, if not in different rooms. The morning—betokening a clear, bright, beautiful day—arrives. On arising, they take their usual morning bath, and dress in loose, bright, enjoyable costume. If they never have heretofore exercised the spiritual of their natures, let them this morning, on bended knees, before the throne of grace, give earnest utterance to their thanks and desires.

O God, our God ! This morning, in the full glory of Thy ever-present presence, we supplicate the aid of Thy love, Thy glory, Thy power, in this our souls' desire. Into this New Life implant, in full measure, the wishes of our hearts. Of and from Thee let the light come that is to guide it into life, through life, and into eternity. Make it—as we so earnestly desire—a bright, happy, loving and beautiful child. Implant in its organism the qualities that will enable it to live and grow toward perfection. Give it, we pray Thee, the elements of a holy life, so that all its thoughts, words and actions will be a reflex of Thy ever-present loving care. And to the end of doing these our desires, impart, O God, strength of will, firmness of purpose, purity of life, and the full measure of Thy daily and hourly presence. And to Thee, O Thou Ancient of Days, be the glory, the honor and praise.

An enjoyable walk and saunter, of an hour or more, into the pleasant morning sunshine. Breakfast at about eight o'clock—a breakfast of plain, unstimulating food. Again into the open air and bright sunshine ; and for a couple of hours the husband and wife should lovingly and enthusiastically exchange thoughts, hopes and desires. Keeping their natures as is the bright sun, with not the smallest cloud intervening to darken their joy and happiness, they enter their chamber, and in the clear light of day the New Life is conceived and generated—a new soul started into eternity.

> " A child is born ; now take the germ and make it
>   A bud of moral beauty. Let the dews
> Of knowledge, and the light of virtue wake it
>   In richest fragrance and in purest hues."

CHAPTER XV.

THE PHYSIOLOGY OF INTRA-UTERINE GROWTH.

 MMEDIATELY the egg is fe-
cundated, the mucus membrane
of the uterus takes on an activity of growth. It increases
in thickness, becomes tumified
and vascular, and projects in
rounded convolutions into the
cavity of the uterus. "In this
process, the tubules of the uterus increase in length, and also
become wider, so that their
open mouths may be readily
seen, by the naked eye, upon
the uterine surface, as numerous minute perforations. The
blood-vessels of the mucus membrane also enlarge and multiply, and inosculate freely with each other, so that the vascular network encircling the tubules becomes more extensive
and abundant.

"The thick, rich, soft, vascular and velvety lining, the result of this process, was formerly supposed to be an entirely
new product, but it is now known to be no other than the
mucus membrane, greatly thickened, but still retaining all its
natural connections and its original anatomical structure."

At the fundus of the uterus, in one of the projecting convolutions, the fecundated egg is lodged. At this point of

lodgment, the mucus membrane takes on a still more rapid development, projecting its folds, and so growing up and around the egg as to inclose and shut it off from the rest of the uterus. This new growth of the mucus membrane is called the Decidua Reflexa, while the original lining membrane of the uterus is called the Decidua Vera.

The egg, which during this time has considerably enlarged, throws out projecting filaments (Fig. 14), which insinuate themselves, as they grow, into the folds of the decidual sur-

FIG. 12. IMPREGNATED UTERUS,

Showing the formation of Decidua. The Decidua is represented in black; and the egg is seen at the fundus of the uterus, engaged between two of its projecting convolutions.

FIG. 14. APPEARANCE OF EGG AT FOURTEENTH DAY.

FIG. 13. IMPREGNATED UTERUS,

Showing how the projecting folds of the Decidua have grown up around and completely inclosed the Egg.

face (Fig. 15) in contact with the egg, and spreading in all directions from its external surface. It is through these filaments the nutritious fluids are imparted for its nourishment.

As the egg increases in growth—a greater supply of nourishment being necessary—the decidua in contact with that part of the projecting filaments of the chorion (Fig. 16) continues to grow, while over the remaining portion of its surface they disappear, and become concentrated and developed at the situation of the future placenta, which it helps to form.

The germ-cell or egg, consisting of a vitellus or yelk, and its cover of vitelline membrane, is fecundated by the sperm-cell, and is then called the embryonic cell.

This embryonic cell absorbs into itself a portion of the nutriment prepared within the ovary for its use, and thus commences its own development.

And now, to quote from Prof. Dalton—to whom I am indebted, in great measure, for the illustrations and subject-matter of this chapter—"a remarkable change takes place in

FIG. 15. IMPREGNATED UTERUS, Showing connection between villosities of Chorion and decidual membranes.

FIG. 16. PREGNANT UTERUS, Showing formation of Placenta, by the united development of a portion of the Decidua and the villosities of the Chorion.

the impregnated egg, which is known as the spontaneous division, or *segmentation*, of the vitellus. A furrow first shows itself, running around the globular mass of the vitellus in a vertical direction, which gradually deepens until it has divided the vitellus into two separate halves or hemispheres (Fig. 17, *a*). Almost at the same time, another furrow, running at right angles with the first, penetrates also the substance of the vitellus, and cuts it in a transverse direction. The vitellus is thus divided into four equal portions (Fig. 17, *b*), the edges and angles of which are rounded off, and which are still contained in the cavity of the vitelline membrane. The spaces between them and the internal surface of the vitelline membrane are occupied by a transparent fluid.

"The process thus commenced goes on by a successive

formation of furrows and sections in various directions. The four vitelline segments already produced are thus subdivided into sixteen, the sixteen into sixty-four, and so on, until the whole vitellus is converted into a mulberry-shaped mass, composed of minute, nearly spherical bodies, which are called the

'vitelline spheres' (Fig. 17, *c*). These vitelline spheres have a somewhat firmer consistency than the original substance of the vitellus, and this consistency appears to increase as they successively multiply in numbers and diminish in size. At last they have become so abundant as to be closely crowded

together, compressed into polygonal forms, and flattened against the internal surface of the vitelline membrane (Fig. 17, *d*). They have by this time been converted into true animal cells; and these cells, adhering to each other by their adjacent edges, form a continuous, organized membrane, which is termed the *Blastodermic Membrane.*

"The next change which takes place consists in the division or splitting of the blastodermic membrane into two layers, which are

known as the *external* and *internal layers of the blastodermic membrane.* They are both still composed exclusively of cells; but those of the external layer are usually smaller and

FIG. 17. SEGMENTA-
TION OF VITELLUS.

more compact, while those of the internal are rather larger and looser in texture.   The egg then presents the appearance of a globular sac, the walls of which consist of three concentric layers, lying in contact with and inclosing each other, namely—first, the structureless vitelline membrane on the outside; second, the external layer of the blastodermic membrane, composed of cells; and third, the internal layer of blastodermic membrane, also composed of cells. The cavity of the egg is occupied by a transparent fluid, as before mentioned.

"The entire process of the segmentation of the vitellus and the formation of the blastodermic membrane is one of the most remarkable and important of all the changes which take place during the development of the egg. It is by this process that the simple globular mass of the vitellus, composed of an albuminous matter and oil granules, is converted into an organized structure. For the blastodermic membrane, though consisting only of cells nearly uniform in size and shape, is nevertheless a truly organized membrane, made up of fully formed anatomical elements. It is, moreover, the first sign of distinct organization which makes its appearance in the egg; and as soon as it is completed the body of the new fœtus is formed. The blastodermic membrane is, in fact, the body of the fœtus. It is at this time, it is true, exceedingly simple in texture; but we shall see hereafter that all the future organs of the body, however varied and complicated in structure, arise out of it, by modification and development of its different parts.

"The two layers of the blastodermic membrane, above described, represent together all the organs of the fœtus. They are intended, however, for the production of two different systems; and the entire process of their development may be expressed as follows: The external layer of the blastodermic membrane produces the spinal column and all the organs of animal life; while the internal layer produces the intestinal canal and all the organs of vegetative life.

"The first sign of advancing organization, in the external layer of the blastodermic membrane, shows itself in a thickening and condensation of its structure. This thickened portion has the form of an elongated, oval-shaped spot, termed the 'embryonic spot' (Fig. 18), the wide edges of which are somewhat more opaque than the rest of the blastodermic membrane. Inclosed within these opaque edges is a narrower, colorless and transparent space, the 'area pellucida,' and in its centre is a delicate line or furrow, running longitudinally from front to rear which is called the 'primitive trace.'

FIG. 18. IMPREGNATED EGG,

With commencement of formation of embryo; showing embryonic spot, area pellucida, and primitive trace.

"On each side of the primitive trace, in the area pellucida, the substance of the blastodermic membrane rises up in such a manner as to form two nearly parallel vertical plates or ridges, which approach each other over the dorsal aspect of the fœtus, and are therefore called the 'dorsal plates.' They at last meet on the median line, so as to inclose the furrow above described and convert it into a canal. This afterward becomes the spinal canal, and in its cavity is formed the spinal cord, by a deposit of nervous matter upon its internal surface. At the anterior extremity of this canal its cavity is large and rounded, to accommodate the brain and medulla oblongata; at its posterior extremity it is narrow and pointed, and contains the extremity of the spinal cord.

"The process of development may be briefly recapitulated as follows:

"1. The blastodermic membrane, produced by the segmentation of the vitellus, consists of two cellular layers—an external and an internal blastodermic layer.

"2. The external layer of the blastodermic membrane incloses by its dorsal plates the cerebro-spinal canal, and by its abdominal plates the abdominal or visceral cavity.

"3. The internal layer of the blastodermic membrane forms the intestinal canal, which becomes lengthened and convoluted, and communicates with the exterior by a mouth and anus of secondary formation.

"4. Finally, the cerebro-spinal axis and its nerves, the skeleton, the organs of special sense, the integument and the muscles are developed from the external blastodermic layer;

while the anterior and posterior extremities are formed from the same layer by a process of sprouting or continuous growth."

From the external layer of the blastodermic membrane is formed the amnion or inner membrane, which secretes upon its inner surface the liquid in which is suspended the fœtus during the whole period of gestation.

From the inner layer of the blastodermic membrane is formed the allantois, which on attaining its full growth entirely surrounds the fœtus, is united with the vitelline membrane and outer lamina of the amniotic fold, and is then

FIG. 19. HUMAN OVUM AT THE
END OF FIRST MONTH.

FIG, 20. HUMAN OVUM AT END
OF THIRD MONTH.

termed the chorion, and thus becomes the sole external membrane of the egg.

The chorion or outer covering (Fig. 14) throws out villi, which after a time gather at one point, uniting with the decidua or inner surface of the uterus, and forms the placenta, by which the fœtus is nourished from the blood of the mother.

Fig. 19 shows the human ovum at the end of the first month.   In the middle of the amniotic fluid is seen the umbilical vesicle, which contains the fluid for the first nourishment of the embryo.   It after a time is absorbed, and after the third month the sac gradually disappears.   Next is seen the amnion, which secretes the amniotic fluid in which the fœtus floats; and lastly, the chorion, which was formed from the internal layer of the blastodermic membrane, and on which is seen the villi, which carry nourishment to the embryo. As the fœtus grows, the tufts of the chorion greatly develop at one point (Fig. 19), disappearing elsewhere, and the quantity of the amniotic fluid continues to increase, to allow the free movements of the fœtus. At the same time, the umbilical cord elongates, in proportion to the increased size of the amniotic cavity. It contains the vein and two arteries through which the fœtus receives its nourishment. A gelatinous matter, covering the vessels with a thick, elastic envelope, protects them from injury.

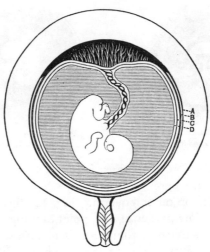

Fig. 21. Gravid Human Uterus and Contents,

Showing the relations of the Cord, Placenta, Membranes, etc., about the end of the seventh month.
A, Decidua Vera; B, Decidua Reflexa; C, Chorion; D, Amnion.

In Fig. 21 is shown the relation of the cord, placenta, membranes, etc., about the end of the seventh month. The decidua vera (A) and the decidua reflexa (B) about this time fuse together and form a single thin layer. The chorion (C), from which is seen the vascular tufts which go to make the placenta. At this period the amniotic fluid has so increased as to fill the cavity of the uterus, and the amnion (D) is seen lying close up to the chorion, and surrounding and forming the umbilical cord.

As already mentioned, during the first weeks of the growth of the embryo it is nourished, as the young chicken is, by the yelk of the egg. But soon the villi of the chorion gather into a compact mass, and become adherent to some portion of the uterus. There is thus formed a placenta, made of two portions—the maternal side (Fig. 22) toward the

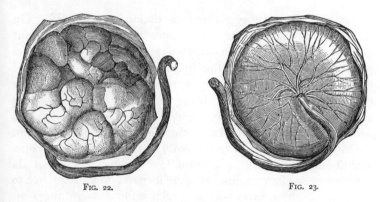

FIG. 22.   FIG. 23.

walls of the uterus, and the fœtal (Fig. 23), in which the vessels unite into two arteries and one vein, which with their envelopments form the umbilical cord and communicate with the fœtal heart. The vein carries red, arterial, nutritive blood from the placenta to the child, to be distributed to all parts of its system. The two arteries carry the dark, venous blood from the child back again to the placenta, there to be purified and rendered nutritious.

The blood itself does not pass from the system of the mother to the child, or from the child to the mother; but, though it has its own individual circulation and life, all its nutriment, from the time this connection is formed until it is severed at birth, comes from the mother.

The placenta is circular in shape, having two flattened surfaces; it is from one to two inches in thickness in its central and thickest part, and six or eight inches in diameter. Its flattened surface, most distant from the child, is closely attached, and adheres tightly to some portion of the inner surface of the womb. It is formed for merely a temporary use, and does not constitute, in any proper sense, a part of either the mother or child.

The placenta, the umbilical cord, and the membranes of the ovum, constitute the after-birth.

The growth of the egg after fecundation is very rapid. On the *tenth day* it has the appearance of a semi-transparent grayish flake. On the *twentieth day* it is nearly the size of a pea, filled with fluid, in the middle of which is an opaque spot, presenting the first appearance of an embryo, which may be clearly seen as an oblong or curved body, according as it is viewed, and plainly visible to the naked eye on the *fourteenth day*. Its weight, at this time, is about one grain.

On the *twenty-first day* the embryo resembles an ant, or a lettuce-seed; its length is from four to five lines, and its weight three or four grains. Many of its parts now commence to show themselves, especially the cartilaginous beginnings of the bones of the spinal column, the heart, brain, etc.

On the *thirtieth day* the embryo is as large as a horse-fly, and resembles a worm bent together. There are as yet no limbs, and the head is larger than the rest of the body. When stretched out, the embryo is nearly half an inch long.

Toward the *fifth week*, the head increases greatly in proportion to the remainder of the body, and the rudimentary eyes are indicated by two black spots turned toward the sides, and the heart exhibits its external form, being a tolerably close resemblance to that in the adult.

In the *seventh week* bone begins to form in the lower jaw

and clavicle. Narrow streaks on each side of the vertebral column show the beginning of the ribs; the heart is perfecting its form, the brain enlarged, and the eyes and ears growing more perfect, and the limbs sprouting from the body. The lungs are mere sacs, about one line in length, and the trachea is a delicate thread, but the liver is very large. The arms are still imperforate. In the seventh week are formed the renal capsules and kidneys, and the sexual organs are speedily evolved, but the sex of the fœtus is not determined until some time after. The embryo is now nine lines or three-fourths of an inch in length.

At *two months* the forearm and hand can be distinguished, but not the arm; the hand is larger than the forearm, but it, is not supplied with fingers; the distinction of sex is yet difficult; the eyes are prominent, but the lids, from being still rudimentary, do not cover the eyeball; the nose forms an obtuse eminence; the nostrils are rounded and separated; the mouth is gaping, and the epidermis can be distinguished from the true skin. The embryo is from one and a half to two inches long, and weighs from three to five drachms, the head forming more than one-third of the whole.

At from *sixty* to *seventy days* the development is rapid, and all the parts are in the course of progressive formation. The eye enlarges, the lids are visible, the nose grows prominent, the mouth enlarges, the external ear is formed, the brain is soft and pulpy, the neck well defined, and the heart fully developed.

At the end of the *three months* the eyelids are distinct, but shut, the lips are drawn together, the forehead and nose are clearly traceable, and the organs of generation are prominent in both sexes. The heart beats with force, the larger vessels carry red blood, the fingers and toes are well defined, muscles begin to be developed, and the fœtus is four or five inches in length, and weighs from two to four ounces.

At the *fourth month* the embryo takes the name of *fœtus;* its growth is not so rapid in the commencement as at the end of this month.   The body is six to eight inches in length, and weighs from seven to eight ounces.   The face still remains but little developed, although more elongated than it has previously been.   The eyes, nostrils and mouth are closed.   The skin has a rosy color, and the muscles now produce a sensible motion.   A fœtus born at this period might live for several hours.

At *five months* the length of the body is eight to ten inches, and it weighs from eight to eleven ounces.

At *six months* the length is eleven to twelve and a half inches, and the weight about one pound.   The hair appears upon the head, the eyes closed, the eyelids somewhat thicker and their margins, as well as the eyebrows, are studded with very delicate hairs.

At *seven months* every part has increased in volume and perfection ; the bony system is nearly complete.   Length, twelve to fourteen inches ; weight, two and a half to three pounds.   If born at this period, the fœtus is able to breathe, cry and nurse, and may live to grow up, if properly cared for.   It is frequently too feeble to endure being either washed or dressed, and must necessarily sleep nearly the whole time, except for the short periods required for the taking of its food.   Its power of generating heat within itself is also extremely feeble ; it should, therefore, be kept wrapped in a warmed, soft flannel blanket, and laid close beside the mother, or held in the lap of some other person, in order that their warmth or animal heat may be constantly imparted to it.

At *eight months* the fœtus seems to grow rather in thickness than in length ; it is only sixteen to eighteen inches long, and yet weighs from four to five pounds.   The skin is very red, and covered with down and a considerable quantity of sebaceous matter.   The lower jaw, which was at first very short, is now as long as the upper one.

Finally, *at term*, the fœtus is from nineteen to twenty-three inches long, and weighs from six to nine pounds.   The red blood circulates in the capillaries, and the skin performs the function of perspiration.

There is nothing more interesting in the growth of the foetus than is the development of the face. Says Dalton:

"From the sides of the cephalic mass five buds or processes shoot out and grow toward each other, so as to approach the centre of the oval orifice (Fig. 24.) One of them grows directly downward from the frontal region, and is called the frontal or intermaxillary process, because it afterward contains in its lower extremity the intermaxillary bones, in which the incisor teeth of the upper jaw are inserted.

"The next process originates from the side of the opening, and, advancing toward the median line, forms, with its fellow of the opposite side, the superior maxilla. The processes of the remaining pair also grow from the side, and form, by their subsequent union upon the median line, the inferior maxilla. The inferior maxillary bone is finally consolidated, in man, into a single piece, but remains permanently divided, in the lower animals, by a suture upon the median line.

FIG. 24. HEAD OF HUMAN EMBRYO, At about the twentieth day. After Longet; from a specimen in the collection of M. Coste.

"As the frontal process grows from above downward, it becomes double at its lower extremity, and at the same time two offshoots show themselves upon its sides, which curl round and inclose two circular orifices, the opening of the anterior nares; the offshoots themselves become the alæ nasi (Fig. 25.) The mouth at this period is very widely open, owing to the imperfect development of the upper and lower jaw, and the incomplete formation of the lips and cheeks.

"The processes of the superior maxilla continue their growth, but less rapidly than those of the inferior; so that the two sides of the lower jaw are already consolidated with each other, while those of the upper jaw are still separate.

"As the processes of the superior maxilla continue to enlarge, they also tend to unite with each other on the median line, but are prevented from doing so by the intermaxillary processes which grow down between them. They then unite with the intermaxillary processes, which have at the same time united with each other, and the upper jaw and lip are thus completed (Fig. 26.) The external edge of the alæ nasi (wing of the nose) also adheres to the superior maxillary process and unites with it, leaving only a curved crease or furrow, as a sort of cicatrix, to mark the line of union between them.

FIG. 25.
HEAD OF HUMAN EMBRYO,
At about end of sixth week. After Dalton.

"The eyes, at an early period, are situated upon the sides of the head, so that they cannot be seen in a front view (Fig. 24.) As development proceeds, they come to be situated further forward (Fig. 25), their axis being divergent and directed obliquely forward aud outward. At a later period still they are placed on the anterior plane of the face (Fig. 26), and have their axis nearly parallel and looking directly forward. This change in the situation of the eyes is effected by the more rapid growth of the posterior and lateral parts of the head, which enlarge in such a manner as to alter the relative position of the parts seated in front of them."

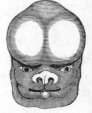

FIG. 26.
HEAD OF HUMAN EMBRYO,
About the end of the second month. After Dalton.

POSITION OF FŒTUS.—The fœtus lies curved within the bag formed by the membranes; usually the head is somewhat flexed, the chin resting on the breast; the feet are bent up in front of the legs—the latter strongly flexed on the thighs; the knees are separated from each other, but the heels lie close together on the back part of the thighs; the arms are placed so as to receive, as it were, the chin between the hands. The fœtus, thus folded on itself, forms an oval, whose longest diameter is about eleven inches. Why the fœtus takes this position in utero has not yet been clearly explained.

CHAPTER XVI.

PERIOD OF GESTATIVE INFLUENCE.

N the fecundated ovum—the size of which is one two-hundred-and-fortieth of an inch in diameter, and a thousand of which could be placed on the thumbnail—is contained the principle of a new life—the elements of a new soul. Embodied in its undeveloped organization is the future statesman or orator, farmer or mechanic. Ingrained in its tissue may be scrofula, consumption, insanity or deformity. This minute speck represents an individual who eventually will be temperate, or else a drunkard or glutton; who will be chaste or licentious; whose life will be a success or a failure, depending alone or altogether on what the parents choose to make it.

From the moment the egg is fecundated there is life—for that matter, there must be life in the germ-cell and sperm-cell before impregnation, else there could be no conception; but when conception does occur, the life of a new being is established, and this new being has within it the elements of a new soul, as well as body. This soul grows and expands with the growth of the body, and in harmony with the quality and character of the body.

The medium of connection between the soul, which is immortal, and the body, which is mortal, is the nervous system. Through the wonderful system of nerves, the soul takes on the impress of the body's habits of thought and action; and through the nervous system does the soul, in its intensity of action, find expression through the body. During ante-natal life, the soul, in harmony with the body, takes on the character transmitted to it by the parents, and this character, in a great measure, clings to it through post-natal life, and after death into eternity.

This birth of the soul in common with the creation of the body is a fact that carries with it great significance, and one that, more than aught else, should determine parents to beget a new being under loving and holy conditions.

There being no nervous connection between the foetus and mother, it is through the blood of the mother *only* that the body of the child is nourished, its character influenced, and its habits of life formed.

This being so, the first great requisite in the mother, during this gestative period of influence—next to right habits of thought and action—is a correct diet. Her food, during this period, makes not only her own blood, but also the blood of the child; and this blood, vitalized by her nervous system, imparts its vitality to the nervous and muscular system of the child, and in this way is the character of the new life influenced. A man or woman's daily thoughts and actions affect and impress the secretions of the nutritive system, and through this the blood; and in this way, through its reaction on the nervous system, the character of the man increases for better or worse, as may be. It might with truth be said, that a drop of blood represents in its elements the character of the individual who manufactured it.

The mother of a gloomy, morose, sullen or fretful disposition impresses these qualities on every globule of blood that comes through her system, and, as a necessity, on the rapid-growing tissues of the child, which after its birth will have embodied in its organization all these undesirable qualities.

Undeniably, the best food for mothers, during this period of pregnancy, is fruit and vegetables, in as nearly their natural condition as possible. When apples, grapes, peaches, plums, etc., are eaten, the skins of such fruit should invariably be eaten along with the substance. One great trouble with pregnant women is costiveness, and this can in a great measure be avoided by the adoption of this rule. Graham bread, so highly recommended as the true staff of life, is to be used in very moderate quantities during this season, for it has a tendency to prematurely harden the bones, causing increased difficulty in parturition. Pure blood being a requirement in the right growth of the child, it is almost unnecessary to say that a clean, sweet, lovable baby cannot be grown by a mother who uses fat meats, pork, spices, grease, tea, coffee, beer, whisky, wine, etc. ; and even lean, fresh or healthy beef or mutton, the least hurtful of flesh diets, are not fit to make babies of the right stamp.

It is a popular opinion with women, during this period, that they require double or treble their usual quantity of food. This is a mistake, and is the cause of much physical suffering. A healthy woman will not and ought not to require (in the early months of pregnancy) more than her usual amount of food, and she will not have that craving after all manner of food that many women have. This craving for and surfeiting with unusual articles of diet proceeds entirely from a disorganized nervous system, and not from the fœtus in utero, and is easily avoided by the adoption of a right life.

A woman, during this period of gestative influence, if she desires to carry out the Law of Genius, should closely follow the Plan of Life given in a former chapter, excepting the farinaceous food, which should be used in moderate quantities.

The only allowable drink to be used during this period is water, and if spices and condiments are abstained from very little of that will be required.

It should be understood by parents that, through the wrong use and abuse of food—over-eating, fast eating, indulging in hot food and hot drinks, eating indigestible food, as new bread, pastry, pickles, sweetmeats, oily and greasy meats, mince pie, condiments, etc.—it is as easy to transmit dyspepsia, with its attendant horrors, to the unborn child, as it is to transmit much less important attributes. Dyspepsia is as often hereditary as is consumption, scrofula, insanity, etc. This of itself is an argument that should influence the mother in a right choice of drink and diet.

Next in importance to proper food is pure air and light. The mother should at all seasons have an abundance of pure air, and especially so during her sleeping hours. Open fire-places are at all times the most desirable ; but where tight-fitting stoves are used, ample arrangements should be made for thorough ventilation. In the room in which the mother lives, the light of the sun should never be obstructed by blind or curtain. Many people, thinking much more of their carpets and furniture than of their own health, keep their houses, by the aid of blinds, curtains or trees, in a state of Egyptian darkness. No more fatal error ever was made. Under the influence of the sun's heat, air and moisture, a new seed or plant will germinate, grow, and gradually develop into health and beauty of leaf and flower ; whereas, if kept in darkness, it may grow to a certain extent, but its leaves and stem are of a sickly yellowish hue, and is in its appearance an undesirable thing. This is applicable, with much greater force, to the human organism. A child of light is a child of joy, of purity, of health ; while a child whose mother has lived in a dark, unventilated room during this period will be a child of many troubles,—deformities, rickets, bad teeth, crooked spine, pale and sickly-looking skin, soft and flabby muscles, enfeebled digestive organs—altogether a most undesirable list of results. Not only should pregnant women, but all mankind should live in the light of the life-giving sun, and only court darkness during the hours of sleep.

The daily bath, during this full term of nine months, should never be neglected. The best time in the day for bathing is in the forenoon, between eleven and twelve o'clock, when the body is at its highest state of health and strength. As before mentioned, the taking of it should occupy as short a time as is consistent with its being thoroughly done. After drying and friction with the hands, the mother for a few moments should allow the full rays of the sun to fall direct on her nude body, and during this time she should take deep inspirations of pure air, filling her lungs to their full extent. This water, sun and air-bath—after dressing in part or in whole—should be followed by a rest of fifteen or thirty minutes in bed or on a lounge.

It is almost unnecessary to again say that the dress of the woman during this period must be perfectly loose, having no constrictions of any kind or nature, and that the extremities be warmly and comfortably clad.

A full measure of sleep should always be secured. A regular hour of going to bed and rising should be established and faithfully adhered to. No feathers are to be allowed near the bed, and the room to be large, pleasant and well ventilated.

This brings us to the habits of thought and action to be observed by the mother, in order to secure in her offspring health and beauty of form and feature, and the elements of character that in their action will constitute genius.

The period of gestative influence is to be divided into two sections—the first four months and the last five months. During the first four months the physical in the mother should predominate, while during the last five months the mental should predominate.

The positive and intense exercise of the mental faculties,

during the period of preliminary preparation, should, immediately following conception, be arrested, and no more intense exercise of the mental power should be essayed until the arrival of the fifth month of pregnancy.

During this first four months of gestative influence, the mother should daily take ample physical exercise, and the best exercise she can have is walking. Alone, or with her husband or other companion, she should, about ten o'clock in the forenoon, go on a walk of from three to six miles. On returning, a bath should be taken as above, and a short rest afterward. It is important that during this walk the mother feel no sense of being tired. By pleasant talk, if with a companion, or, if alone, by pleasant thoughts of her plans and purposes in the growth and life of the new being, the time in walking will pass unperceived—otherwise there may be present a feeling of lassitude, which ultimately may do her more harm than good. Having a free, loose, comfortable dress, with well-fitting, heavy shoes, and no vail, she should give full swing to her arms and legs, when every muscle, nerve and artery in her body will feel the electric effects of motion and rapid, renewed life. This walk should, rain or shine, be taken every day of this period of gestative influence, up to within a few days of parturition. If faithfully observed, it has a wonderful happy effect on the whole process of gestation and parturition.

Otherwise, during this four months, the mother should live what might be termed a negative life—that is, without employing in any great measure her intellectual faculties, she should carefully avoid all the bad qualities she does not wish to transmit to the child. If she have a fretful or irritable disposition, she should carefully guard against it, and endeavor to cultivate only the bright and cheerful of her nature; and so of any other greater or smaller idiosyncrasy of character that she would not desire to have incorporated in the life of the child.

To impress the matter more fully on the minds of parents,.

13

I will again repeat that, during this full period of gestative influence, as well as during the period of nursing, *sexual congress should not be had between husband and wife.* This is the law of Nature, the law of God, and outside of Christendom it is never violated. Animals will not permit it—savages will not permit it, and over three-quarters of the world it is looked upon as infamous by our own species. A man acting out the licentious of his nature with his wife during gestation is worse than a brute—in fact, there is no species of the animal to which he can be compared, unless it be the tobacco-flavored, whisky-steeped hanger-on to a rum-shop —whose life is an epitome of tobacco, whisky and licentiousness. Do not, I pray you, O parents, do this unclean thing. Do not taint your clean bodies, do not foul your pure souls with the lustful of your natures, while a new body is being developed, a new soul being organized ; but by sweet words, loving caresses, endearing actions and warm kisses, cultivate within you the love-element that, in its pure exercise, joins together two souls, and brings in its path such a measure of peace and happiness as must be realized ere it can be appreciated.

When the fifth month has arrived, the mother should carry out, by persistent mental effort, the plan of life decided on for the child's post-natal existence, and this effort should be continued up to the day of its birth. To this end, all the thoughts and suggestions given in Chapter XIII. should be closely observed and followed. If it is the desire of the parents that the child be a carpenter, a minister, a fruit-grower, a novelist, an inventor, a house-builder, etc., this later period of gestative influence is *the* period in which to impress on the child's organism the qualities that will, when he or she arrives at manhood or womanhood, constitute in their action the desirable quality of genius, so necessary to success in any line of life chosen.

During this period the father should, when absence from his daily avocation is permissible, lovingly think and act in harmony with his wife. They together should by repeated expression strengthen their will-power in the direction desired. They should help each other to avoid all that is uncongenial in their nature, and cultivate only desirable qualities of head and heart, so that the growth of the new being will tend toward perfection, rather than back into barbarism —for it should be noted that there is no mid-way in life's endeavors—mankind must either recede or advance.

In their efforts to conform to the Law of Genius, the parents, and particularly the mother, must carefully avoid anxiety of mind for desired results, for over-solicitude will in the child work anomalies. Over-anxiety, vastly increased, will be transmitted to the New Life, and be to it a source of life-long trouble. This undesirable quality can easily be avoided by the cultivation of a bright, cheerful, reliant disposition, a belief in the law of transmitted influence, and trust in God's care and presence. The parents must not only have faith in this law, but in its practice they must feel confident of success, for people who have no faith care for nothing, and as an inevitable consequence accomplish nothing.

To the end that faith, in the minds of doubting parents, may grow and increase in the direction of the wonderful power of pre-natal influence, I will here give some illustrations of the results of chance acts, as well as of intelligent obedience to law, in the propagation of offspring.

Some years ago a man, one of whose hobbies was that unless an individual was a musician there was something radically wrong in his make-up, married a woman who did not know the first elements of music. This woman, his wife, knowing his desire for musical abilities in children, and his utter carelessness or want of interest in children who did not possess such, at first had a dread that she would bear a child wanting in his desires. But she made up her mind that such should not be the case, and to this end she obtained a piano, practiced upon it for a certain number of hours daily, and daily cultivated what voice she had in singing. Coupled with this was the strong desire of her whole soul to have a child possessing a genius for music, so that in its birth and growth it would be a well-spring of pleasure to the father, if not to her. This mother has now two children, both of which are born-musicians. They can sing any tune they once hear, and can already play the most difficult music placed before them. They delight and revel in it. This mother, in a measure, accidentally observed the Law of Genius, as the results so plainly prove. She, it must be noted, never did, and never possibly can, excel as a musician. As already mentioned, this is not necessary, the principal requirement being *the whole-souled desire, and the determined, persistent effort in the direction required.* This mother had no other wish in transmitting musical capacities to her offspring, than the pleasing of her husband. In no other quality were the children improved, in mental or physical peculiarities, than the single one of music; for otherwise they have inherited characteristics from their parents which in themselves are not desirable. Yet she done much in having children with such a love and genius for music, for music should be much more cultivated than it is. " Every heart should be the home of music. Every home should be an orchestra for sacred, and an opera for sprightly, gladsome music. The richest sentiments of the heart are to be sung. The holiest feelings of the soul find their best utterance in music. The warmest, purest affections express their fervor in song. Music is the natural language of a full soul. The mourner—yes, even the mourner loves the mellow, grief-laden cadences of slow and solemn music. The patriot expresses his bursting joy in the rich notes of the bugle ; the warrior shouts in answer to the stirring fife and drum ; the worshiper rises in praise with the swelling strains of the orchestra ; the lover melts to the soft tones of his ravishing lute, whose very melody seems the sweet breath of love. It is proper, then, that all should be masters of this glorious science One day, which is to come, all must be taught, and will willingly—yea, gladly join in the anthem of redemption. All souls will one day be full of love and praise, of heavenly aspiration and glorious sentiment. At once, then, they should enter upon a preparation for that great day of the fullness of glory; at once they should begin to taste a prelibation of that flood of angel-music which is to be poured into the ear of creation's King. While the infant mind is untarnished with sin and corroding care, this heavenly element should be awakened to a chorus of harmony that shall ever swell above the harsh discord of life. Early should the soul's great powers be developed for the work of the immortal world, and the enjoyment of immortal felicities."

As another illustration of inherited musical abilities—abilities, I presume, that were transmitted accidentally, and not knowingly or designedly—I give the following, taken from a Connecticut paper:

" A YOUNG PRODIGY.—There is a little child living in the village of Baltic, only four years old, who plays more than forty tunes correctly on the piano. Her name is Susa M——, daughter of George M——, chorister in the Baptist church. She played, a few Sabbaths since, all the tunes sung in the Sabbath-school concert, to the delight and astonishment of a large concourse of people. But what is more wonderful, perhaps, in the case of the little musician, is that she has never been taught to read. Her knowledge of music seems to be intuitive."

A man who by profession was an engineer, and who had just started business on his own account, received a commission from a prominent and wealthy firm to construct a large and peculiar steam engine. So desirous was he to succeed, and please and satisfy his employers, that he worked whole days and evenings, in concentrated study, to perfect the design. In doing this, his wife, who was along in pregnancy, got interested, and together they thought, talked and planned.   When the time arrived a daughter was born, who, in growing, developed in an unusual degree a talent to invent and construct—great mathematical and mechanical powers. The parents, no doubt, will make of this girl an ordinary every-day woman, having no special aim or object in life.   I would advise that she follow and attain those qualifications necessary to her success as a designer and constructor of engines, the genius for which was transmitted to her during the period of gestative influence.   "An unwomanly employment," you say.   Yes, if you decide by old-established usages ;   No, if you decide by the Law of Genius, which implies fitness.   "A dirty business," you say.   Not necessarily more so than washing dishes or peeling potatoes.   "Would not woman's dress interfere with the practical details of constructing or superintending mechanical work ?"   Yes, if such women dressed as at present, which mode is as unnatural in its form and purpose as it is destructive to the wearer's life and health.   A perfectly physiological dress for woman will in no way prevent her from adopting *any* of the departments of work occupied by man.

Another, and perhaps the only other objection that can be advanced, is that it would place woman out of her true sphere of life—that of mother, companion to her husband, and educator of her children.   This objection might hold valid if there were no inequality in the number of the sexes —if there were no more women than men.   But unfortunately this is not the case.   In Great Britain, many parts of Europe, parts of the United States—not mentioning China and other Asiatic countries—women largely predominate, and, judging by past records, they will continue to do so. Now these women must live, unless the Chinese plan of killing them off in their infancy be adopted.   Already there are thousands of women on this comparatively new continent who do not live—they only exist, and a wretched existence it is at that.   This being so—and it cannot well be denied— there must be through all time a preponderance of unmarried women, and these unmarried women should possess the privilege, if they have the genius, to fill any sphere in life that will allow them not only to be independent, but that will enable them to cultivate and perfect the imperfect that is within them. Again, there are, very often, women who, at the death of their husbands are thrown upon their own resources

And, allowing that a woman be born with a genius for an employment that is pre-eminently fitted for man, it does not follow that she, in pursuing that employment, need part with the qualities that constitute a true woman, a loving and faithful wife, and a pure and good mother.

Originate a woman having in full measure the quality of genius, and place her in any department of life's workshop monopolized by man, and she will much more naturally fall into that particular station than will a man possessed of second-rate talents. And notwithstanding the custom that confines her to particular spheres—which custom was born of her slavery—she will be admired for her genius and sought after for her ability.

And yet there is much that women, or the mothers of women, can perfect themselves in, before it will be necessary for them to largely infringe on masculine occupations. Why is it that there is so much want, misery, and ultimately lives of shame among women—especially women in large cities ? Simply because of a lack of ability, capacity, genius. And this lack of ability, mind you, is in employments that are or have been allotted to women. The most successful and most fashionable bonnet and dressmakers at this time in Paris are men. A woman requires the training, the ability and the element of genius as much in cleaning and making up a shirt, as in carving from marble an idealized fancy ; as much in making a loaf of bread, as in writing a novel ; as much in cooking a dinner, as in singing an operatic air. Yet this is lamentably not the case, and until women are educated, trained, and born to some particular employment, so that they will be masters of its every detail, so long will they be dependent on the first offer of marriage that comes along, be the man what he may ; so long will they be dependent on friends or relatives for a home ; so long will they be dependent on the grasping avarice of moneyed monopolies ; and, failing in husband, friends and low wages—a life of shame. Much more might be said on this woman-question, but I will refrain ; except so far as to advise mothers who are rearing girls, that they from the beginning bequeath them in full measure the quality of genius in some department of life's efforts, and that after birth they continue in full measure the plan of life intended for the unborn, even allowing the child should prove a girl when a boy was desired, and up to the full age of womanhood, allowing no present thoughts of marriage to intervene, the education be continued and completed. In this way can you have a woman who will be an honor and glory to her parents, and a bright and shining star among womankind.

The genius of Napoleon I. affords another instance of the effects of pre-natal influence.   The mother of Napoleon, some months previous to his birth, shared the fortunes of war with her husband.   On horseback most of the time, she acquired active and health-inspiring habits.   During this time she was in constant peril and danger, and not only surrounded with, but intensely engaged in, all the pomp and circumstance of war, and in this way not only became familiar with the horrors and anguish of war, but also became reconciled to it, and in a measure enjoyed it.   This being so it could not possibly be otherwise that in her son was implanted that indomitable spirit, that unbounded ambition and passion for warlike pursuits, that in its exercise did not stop short of the subjugation of a world.

In the mode of life necessary to transmit the quality of genius, much may be gleaned from a perusal of the pre-natal life of the poet Burns, who was from and of the people, and whose efforts are and ever will be regarded with wonder and delight by the Saxon race.

" The mother of Burns was a native of the county of Ayr; her birth was humble, and her personal attractions moderate; yet, in all other respects, she was a remarkable woman. She was blessed with singular equanimity of temper; her religious feelings were deep and constant; she loved a well-regulated household; and it was frequently her pleasure to give wings to the weary hours of a checkered life by chanting old songs and ballads, of which she had a large store. In her looks she resembled her eldest son; her eyes were bright and intelligent; her perception of character quick and keen. She lived to a great age, rejoiced in the fame of the poet, and partook of the fruits of his genius."

And of the father it is said that—

"Amid all these toils and trials, William Burns remembered the worth of religious instruction, and the usefulness of education in the rearing of his children. The former task he took upon himself, and, in a little manual of devotion still extant, sought to soften the rigor of the Calvinistic creed into the gentler Armenian. He set, too, the example which he taught. He abstained from all profane swearing and vain discourse, and shunned all approach to levity of conversation or behavior. A week-day, in his house, wore the sobriety of a Sunday; nor did he fail in performing family worship in a way which enabled his son to give to the world that fine picture of devotion, the 'Cotter's Saturday Night.'

" The education of Burns was not over when the school doors were shut. The peasantry of Scotland turn their cottages into schools; and when a father takes his arm-chair by the evening fire, he seldom neglects to communicate to his children whatever knowledge he possesses himself. Nor is this knowledge very limited; it extends, generally, to the history of Europe, and to the literature of the island—but more particularly to the divinity, the poetry, and what may be called the traditionary history of Scotland. An intelligent peasant is intimate with all those skirmishes, sieges, combats and quarrels, domestic or national, of which public writers take no account. He has by heart, too, whole columns of songs and ballads; nay, long poems sometimes abide in his recollection; nor will he think his knowledge much, unless he knows a little about the lives and actions of the men who have done most honor to Scotland. In addition to what he has on his memory, we may mention what he has on the shelf. A common husbandman is frequently master of a little library; history, divinity and poetry—but mostly the latter compose his collection. Milton and Young are favorites; the flowery meditations of Hervy, the religious romance of the ' Pilgrim's Progress,' are seldom absent; while, of Scottish books, Ramsay, Thompson, Ferguson, and now Burns, together with song and ballad-books innumerable, are all huddled together, soiled with smoke, and frail and tattered by frequent use. The household of William Burns was an example of what I have described; and there is some truth in the assertion that, in true knowledge, the poet was, at nineteen, a better scholar than nine-tenths of our young gentlemen when they leave school for college.

The great number of literary and scientific men Scotland has produced, when compared with her sister kingdoms, is, to many reflecting minds, matter of surprise and wonder. The preceding account of the general literary taste and acquirements of the people, together with the following opinion of one of the most original thinkers of the age, may furnish an explanation, and, at the same time, support the theory of transmission and inheritance contended for in these pages:

"A country where the entire population is, or even once has been, laid hold of, filled to the heart with an infinite religious idea, has made a step from which it cannot retrograde. Thought, conscience—the sense that man is denizen of a universe, creature of an eternity—has penetrated the remotest cottage, to the simplest heart. Beautiful and awful, the feeling of a heavenly behest, of duty God-commanded, over-canopies all life. There is an inspiration in such a people; one may say, in a most special sense, ' the inspiration of the Almighty giveth them understanding.' Honor to all the brave and true; everlasting honor to the brave old Knox, one of the truest of the true! That in the moment while he and his cause, amid civil broils, in convulsion and confusion, were still but struggling for life, he sent the schoolmaster forth to all corners, and said: 'Let the people be taught' —this is but one, and, indeed, an inevitable and comparatively inconsiderable item of his great message to men. His message, in its true compass, was: *' Let men know that they are men, created by God, responsible to God ; who work in any meanest moment of time what will last through eternity.'* It is, verily, a great message. This great message Knox did deliver with a man's voice and strength, and he found a people to believe him. Of such an achievement, we say, were it to be made once only, the results are immense. Thought, in such a country, may change its form, but it cannot go out; the country has attained *majority*, thought, and a certain spiritual manhood, ready for all work that man can do. It may take many forms—the form of hard-fisted, money-getting industry, as in the vulgar Scotchman, the vulgar New Englander; but as compact, developed force, and alertness of faculty, it is still there. It may utter itself as the colossal skepticism of a Hume (beneficial, this, too, though painful, wrestling, Titan-like, through doubt and inquiry, toward new belief); and again, in some better day, it may utter itself in the inspired melody of a Burns; in a word, it is, and continues in the voice and the work of a nation of hardy, endeavoring, considering men, with whatever that may bear in it, or unfold from it. The Scotch natural character originates in many circumstances; first of all is the Saxon stuff there was to work on; but next, and beyond all except that, the Presbyterian Gospel of John Knox."

Mrs. Hester Pendleton says:

"Two of my early friends, of very dissimilar characters, married about the same time, and their children have partaken strongly of the peculiarities of their mothers—one of whom was of a dull, sluggish nature, and as much averse to mental as to physical activity. Her conscience appeared quite at ease if her fingers were employed, even in the most trifling occupation; and the less mental effort her work required, the more pleasing it was to her. While thus employed, she frequently beguiled the time by caroling sentimental songs and ballads. The phrenological developments of her eldest daughter correspond perfectly with the habits and pursuits of the mother during her pregnancy: tune, large—domestic sentiments and animal propensities, large—reflective organs, moderate—perceptive ones, small—quite deficient in the organ of weight, and very near-sighted. That the last two defects were caused by the personal inactivity of the mother, and by her sight being constantly confined to small and near objects, appears the most probable, as her last children's organs of weight and vision were perfect—she having removed to the country, and been obliged to perform the active duties of her family.

"The other youthful mother was blessed with a most happy, joyous temper, and possessed of mental and personal activity in a high degree—passionately fond of dancing, walking, riding on horseback, and all other exercise requiring action, skill and grace. She was a perfect economist of her time, allowing no portions of it to be wasted. Her household was regulated with order, neatness and taste. By her habit of early rising, she was enabled to arrange all her domestic matters before breakfast; after which, she usually occupied herself with plain needlework, while her husband read aloud the morning papers. She would then accompany him in a walk of three miles to his office; and on her return, devote the remainder of the morning to pursuits congenial to a highly cultivated literary taste; and thus, on her husband's return to dinner, she had something new, interesting, and amusing to read or relate to him. A portion of the afternoon was generally devoted to exercise in the open air; or, the weather not permitting, to a game of battle-door, or the graces at home ; or to chess, reading or needlework. Born under such pleasant influences, the children were sprightly, active and graceful—perfect emanations of joy—their perceptions quick, their sensibilities acute, their understanding vigorous—no lesson a task, no duty a burden. Their father was a man of sense and feeling, who perfectly understood the influence of the mother's mind, during the period of gestation, on the temper and disposition of her child ; therefore, never allowed her feelings to be disturbed, irritated or annoyed. Hence, the sweetness, docility and tractability of their children ; and hence their dissimilarity to those first mentioned, whose parents allowed no such influence, nor gave themselves any trouble or thought about the matter— and their children were perfect clods of dullness, ill temper and stupidity."

The same writer gives another remarkable instance of the effects of the habits and pursuits of the mother on her offspring :

" Mrs. A—— was a melancholy instance of strength of mind perverted to selfish ends. Ambitious of power and influence, she was unscrupulous in the means by which they were obtained. Owing to her plausibility and pertinacity, she once was elected to an office of trust in a benevolent society of which she was a member. This was a situation of great temptation to one in whose head the selfish sentiments predominated, as the event proved ; for, at the expiration of the year, she was dismissed, under the imputation of having appropriated a portion of the funds of the society to her own use. During the year in which she held this office, Mrs. A—— gave birth to a daughter, whose first manifestations were acquisitiveness and secretiveness in excess, or a propensity to theft. That the great development and activity of those organs in the head of the child were the effect of the dishonest practices of the mother, previous to her birth, there can be but little doubt."

These illustrations of the tendency of perverted influence

on the New Life might be continued interminably; but this is unnecessary—for any reader need but knowingly observe the offspring of families in his immediate neighborhood to be convinced of these indisputable facts—to be convinced of the truth that the great law of pre-natal influence is based on the principle that like produces like. As are the parents' lives during the period of preliminary preparation—as is the life of the mother during the period of gestation and nursing, so will be the child, a duplicate in physical, mental and moral peculiarities. It is only necessary, in the proving of the fact that like produces like, that parents but compare their lives, in thoughts, words and actions, during these seasons of preparation, to account for the character of mind and body of any of their offspring.

Now the right observance of the laws and rules laid down in these pages will—cannot help—resulting in beautiful, talented, healthy offspring; and yet, if any parents doubt these truths or assertions, let them follow their old ways.

Let them—if they have no desire for pure, bright, and more perfect offspring—adopt the opposite plan, and see for themselves the result.

Let them—the husband and wife—during this period of gestative influence, disagree as much as possible—fall out and quarrel about the most trifling subjects, and the results will be, in a measure, as was the case with a boy in Vermont, whose parents previous to his birth had a difficulty, resulting in the mother for a time refusing to speak to her husband. After awhile the child was born, and in due season began to talk, but when sitting on his father's knee was invariably silent. It continued so until the child was five years old, when the father, having exhausted his powers of persuasion, threatened it with punishment for its stubborness. When the punishment was inflicted, it elicited nothing but sighs and groans, which told but too plainly that the little sufferer could not speak, though he invariably endeavored to do so. This child has reached manhood, and even now his efforts to converse with his father can only produce the most bitter sighs and groans.

Let the parents, during this period, lead untruthful lives. Let the mother lie whenever the least opportunity offers. It is not necessary that she tell positive lies, for the effect will be the same if they are of a negative character—whether they be "white lies" or society-lies—yea, even unexpressed untruths, are as efficient as would be a lie under oath. Doing this, can you have a child that will be the embodiment of truth and honor? Oh, no; you will have a child similar to a very large class of mankind, who by thought, word or action live untruthful lives; who are, every day of their existence, in a very small or very great measure—to use a plain Saxon word—liars; and of whom, because of their great number, no individual illustration need be given.

Apropos to this subject is the following anecdote, which I have noticed drifting through the papers :

"A Canadian boy—too young to fully comprehend the doctrine of total depravity (?), but old enough, at least to have a vague idea of the hereditary principles of mankind— was recently detected by his paternal ancestor in a falsehood, and punished therefor by solitary confinement. The punishment over, the youngester accosted his father with the question :

" 'Pa, did you tell lies when you were little ?'

" The father, perhaps conscience-smitten, evaded an answer; but the child, persisting, again asked :

" 'Did you tell lies when you were little ?'

" 'No,' said the father; 'but why do you ask ?'

" 'Did ma tell lies when she was little ?' he then asked.

" 'I don't know, my son ; you must ask her.'

" 'Well,' retorted the boy, 'one of you must have told lies, or you would not have a boy who would.' "

If to an untruthful life be added a disrespect for God's name—a breaking of the third commandment—a combination will be transmitted to the child's organism that will greatly tend toward making it an essentially bad character. Let the parents during this period—if they desire pale, weak, scrofulous, consumptive, short-lived children—carefully live a confined life, in a close, dark, stove-heated, unventilated house; avoiding all out-door exercise and amusement; eating all manner of rich, greasy and concentrated food, spices, hot and sweet drinks, carefully abstaining from daily baths, and they will have, with a tenfold increase, their desire fulfilled, as did the following parents, who certainly did not desire offspring with such peculiarities:

"I was married at the age of twenty-five, inheriting from both my parents a most vigorous constitution. My husband was four years my senior, and alike blessed with most perfect health. But we started wrong after all, for we both determined to be rich, let what would come. We occupied a large farm, and I, in my eagerness to amass wealth, which has been a canker to my happiness, would never employ help for a day, frequently doing all the labor for a family of twenty during the period of gestation. My first children were twins. My living at the time was what is commonly called the plain living of farmers, but what I now consider as much too luxurious for health.

"Previous to my accouchment, a cutaneous eruption appeared on my face, neck and hands, together with swelling of the joints. This I looked upon as the effect of heat, which would soon pass off; but what was my disappointment, at the birth of my babes, to have presented to me two emaciated little beings, covered with this eruption, which was found to be scrofula, induced by wrong living. I had most ardently desired children, and my love of riches gave way to my maternal feelings; but in less than four months both the little sufferers were carried to their resting place. I regarded myself as stricken of God; I sought to submit to my trying fate as a Christian—for I did not regard myself as having anything to do with my affliction. A third, fourth and fifth child followed, diseased in the same way, and only lingered for a short period. At length my desires were gratified in everything except living children. I wept and prayed much for a child that might bless our old age.

"At length the illness of a beloved parent called me to a different scene, and during almost the entire period of pregnancy with my sixth child I was occupied in her care. Being no longer actively engaged, my mind turned naturally to investigating the causes that had co-operated to produce such painful results, if causes there were. Does God, I asked, arbitrarily punish us in this world for infringements of His moral law ? If so, of what use is the atonement or death of Christ ? Then first dawned upon my mind the belief that there were natural as well as moral laws given to govern us, and that an infringement of them would meet with punishment. The period of parturition arrived. Conceive, if you can, the joy and gratitude of my heart to find myself the mother of a fair and beautiful boy, which still lives to bless and comfort me ; but although he lives, and the three daughters which followed him, yet they too partake of the feeble constitution which I have entailed upon them, for my own health had become greatly impaired by my wrong mode of life and struggle after riches."

Or, if any parents have an antipathy to following the laws given for the production of beautiful children, they can—by the avoidance of the beautiful in art and nature, and the cultivation of the homely, rustic and coarse embodied in their immediate surroundings ; the exercise of the propensities of their natures ; the living on rich food, and in unlighted and unventilated rooms ; but especially by the wearing of corsets by the mother, and general constriction of dress—secure not only homeliness of feature in the offspring, but deformity of soul as well as body. In no way does the fashionable or unfashionable mother so influence the appearance of the child, during and immediately preceding gestation, as by constriction of the body by corsets, tight dresses or bands. By this unnatural habit the circulation of the blood through the ab-

14

domen is impeded, the regular nourishment of the fœtus is also checked, and so the child is born with not only high shoulders, awkward figure, pinched up and painful expression of countenance, but also with a weak and sickly organization. The Romans were so well aware of the mischief caused by compression of the waist during gestation, that they enacted a positive law against it; and Lycurgus, with the same view, is said to have ordained a law compelling pregnant women to wear very wide and loose clothing.

Or if the parents wish a child that will possess a desire for using tobacco, or a fondness for alcoholic liquors, it is only necessary that the father—during the period of preliminary preparation—use moderately or in excess tobacco, wine, whisky, beer, etc. If the mother have her morning or evening glass of beer, ale, wine, cider, or whisky—spiced, hot or plain—the effect on the character of the New Life will be much more positive. The children born of parents under these conditions will, long before they have grown to manhood (or womanhood), take as naturally to alcoholic liquors and tobacco as does the father. This is an undeniable fact, and people have only to glance around them to be convinced of it. A boy, man or woman, born of parents who are healthy and perfectly free from these curses of modern civilization, will not only not adopt these debasing practices, *but cannot be made to do so.* Born of a clean, pure, holy conception, he will remain while he lives clean, pure, and free from the body-corrupting, soul-destroying practices of smoking, chewing or snuffing tobacco, or the use of alcoholic liquors.

Or if the parents desire a child that will be the embodiment of licentiousness, it is only necessary that during these periods of preparation and influence—beside eating of rich food and using hot drinks, alcoholic liquors and tobacco—they practice the abnormally amative of their natures—that they together lead incontinent lives—that they put to shame the beasts of the field in their unnatural lust. By doing this they will not fail to have children whose unnatural desires will crop out very long before they have reached manhood or womanhood—long before their bodies are so grown and perfected as to be prepared to take on the holy duties and responsibilities of a loving and pure married existence. Think you I harp too much on this theme of the abnormal exercise of amativeness, and especially at these seasons of the birth and growth of a new life? You cannot so think, if you are of an observing and reflecting nature. Ask any discreet, watchful and observing male or female teacher of any one of the primary schools in town or country, and you will be told that the practice of self-abuse is next to universal in children ; that it is practiced by girls as well as boys ; that children before they reach the age of five years practice it—practice it in company and alone ; that these children, as they grow up, become pale, weak and sickly—caused, as the fond parents suppose, by hard study ; that eventually many of these young men become insane, while others die of some unpronounced disease—consumption or general debility—when *the* cause of death was the body-disintegrating, soul-destroying habit of self-abuse. And the great underlying cause for the practice of self-abuse in the child was the fact that it was transmitted by the parents, during some one or other of these seasons of pre-natal influence.

This transmitted sexual desire may not take on the form of self-abuse, for the child may grow up to manhood without doing this great wrong to his body—though this seldom or never happens ; but when it does, as well as when it does not, his inherited licentiousness is exercised in a comparatively legitimate way—legitimate, if the using of his wife as a chattel or the sexual acquaintance of harlots be a legitimate way. And yet the results are almost the same : a sickly, diseased, unnatural life, and an early death.

" J. P. finished early his college course, and with a rapidity surpassing even the most sanguine hopes of his friends acquired the profession of law. The evening that he was admitted to the bar saw him the husband of a lovely and pure-hearted woman. He rose in his profession with a rapidity unequalled; but his wife drooped in spirits and health; her happiness had been evanescent as the dew, for she had too late learned that her husband, like his father, was a profligate, licentious man. A few months previous to the birth of their son, he had abandoned the young and tender wife. That son, at the age of nineteen, when I first knew him, was the most brilliant young man in mind, the most noble in form and feature, of any person I had ever known; but he was pursuing a reckless, licentious course, and was self-indulgent in all his appetites to a degree unparalleled. The child was trained, with the exception of proper physical training, with great care. Often, after receiving a letter from his mother, in which she gave excellent advice, and much religious counsel and exhortation, have I known him to shut himself up for days, and fast and pray, and weep like an infant over his transgressions. I have heard him make the most solemn promises before God of entire reformation. Again and again I have seen this strong man bowed to the very earth under a sense of his transgressions. But when he went forth it was to eat and drink, and again to go out and commit the same sins, perhaps to a more fearful extent.

"Now did not that father stamp his character upon his child most perfectly. The mother was a noble, highly gifted woman; but the baser passions of the father were stronger than the moral ones of both. But had one-half of the study of the mother been directed to acquiring a knowledge of the laws of Nature, she might have saved him much suffering; she might have given to his constitution a shield that would have protected him from temptation to which he was exposed. For she would have taught him that, by living on a mild, unstimulating diet, together with bathing, air and exercise, those baser passions might be controlled and brought into due subjection to his higher nature. But ignorantly she fed the volcanic fires in him, which in after life she vainly sought to quench. She loved, when her fair boy came home from school, to have something prepared to please and pamper his vitiated appetite. Thus she, like thousands of others, took the most sure means to prevent an answer to her daily—nay, almost hourly prayer, that God would keep pure her son. Would that parents—when they surround their luxurious boards, furnished with tea, coffee, flesh-meats, condiments, etc., and lift up their voices and ask of God to bless the food to the strengthening of their bodies, and then rise with those bodies stimulated and unnaturally excited, and their spirits groveling and fleshly—could but see their inconsistency. To a mind truly enlightened such scenes are most revolting. They savor strongly of Pagan idolatry. It is, at least, mocking God with lip-service, while the heart is so debased, low and sensual, that the higher natures are dormant, and their religion sensualism."

The following single paragraph, from a late daily paper, gives, in strong relief, three instances of the effects of the parents' licentiousness during the ante-natal life of the child :

"Within a short time the Police have become acquainted with the facts connected with the abandonment by three young girls of their homes, and their deliberate entry upon lives of prostitution. In one instance, the father came to this city, and finding his daughter in a house of ill-fame, prevailed upon her to accompany him home. She remained there, however, but a short time, when she again deserted her family, and is now leading a life of infamy. A second case was that of a young girl, who came to this city and was admitted into a house of improper character, but only after she had brought from her mother a written document, stating that she had abandoned her, and had no objection to her leading a life of shame. The paper was probably a forgery. Last night, in a cell in one of the Station-houses of the city, a very beautiful girl, only 17 years of age, was confined for having deserted her mother, and voluntarily entered upon a career of crime and dissipation. The mother had been in search of her for some weeks, and yesterday succeeded in finding her in a fashionable place of resort on Sixth street. The young girl stated that the woman at whose house she was discovered and the *habitues* of the place had all urged her to go home and lead a pure and virtuous life, and had pointed out to her the inevitable and certain end of the career upon which she was embarking, but that she had thought the matter all over, and had fully determined to continue on her course."

Where there are three such cases as the above come to the knowledge of the public, there are thousands that do not. And substitute three young men in place of the above three young women, and you can substitute millions for thousands, so great in number are they who live other than pure lives. Live a licentious married life, and you cannot possibly expect to have children that will be other than licentious and incontinent. Live a pure, chaste and continent married life, and your children will be—as God intended they should—embodied reflections of His love, purity and goodness.

Or, if the parents desire a child that will not only be deficient in mental or moral qualities, but will be idiotic, it is only necessary that, immediately preceding the period of conception, the parents judiciously combine some of the principal bad conditions enumerated above— that, beside living on wrong food—living in dark, unventilated rooms, they use in excess alcoholic liquors, and the abnormally amative of their natures, and they will not fail in producing children that will be blots on this beautiful earth. The fact is established, that the parents who use alcoholic liquors, tobacco or opium, either moderately or in excess, and otherwise misuse the laws of life, have generated children who were partially or fully idiotic.

Or, if the parents desire to generate a child that will possess the qualities that will go to make it a murderer, it is only necessary to add to some one or more of the above enumerated abnormal characteristics the one—on the part of the mother—to desire to get rid of the unborn child, the attempt to do so, and its failure.   Somewhere I have read of a child, whose mother so desired to get rid of it, to murder it, in the early months of pregnancy, but without success.   From the time the boy was five years old, he was not allowed to play or associate with other children unless carefully watched, as already he had made several attempts to kill his fellow-play-mates.   Of course, the hate, loathing, and desire for the death of the unborn, must be deep and positive to produce such an effect as this.   The pain, grief and sorrow of that mother might be imagined, but not described.   She longed for and prayed that her boy, in some way, might die an early death, so that no harm should befall others through the murderous propensities bequeathed him.

Happening into a court house, where a crowded and anxious audience filled every seat and aisle, I ascertained that the prisoner at the bar was arraigned for murder.   Presently the jury appeared, the foreman of which, in a clear voice, returned a verdict of murder in the first degree.   The judge asked the prisoner if he had aught to say why sentence of death should not be passed on him.

The prisoner, a man in the prime of life, well formed, and of rather prepossessing appearance, lifted his eyes toward the judge, and, in a voice husky with emotion, said :

"I am guilty, and have no hopes of other than suffering death—for has not my life been one great record of sin ? Only in the prime of life, I have been arrested times without number.   I have led a licentious, wicked life.   I have done all manner of positive wrong—lied, robbed counterfeited, and now murdered.   And yet I should not suffer death, for I have not done one of these things willingly.   The wickedness that was transmitted, bequeathed, and that is in me, I have striven against, fought against, yea, even prayed against.   Where is my father, who bequeathed me this deformed soul ?   Where is my mother who nurtured and more firmly implanted in me this wicked nature ? For it is they who embodied these qualities in my organization that have culminated in murder, and it is they to whom this sentence of death should be addressed, and not to me. Oh ! not to me for have I not wrestled and fought against it all the days of my life ? But do what I would, strive as hard as I might, it would assert the individuality of its transmitted nature. In saying this, I have said all that I have to say in extenuation of my guilt."

This argument—an argument that can be used and applied by nearly every wrong-doer brought before the dispensers of law and justice—of course availed nothing with the judge. A jury of his countrymen had found him guilty, and he must suffer the extreme penalty of the law—death.

And yet, was he guilty ?

On you, O parents, in the generating of a new life, rests a great responsibility—a responsibility that, if assumed in a right, loving and holy endeavor, will produce fruit that will redound to your honor, the world's happiness, and God's glory. Assume it in a wrong, unloving and unholy spirit, and O the trouble, the anxiety, the pain, the penalties that will result will be more than a single soul can bear.

See to it, therefore, that you faithfully read, diligently study, and ever obey the laws that govern your sexual organism, in the production of souls in the image of God.

CHAPTER XVII.

PREGNANCY—ITS SIGNS AND DURATION.

HEN a new life is started on its growth toward perfection, the whole nature of the woman takes on, or seems to take on, new life and vigor. She enjoys better health, and feels more cheerful and buoyant in spirits, and often becomes more fleshy than is usual with her. This fact is especially noticeable in those women who possess a delicate constitution and somewhat feeble health. Others, again, go through the various stages of pregnancy without experiencing any marked change in the general state of their systems ; while others, still, suffer more or less severely from a variety of harassing and painful symptoms. But all, or nearly all, upon becoming pregnant, or very soon after, experience changes from their previous condition more or less diversified, numerous and important.

A woman in perfectly good health, having her stomach and other digestive organs properly performing their appropriate functions, and hitherto having been constantly regular in menstruating, will have, as a first intimation that pregnancy has taken place, *failure in the recurrence of the menses* at the expected period.   This is a good and positive sign in a woman who hitherto has been strong, healthy and regular. In weak and sickly women the cessation of the menses may be owing to other causes.   It is asserted by some physiologists that this is not a reliable sign, as a woman may be pregnant and menstruate at the same time.   This I believe to be wrong; for, when such an exception occurs, it has its source in ulcers or abrasions of the mouth and lips of the womb, and not from the interior of the womb, where the impregnated egg is located, and from whence the true menstrual flux has its origin.

Nausea, or "morning sickness," occurs about the third or fourth week, although it may be present almost immediately after conception.   Nausea, depending as much, and perhaps more, on the morbid condition of the patient than on pregnancy, is not an ever-present sign; but when it occurs and is unaccompanied by any other derangement of the health, it may be regarded as a sign of no inferior importance.

Salivation of a very peculiar character affects some women during pregnancy.   The saliva is extremely white, a little frothy, very tenacious, and difficult to deliver from the mouth. As a sign of pregnancy, it is to be regarded as an exception rather than the rule.

Mammary changes.—From the fourth to the twelfth week after pregnancy the breasts will be found to have increased in size, and to have formed round the base a circle of darker color than formerly, with here and there scattered upon the surface a number of prominent points or pimples.   As time advances, the circle will be found to increase in its dimensions, to become of a still darker color, and the little prominences to have increased in size.   In some these changes begin to appear within two or three weeks after conception; in others they appear at a much later period; and in many none of them are ever manifested; so that—although their appearance, and particularly the appearance of these little prominences, is considered as almost a positive indication of pregnancy—their absence is very far indeed from being any important evidence to the contrary.

Secretion of milk.—At the time when the breasts begin to enlarge, milk, or rather a milky fluid is secreted ; but the secretion of this fluid takes place under many conditions where pregnancy does not exist. Any derangement of the health, causing the interruption of the menses, may result in the enlargement of the breasts, and even the secretion of milk.

Enlarged womb.—From six to ten weeks after conception, women who are thin and not fleshy can, by pressing the fingers upon the lower part of the abdomen just above the frontal bone, feel the enlarged womb, in the shape of a hard, round substance or ball, about the size of an orange. This can only be done when the abdominal muscles are relaxed, by lying down on the back, with the shoulders slightly raised and the knees drawn up.

Enlargement of the abdomen takes place about the third month. During the second month it is usually much flattened. From the third until the eighth month it continues to enlarge—at first along the median line, or directly in front, and at quite its lower part. Until the fourth month the sides, between the ribs and hips, appear to diminish, instead of enlarging—the growth being from below upward, directly in front, while the sides are for a long time considerably flattened. Enlargement of the abdomen may be caused by dropsy, ovarian disease, or tumors, but differs materially in its growth from the enlargement caused by pregnancy.

Quickening, which occurs about the fourth month, when the motions of the child are first observed by the mother, is commonly regarded as an unequivocal sign. These motions, which may occur as early as the third month, are at first very feeble, and are described as producing a feeble, fluttering sensation, causing the woman to experience an uncomfortable feeling of nausea and faintness. After a time the motions are more quick and elastic, and are usually felt very frequently during the remainder of the time, until confinement puts a termination to them.

Pregnancy may exist with none of the above signs, or with all of them ; but in a woman who is healthy, and who has led a regular life, the appearance of any or all of them is almost proof positive that pregnancy does exist. In cases where character is at stake, and doubts prevail, there are less equivocal sources of evidence, by which any well-informed physician can solve such doubts.

Duration of pregnancy.—Owing to the fact that conception is, as a rule, a chance act, having in it no educated desire, preparation or method, and therefore an impossibility to fix the exact period of conception, there is much discrepancy of opinion with regard to the duration of it. Nine calendar months, or two hundred and eighty days, is the generally accepted length of this period. If women who lead continent lives, and who adopt the laws of generating a new being laid down in these pages, would make a note of the period of conception, they could not only tell to a day the duration of pregnancy in their cases, but would know of a certainty the next time they were pregnant (under like conditions), the very hour they would be confined, which of itself would be a wonderful satisfaction to the mother. Of course, this only can be done by women who are allowed by their husbands to live pure and healthy lives, and who generate offspring under true and lovable conditions.

It sometimes occurs that the period of pregnancy extends to more than two hundred and eighty days.

"Some years ago there was held, in England, a legal trial of a case involving the question of the duration of pregnancy. It was called the Gardiner Peerage case, and was instituted for the purpose of settling the title of a claimant of that peerage. Many eminent medical men were examined on the occasion, and the result was that no absolute term of pregnancy was ascertained. Moved by the interest excited in that case, Dr. Merriman, of London, took the greatest pains to ascertain the duration of pregnancy in a great number of women, and succeeded in satisfying his mind of the great correctness of the computation for one hundred and fourteen cases of mature children. He gave a tabular statement, designating the number of days' duration of each case, from which it appears that there were—

   3 born during the thirty-seventh week.
 13   "   "   thirty-eighth week.
 14   "   "   thirty-ninth week.
 33   "   "   fortieth week.
 22   "   "   forty-first week.
 15   "   "   forty-second week.
 10   "   "   forty-third week.
  4   "   "   forty-fourth week.

" From this, as well as from a great amount of other testimony to the same effect, it appears certain that the term or duration of pregnancy is far from being absolutely fixed ; that, while in some cases the fœtus may become mature in less than two hundred and sixty days, in others it does not become so until the completion of the three hundred or more—the time varying much, according to the vital force with which it is endowed and other circumstances perhaps unknown."

Viability of the child.—It sometimes happens that the child is born before its natural time. This occurs generally in first pregnancies, when the womb, on account of its being unaccustomed to distension, or from other causes, takes on the expulsive contractions of labor, and terminates the pregnancy before the fœtus has arrived at maturity. The earliest period at which the child is enabled to carry on an independent existence is involved in much uncertainty. The period generally assigned is the end of the seventh month.

A case is given by Dr. Rodman, of a woman who gave birth to a child, the period of her gestation being less than *nineteen weeks.*   She had borne five children previously, and in this instance premature labor came on in consequence of fatiguing exertions, and she was delivered of a living male child.

"Not daring to allow the washing of the infant's body, he was speedily wiped, and wrapped in flannel, with only an opening in the dress around his mouth for the admission of air ; and by the time the dressing was over, the mother was ready to take him into the warm bed with herself. It is common, if there be much apparent weakness, to feed a child the first twelve hours after birth very frequently ; yet, in this instance, although the child was weak, no feeding was attempted until beyond that time ; the nourishing heat with the mother in bed was relied on.   On the following day, the head, body and extremities of the child were surrounded with fine cotton wool, pressed to appear like cloth, to the thickness of two or three folds, and over that the flannel, as before ; and again the child was given to the mother in bed. His vital energy was so deficient that, even with this dress, of himself, he was unable to support the degree of warmth which was necessary to his existence.   The heat of a fire was evidently injurious, as he soon became weaker when exposed to it ; while the warmth of the mother in bed enlivened and strengthened him.   Too much heat induced a sickly paleness of the face, with an obvious expression of uneasiness in his countenance ; and the abstraction of heat, even by tardily undressing his head, brought on a nervous affection, or starting of the muscles all over his body.   From seeing how these morbid affections were induced, the child was kept regularly and comfortably warm, by the mother and two other females alternately lying in bed with him, for more than two months.   After that, he could be left alone from time to time, but was still undressed very cautiously, and only partially at any one time.   It was not till the child was three weeks old that the length or the weight of the body could be ascertained.   The length was found to be thirteen inches, and the weight one pound and thirteen ounces, avoirdupois. It was extremely difficult to get the child to swallow nourishment the first week; the yellow gum soon came on, and the thrush seized him severely on the eighth day, and was not cured till the end of the third week. During the first week, he was fed with toasted loaf bread, boiled with water, sweetened and strained through fine linen; in the second week, twenty drops of beef tea were added to the two or three tea-spoonsful of his mother's milk, and in two days afterward he made exertions to suck. His mother's milk was gradually substituted, at least in part, for the panada, though this was still continued occasionally. Under this careful management he attained the age of four months, at which time his health and excretory functions were peculiarly regular."

A child born at the expiration of the seventh month is usually so far developed as to survive, if properly taken care of; and it is possible for a child born of a healthy mother, at the end of the sixth month, to live, if very great care is taken of it.

CHAPTER XVIII.

DISORDERS OF PREGNANCY.

EFORE noticing the requirements that go to make childbirth natural, and therefore easy, it may be well to glance at some of the disorders incident to pregnancy.

It should in the commencement be understood that the bearing of children is a *natural* process—that the pre-natal growth and birth of the child should not—cannot—in a perfectly healthy woman, entail any disorder, disease, or even pain, and the prevailing opinion that suffering and danger are inseparable from parturition is a reflection on God's loving justice and mercy. It is as natural for a woman to have a child as it is for a tree to bear fruit, or an animal to bring forth its young; and, being natural, the process should be one of pleasure rather than pain —one of desire rather than dread.

We are told that Indian women, whether at home or marching, without physician or even companion, will give birth to a child, and immediately after are ready for the observance of their duties, whether it be the drudgery of their home-life or the fatigues of a long march.

It can be offered in argument against this fact of easy births in native women, that they belonging to a low scale of civilization, the heads of their children are very moderately developed, which allowing of easy birth, might account for their general freedom from accident and pain; whereas, when the mother belongs to a grade of society who are highly intelligent, well learned, and progressive in their modes of thought, the head of such a child will be from a quarter to a third more in size than that of the child of the uneducated mother. And yet, making all due allowance for this fact, if the civilized mother be endowed with perfect health, and closely follow the laws of life, child-birth will be as easy and painless as Nature intended it should be. The period of pregnancy should be one of increased health, rather than one of increased disorders. The mother who has hitherto led a true life will, during this period, experience an exhilaration of spirits, a redundancy of health and cheerfulness of mind that is not to be enjoyed or experienced at any other time of life. But such is lamentably not the case, else there would be no need of including this chapter on the disorders incident to this period.

The underlying source for much of the ill health during pregnancy, may be discovered in the nervous system. The nerves of organic life with which the uterus is supplied are never sensitive in a healthy state; it is only in disease they have pain. During pregnancy, while the evolution of a new being is going on in the uterus, a large supply of nervous power is drawn from the rest of the system to supply the deficiency in the diseased or weakened nerves of the uterus— hence the outlying organs of the body suffer. The stomach has less power of digestion, and consequently there is nausea and vomiting; and low spirits and hysterical feelings arise from the limited supply of blood to the brain.

Nausea and vomiting—usually called morning sickness, because occurring in the morning when the woman first assumes an erect posture—is one of the first signs of preg-

nancy in most women who are not of perfectly healthy natures. It usually commences from two to three weeks after
the beginning of pregnancy, although it may begin on the
very day after conception. On rising from her bed, the
woman will not feel ·as well as usual—she will have nausea
followed by retching. It may not occur until after breakfast, which, eaten with a good relish, will almost immediately
be thrown up again. This may continue more or less constant and severe for several weeks, and in some instances until near the time of quickening. Some physicians assert
that morning sickness is of a serviceable nature, in its opera-
ting as a safety-valve for its protection from actual disease,
and in exciting a more vigorous action of the uterus. This
is wrong, for these symptoms are unnatural; and it is possible so to live that a pregnant woman need not have them
any more than any one else. The women of savage nations
never experience it. A close observance of the rules for
living, mentioned in a former chapter, will enable women to
greatly palliate, if not altogether avoid, morning sickness.
They should be very careful what food they use, eating small
quantities at regular intervals—say, twice a day. All longings for all sorts of things should be kept down, and absolutely nothing eaten between meals. In the morning a glass
of pure, cold water should be swallowed, a quickly-taken
bath, with rapid friction of the skin by the hands of the woman or an assistant. After dressing, a brisk, enjoyable walk
in the open air, and on returning a very light breakfast. As
little plain food as possible, eaten at regular intervals; the
daily sponge, air and sun bath, and active daily out-door exercise, will do all that can be done to ameliorate or prevent
this distressing disorder of morning sickness.

Longings.—Many pregnant women experience odd desires and longings for particular and often out-of-the-way articles of diet. These longings never occur in women who
are healthy. On examination it will be found that it occurs
particularly among those who have little or no physical or

mental exercise, who find it difficult to "kill time," and who altogether are constitutionally indolent in their habits. Again, it occurs in those who are or have been pampered and indulged on every occasion by a lenient husband or over-kind friend, with the supposition that in so doing they help to a better life, while in fact they adopt the plan that will surely culminate in a sickly wife and scrofulous offspring. Many of these women believe that, if their longings are not satisfied during pregnancy, they will in some way be incorporated on the child's body. This belief in general cases is erroneous; for the majority of women, especially such as belong to the class described above, do not exercise in their longings a sufficiency of energy, strength of character, or force of will, to transmit any deformities or idiosyncrasies. The only way they do affect the child is imparting to it a more or less sickly and diseased organism. The remedy for these abnormal desires is active exercise, plain and unstimulating food, and altogether living out the Plan of Life laid down in a former chapter.

Fainting.—In women of a weak, nerveless body, fainting sometimes happens, caused in some manner by the derangement of the heart's action through the nervous connection with the gravid uterus. Some women are very subject to it, from the slightest causes, during the whole period of pregnancy, while others experience it only occasionally, and some periodically. When it occurs, the patient should be laid down with the head low, plenty of air admitted, the dress loosened, and the face sprinkled with water. The restoring of the general health will prevent its re-appearance.

Sleeplessness, in a greater or less degree, often occurs during pregnancy, and it is sometimes so troublesome as to altogether prevent sleep. It "most frequently affects the weak, nervous and irritable, occurring sometimes early in pregnancy, but oftener toward the end of the term. The limbs are agitated by involuntary contractions of the muscles, which, by the frequency and suddenness of their motion, instantly interrupt the sleep to which the woman was at the moment strongly inclined. Those who bathe daily, exercise judiciously, and, when possible, in the open air, drink only pure soft water (and all can have this from the clouds), partake only of plain and unstimulating food, and sleep upon hard beds and pillows, in cool, fresh air, will rarely, if ever, be troubled with want of sleep."

Costiveness is very apt to be present during nearly all periods of pregnancy. This is caused in a measure by the pressure of the enlarged womb upon the lower bowel, but primarily by the quality and quantity of food used—superfine flour, butter, fat meats, tea, coffee, cakes, sweetmeats, pastry, etc., coupled with physical and mental inactivity.

"This condition of the bowels induces of itself numerous other difficulties. Headache is often brought on solely by constipation—that is, in many cases we remove the constipation, and the headache is sure to leave with it. Sickness of the stomach is always aggravated and often caused by it. The same may also be said of heartburn, palpitation and fainting. Sleeplessness, and, in fact, almost every one of the disorders of pregnancy, may be said to be caused directly, or greatly aggravated, by constipation of the bowels. Even miscarriage has been known to be induced by it."

Constipation can always be cured by the simplest means. The use of fine flour should be entirely dispensed with in such cases, and the unbolted wheat meal or Graham flour used in its stead. The cracked wheat, cooked in various ways, is also an appropriate and excellent article of diet. All kinds of sweetmeats, cakes, pastry, tea and coffee must be rejected. The laxative fruits—such as figs and dates; apples, either raw or very plainly cooked; vegetables; a very moderate use of milk, if the patient desire it, although pure water should at all times be the only allowable drink. This diet, in connection with regular exercise, an occasional hip-bath, and, if required, an injection of tepid or cool water, will cure and prevent this most troublesome complaint.

Diarrhœa.—It occasionally happens that diarrhœa occurs in place of costiveness. When such is the case, it should be treated on the same general principles as constipation—a careful diet, the hip-bath often repeated, and cold injections taken as often as there is any disposition of the bowels to act, are effectual means.

Piles.—Pregnant women are often subject to piles. Of all the causes which operate in their production, habitual constipation of the bowels is most frequent. If this is avoided by the means already pointed out, there will not often be any suffering from them; but if this is permitted to exist, the woman may during the whole remainder of her life be more or less annoyed by them, and may suffer far more than the inexperienced can easily imagine; for they are often exceedingly painful and troublesome, and daily so. Hence the importance of keeping the bowels in their proper condition at all times, and especially during pregnancy; for it is in this way, and in this way only, that the beginnings of the evil may be prevented.

Pruritus, or Itching.—A great many women, when pregnant, are most sadly annoyed with a severely distressing pruritus or itching. The cause of this affection cannot always be ascertained, but a want of proper cleanliness is no doubt one of the principal sources of it. The most effective remedy is the use of cold, shallow hip-baths, the vaginal injection of cold water, the application of cold, wet cloths, or the application of ice, as often as is required. Some physicians advise the washing of the affected parts several times a day with a strong solution of borax, made by dissolving one ounce or more in a pint of soft water. But the cold water alone, no doubt, is as equally effective in palliating, if not curing the disease.

Heartburn.—Perhaps there is no more frequent trouble during pregnancy than that which is experienced from heartburn. This distressing complaint frequently commences immediately after impregnation. It is caused by the acidity of the stomach, and acidity of the stomach comes from improper food. Seldom or ever will a pregnant woman be troubled with heartburn who adopts correct rules for eating and living, and especially as relating to the quantity of the food eaten ; for it is an indisputable fact that ninety-nine out of every one hundred women eat too much food while in the pregnant state. When heartburn first shows itself, the woman must diminish the quantity of food taken. If she on rising in the morning experience its symptoms, she may conclude that portions of the food eaten the day before, instead of digesting, have passed into acetous fermentation, and thus caused the difficulty she experiences. The introduction into the stomach of more food at this time will but make matters worse ; therefore, fasting a meal, or, if required, two meals, with water-drinking in place, is the best possible thing to do, for the absence of food will allow the stomach to regain its vigor. If a quick succession of tumblers of warm water are swallowed, vomiting will take place and relief follow. If vomiting should not follow, the water, by diluting the offending matter in the stomach, will still afford relief. This is the only rational way of treating heartburn, and is at all times to be preferred to the use of lime-water, lemon-juice, soda and other alkalies, which in the end do more harm than good.

Toothache.—Owing to the increased irritability of the nervous system in pregnant women whose bodies are out of order, erratic pains in the face, but especially in the teeth, often occur. The toothache may occur in decayed teeth or perfectly sound teeth. If the tooth is a decayed one, no harm will follow in having it extracted ; but the legitimate method of cure is by proper attention to eating, drinking, exercise, etc.

Headache.—This same nervous irritability, caused in a measure by disregarded hygienic laws, is early indicated in pregnant women by headache, which may appear and disappear at any part of the period. Caused as it is by wrong living—the use of tea and coffee, improper food, unventilated rooms, and want of judicious exercise—it is only required in its treatment that the woman avoid the wrong in her living and adopt the right, when, as a sure result, the headache will disappear.

Palpitation of the heart, occurring for the first time during pregnancy, is rarely connected with any disease of the heart itself, and should therefore cause no alarm. The heart being in direct nervous sympathy with the stomach, palpitation is generally caused—as is nearly every other disorder during this period—by wrong dietetic habits, and therefore the remedy is to adopt and carefully follow right dietetic habits.

Swelling of the feet and limbs.—During the latter months of pregnancy, the feet and legs generally become much swollen, particularly in the after part of the day. In the great majority of cases this is a trifling disorder, requiring simply the strictest temperance in eating, even a spare diet, and a loose state of the bowels, procured by the means recommended when speaking of costiveness.

Pain in the breasts.—When there is pain in the breasts, as often occurs during the first pregnancy, washing the parts with cold water, and wet cloths worn upon the parts, are the means to be employed for relief. Compression by clothes should be avoided, as this is often the cause.

Hysteria.—In women who live a life of excitement, attending frequently balls, theatres and public exhibitions late at night, and especially such as are much addicted to tea and coffee-drinking and the use of stimulating food, there appears during pregnancy a greater tendency to hysterical symptoms than at any other time. Women can and should avoid these causes of so pitiable a disease—for, whether in pregnancy or at other times, hysteria cannot come upon those who live correctly, and maintain at all times good and permanent health.

Irritation of the bladder.—Pressure upon the urethra or neck of the bladder is one of the mechanical evils of pregnancy, rendering the evacuation of the urine difficult and sometimes painful. To prevent this, the patient should be exceedingly careful to evacuate the bladder frequently, and never to allow the calls of nature to go unanswered.

Jaundice is another disorder of pregnancy that occasionally makes its appearance between the fourth and eighth month. It is generally preceded by a disorganized state of the stomach and alimentary canal. When it is attended with violent symptoms, as is sometimes the case, active measures must be employed, but, in the majority of cases, a few days of abstemious living, alternating, now and then, with a day of entire fasting, together with the daily bath and drinking of pure water, will suffice to effect a cure.

Vaccination.—Women during this period should not be vaccinated, or, for that matter, at any other period.

Salivation.—Probably most women experience at this time a more than ordinary flow of the salivary fluid. It is usually simply an observable phenomena, not demanding any treatment whatever. Yet it sometimes becomes very excessive and troublesome to the patient, especially at night, when the sleep is disturbed by the frequent necessity of emptying the mouth. Those women who follow a right mode of living will be troubled very little, or not at all, by salivation.

Vomiting of blood sometimes occurs when there is a general fullness of the system, or perhaps from the cessation of the menstrual function in the earlier periods of pregnancy. It is generally small in quantity, and continues but a short time. If it arises from too great fullness of the system, it can be prevented by abstinence and fasting. Failing in this, cold, wet compresses should be placed upon the abdomen, and otherwise proceed upon the same general principles as in any other case of hemorrhage.

Abortion or miscarriage.—By abortion is meant the expulsion of the fœtus before the seventh month (should it take place between the seventh and ninth months it is called a premature birth.)

" There is no accident befalling female health which forms a greater source of dread, anxiety, and subsequent regret to a married woman, than miscarriage or abortion. When this occurrence becomes habitual, there are no circumstances the consequences of which are productive of more serious injury to the constitution, blasting the fairest promises of health, and oft-times laying the first seeds of fatal disease."

It often occurs within three or four weeks from the period of conception, but it more frequently occurs from the eighth to the twelfth week than at any other time, and is most likely to occur at the time the catamenia should have appeared, if pregnancy had not taken place.

What are the causes for this unnatural and undesirable accident in the pregnant woman ? In the first place, there are certain classes of females more subject to it than others. Those who are fleshy or excessively fat; those who experience excessive menstruation ; those possessed of a scrofulous organization ; and those who have dropsy or are affected with cancers, are all in a measure, unless very guarded as to their mode of life, predisposed to miscarriage during pregnancy. It is often brought on, or in a remote way caused by excessive drinking of strong tea and coffee, eating habitually highly concentrated food, living a life of excitement, frequenting balls, parties, and theatres late at night ; constant novel-reading, and especially in those women who during this period are used by their brutish husbands in the sensual exercise of what they are pleased to term *their* marital rights.

Again, the death or premature expulsion of the fœtus may be caused by extreme costiveness, purging, vomiting, tight clothing, acute disease, terror, fright, falls blows, or excessive fatigue.

And lastly, it may be caused designedly, either by medicine or violence, which of all the causes entails the most danger to the life of the mother, as by the resulting excessive flooding or inflammation of the bowels it frequently terminates fatally. Under the head of Fœticide (Chapter XXII),

I have fully enlarged on this great sin and its undesirable penalties.

The effects of abortion on the woman are serious and lasting. There is a stronger tendency to a recurrence of the evil, for those who miscarry once are apt to do so again; menorrhagia, or an immoderate flow of the menses, always results, as does also irregularity of the monthly periods, these occurring either too often or too seldom; menstruation with more pain and suffering than attend labor itself; hysteria; dissatisfaction with the pursuits and pleasures of life, with an habitually melancholic state of the mind, are nearly always present. All women should earnestly strive to guard against and prevent miscarriage, when it is affirmed that one abortion is far more trying and worse upon the constitution than half-a-dozen natural labors at the full term.

Abortion always indicates a bad state of the system generally, and the first thing a woman should do to prevent its occurrence during pregnancy, is during the period of preliminary preparation to place herself in as close relations to a sound mind in a sound body as is possible for her to do. A healthy woman, following closely the Plan of Life and Law of Genius already recorded, cannot possibly miscarry. For this reason, the woman, to prevent the possibility of this serious accident occurring, should carefully eat only plain, simple food, drink only pure water, bathe daily, exercise daily, breathe pure air, and live much in the light of the sun. She should also avoid feather beds and pillows, over-heated rooms, tea, coffee and alcoholic liquors, all manner of medicines, all undue mental excitement, and, above all, sexual indulgence. The following this line of life will make assurance doubly sure.

In those women who have not lived natural lives, on the threatening of miscarriage, the symptoms noted are, to quote Dr. Tracy:

"When, at any period of pregnancy, we have regular pains in the back and region of the womb, more especially if attended with a feeling of weight, griping, difficulty in passing water, and it coming away in drops, and a feeling of descent of the womb, we may infer that abortion will take place.

" Now and then, particularly when it occurs for the first time, the whole process of a miscarriage does not occupy more than six or seven hours from the very earliest symptoms of its approach to its final completion. But in by far the greater majority of cases, more especially when it has become 'habitual,' its progress is not terminated in as many days or even weeks.

" When this is the case, it may be clearly separated into three distinct stages. By adopting this division, I shall be able to bring the most important portions of this subject before you in a clear light, and to give with more brevity and distinctness those directions which are to be followed.

" *First stage.*—I shall speak of that as the ' first stage' in which the child has as yet received no essential injury—in which the symptoms are only those *menacing* a miscarriage. This is the stage of *warning*, and by improving it in time the unhappy event *may* frequently be avoided.

" The first symptom, frequently, is a feeling of great depression of strength and spirits, for which no assignable cause can be given. The patient loses her appetite, and has a little fever; pains about her back, loins, hips, and the lower part of the abdomen soon follow. These are at first very transitory; they come and go, and, after a while, increase in frequency. Or, in case she has a strong and vigorous constitution, there will be an excited condition of the circulation, manifested by increased frequency and fullness of the pulse, throbbing in the temples, followed by headache, a hot skin, thirst, and no inclination for food, and, united with the pain in the loins, a feeling of weight and tension in the region of the womb."

These are so many symptoms threatening abortion, but, of course, they are always modified by the constitution and previous state of health of the individual. For instance, some will experience only an indistinct, dull, aching pain in the loins, or back, or some other part, either constant or coming and going, with or without slight languor, continuing many days, without any other or more severe symptoms.

Such symptoms, however slight, should receive prompt attention, especially if they come on about the same period of pregnancy at which the patient has previously miscarried; if they do not, she has every reason to expect that the same event will again befall her.

In the treatment of this stage, the woman should retire to bed, and confine herself strictly to it, resting on a mattrass, with but few clothes upon her, in a cool room. If she eat anything, it should be simply cold gruel, and her drink should be cold water alone. This is the time when means can be used with the most prospect of success, and almost everything depends upon their being put in operation at a sufficiently early period. It is best, after observing the above directions, to send for the family physician, whose rules should be carefully followed.

"*Second stage.*—But suppose the patient has not heeded these symptoms; that, never having miscarried, she has thought nothing of a little pain in the back, etc., and has treated them as of no importance, what will be the consequence? In all probability the local pains will increase in frequency and severity, and soon a small discharge of blood, perhaps in clots, will be discovered. This indicates that a partial separation of the ovum from the womb has taken place, and marks the arrival of what I call the 'second stage.'

"*This* is a stage of *hope*, and with *strict attention* that hope *may* be realized. But in order for its realization, in a situation so critical, a prompt and vigorous practice on the part of the medical attendant, and an equally decided and vigilant conduct on the part of the patient herself will be required.

"If the premonitory symptoms already described as constituting the 'first stage' have been present for any length of time, it is comparatively seldom necessary that the process should advance to this second stage, unless there has been a death of the fœtus, or the ovum is diseased; but it not unfrequently happens that the flowing of the second stage appears almost from the first; this, indeed, is most frequently the case when a sudden shock or fall causes the threatening symptoms."

In the treatment of the second stage, the patient should, until the physician arrives, pursue the same course as already pointed out to be followed in the first stage, with the addition of keeping a linen cloth wet with cold water upon the lower part of the bowels, and extending downward between the limbs; this should be frequently exchanged for another, so as to keep a cold one upon her constantly, and ice water may be injected up the vagina. She should lie upon her back, with the hips a little raised, and her head and shoulders lower than usual, and lower than the hips, if it can easily be done.

" *Third stage.*—The third stage is indicated by an increased flow of blood. Sometimes the flooding is truly alarming. The pains, too, increase in frequency and severity, and become expulsive and bearing down, indicating an entire separation of the ovum from the womb. When the process has arrived at this point, there, of course, remains no hope of preventing a miscarriage, and it only remains for the medical attendant to conduct his patient safely through to the end."

The habit of aborting is to be avoided by maintaining the general health in as good a condition as possible, agreeable to the directions already given in the preceding pages, and avoiding the causes named above, or any other causes that have been known to produce it previously; and maintaining the recumbent posture upon the bed or sofa most or all of the term, for a few weeks during that stage of pregnancy at which previous miscarriages have taken place.

CHAPTER XIX.

CONFINEMENT.

T is asserted by some reform physiologists that in giving birth to children women should not suffer *any* pain. This, I think, is going to extremes, although many every-day evidences seem to bear out the assertion. Be this as it may, the pregnant woman can, by the adoption of a right life, so fortify and strengthen and prepare the system for its labor of gestation and parturition, that the pain will be greatly ameliorated, if not altogether avoided, and accidents or after-disorders cannot possibly happen.

In Chapter XVI., and previous chapters, is given the mode of life that should be adopted by the pregnant woman. But to impress the matter more fully on the minds of those interested, I will here briefly recapitulate the requirements necessary in the life of those women whose desire it is to have a natural and easy child-birth :

Clothing.—The clothing should be light, loose and comfortable during the whole period. There must be absolutely no constriction of any kind—by corsets, bands, or even garters. Especially should great care be taken to keep the breasts from being in the remotest manner compressed by the clothing, and the nipples should be effectually protected from any influences that will tend in the least to prevent their enlarging and standing out prominently from the breasts as they should do. Much suffering has been caused by lack of proper attention in this respect.

Do not let a falsely educated modesty interfere with the full, free, and loose mode of wearing the dress. Women— especially those who court the pleasures and flatteries of the great hollow sham, Society—have been known, by tight lacing and dressing—so as to avoid the appearance of their natural condition—to bring forth children that were greatly deformed, and of sickly, pale and weak organizations. The woman pregnant with a new life, instead of assuming a modesty that is as wrong as it is unnatural, should glory in the opportunity and privilege of being the mother of a new being, the developer of a new soul.

Food.—The food used exerts a wonderful influence on the health and strength of the pregnant woman and on the easy birth of the child, and therefore all care should be taken to follow as closely as possible correct dietetic laws. Flesh-meats, tea, coffee, grease and spices should be avoided, and a judicious use of the grains, vegetables, and especially fruits, made. It should never be forgotten that a pregnant woman, in a perfect state of health, does not require any more food because pregnant than she should if otherwise. Women would add much to their health during this period if they would adopt the two-meals-a-day system. When this cannot or will not be done, the last meal should be very light and very simple. Altogether, the Plan of Life given in a former chapter should as closely as possible be adopted.

A too early consolidation of the bones of the fœtus is one of the reasons for dangerous and painful child-birth. This in a great measure can be avoided, and the pain and labor greatly lessened, if the woman will, for about two weeks previous to confinement, abstain from all food having in it the bone-forming material—phosphate of lime and magnesia —as Graham or white flour, beans, peas, barley, and all farinaceous substances, and milk, butter and cheese; in the place of these, using only fruits and vegetables; and of the former, the apple is at all times the most palatable, most healthy and nutritious. The child born under these conditions will be softer and smaller than usual, but will soon grow into strength and beauty.

Rickets, spina-biffida, etc., in the infant, originating, as is generally supposed, from want of earthy matter in the bones, may lead thinking persons to infer that the adoption of this plan would be at too great an expense to the health of the child in comparison with the freedom of pain it would allow the mother. This would surely be so if it were certain that such diseases of the bones were altogether caused in this way. It will be found on inquiry, that the parents of children having rickets or kindred diseases, disobey the laws of life in scores of ways that would produce these undesirable diseases, as living in unlighted, unventilated rooms, lack of exercise, uncleanliness of body, *unwholesome and unhygienic food*, and irregular habits. A woman who has suffered much in parturition, who closely obeys the rules laid down in these pages, and who observes this precaution, of avoiding food, containing in it the bone. forming element, for two or three weeks previous to confinement, will experience much freedom from suffering, and the child will in no way be abnormal. A woman who has heretofore had a succession of still-born children, caused by the large size of the fœtus, or the small size of the pelvis, if this rule is adopted, and all the other requirements of baths, exercise, etc., be observed, will not fail in giving birth to a living child.

The last day or two previous to confinement, it will greatly help the woman, if she abstain from food in part if not altogether. *The Drink* should be only pure water.

Baths.—If the woman desires to experience the pleasures rather than the pains of maternity, the daily water, air and sun-bath, taken under conditions already mentioned, must not be omitted during the whole nine months of pregnancy. At the time the bath is taken the breasts should be well bathed, dried, and thoroughly rubbed with the dry hand. This rubbing commencing with the commencement of pregnancy, and repeated at every daily bath, will strengthen and toughen the parts and so prevent that chapped and fissured state of the skin, and the sore and cracked nipples that very often trouble and distress the poor mother every time the child is applied to the breast. Twice a week, not less than once a week, a sitz-bath should be taken. The mode of taking the sitz-bath is to fill an ordinary common-sized tub with sufficient water of cool or cold temperature, so that when the person sits down, the water will cover the hips and lower portions of the abdomen. When convenient a vessel should be made for the purpose, having the bottom raised a few inches from the floor, and the back raised to rest against. All clothing being removed, the woman should be wrapped up in her bath with a blanket or comfortable. Sometimes it is necessary that the feet should be placed in a warm foot-bath; when this is done, they should be dipped in cold water when taken out of the warm bath. The best time for the pregnant woman to take this bath is just before taking her daily bath at noon; although should circumstances not allow, it may answer to take it just before going to bed. The woman can remain in her hip-bath from fifteen minutes to half an hour, as her feelings may decide. These baths at all times must be taken in a room of a natural and pleasant temperature, for when they cannot be taken under pleasant and enjoyable conditions they do more harm than good.

Injections.—It is desirable through the whole period of pregnancy that the bowels be moved daily. When this does not occur naturally an injection of water of a cool temperature should be employed at or about the time the natural passage should have occurred. During the last weeks of pregnancy the daily movement of the bowels should never be neglected. The injections are made with any one of the patent elastic rubber syringes, which can be obtained of any druggist.

Air and light—the importance of which has been so plainly stated—must not be neglected. Especially should the bed-chamber, at all periods of the day and night, be thoroughly ventilated, and no curtain or blind be permitted to obstruct the sun's rays.

Exercise.—Daily physical exercise, so important in ameliorating the pain of confinement, should never be omitted.

PREPARATIONS FOR CONFINEMENT.—In the preparation for confinement, the room, bed and clothing for the infant should all be put in perfect order and readiness.

Notice should be given to the friend who is desired to be present. She should have some knowledge and personal experience in such matters. The medical attendant should also be apprised. Many women, when in this condition, dread the presence of a male accoucheur, and perhaps justly so ; whenever the opportunity presents itself, the preference should be given to an educated and experienced female midwife. If women closely obeyed the rules laid down in these pages for the right government of the sexual organism, they would not require the attendance of either male or female midwife. These persons—the female friend and medical attendant, and perhaps the husband—are all that should be allowed in the room during confinement. A crowd of women in the lying-in chamber, as is often the case, is at all times to be deprecated and avoided, for they oft-times exceedingly irritate and annoy the patient, and otherwise in a variety of ways do much harm.

Some days previous to the commencement of labor there is a diminution in the size of the body and a subsidence of the abdomen, caused by the sinking of the womb and its contents into the brim of the pelvis. When this takes place, the stomach is more or less relieved, and there is a much more general feeling of comfort and elasticity than has been experienced for a long time. If, after a week or ten days following this " settling down" of the womb, the woman feels unusually well, she may expect to become a mother within twenty-four or forty-eight hours.

The remainder of this chapter I abridge, in a great measure, from a work entitled "The Mother and her Offspring," by Dr. Tracy.

The commencement of labor is usually first indicated by the occurrence of one or more of the following symptoms, particularly the last named :

1. An irritability of the bladder, and perhaps of the lower bowel, causing the patient to have an almost constant desire for their evacuation.

2. Rigors or shiverings, unattended with any sensation of cold.

3. An increased mucus discharge or flow, sometimes streaked with blood.

4. Nausea and vomiting. The occurrence of this is regarded as a good sign, as it is known to indicate that the mouth of the womb is rapidly dilating.

5. The occurrence of true labor pains.

These frequently commence in the back ; sometimes they are first felt in the uterine region, or lowest and front part of the abdomen, and extending from thence to the loins, the lower part of the back, and the inner sides of the thighs. They are not constant, but periodical or intermittent—that is, pain is felt for a moment or two, and then it entirely ceases for a considerable time. At the commencement there is often merely a feeling of uneasiness ; and when active pains first begin they are short and slight, having long intervals between them, of perhaps half an hour or more, each pain lasting but a few moments. By degrees, they become more and more frequent, longer and harder, till the termination of labor.

During the last weeks of pregnancy, women are not unfrequently troubled with irregular pains in the bowels, back, and other parts, which are called false pains, because they so closely simulate those of true labor.

When the labor-pains commence in the manner described, the woman may either sit in an easy chair, or lie down, as may be most agreeable to her feelings. There is usually no occasion for sitting still or lying down at once when the pains first commence, as many do, and perhaps some are compelled to do. It is much better to keep about and busy one's self in some way as long as may be.

It is, in most cases, several hours after the pains commence before the mouth of the womb becomes sufficiently dilated for the " sac of waters" to be formed ; and in first labors it is usually, but not always, much longer than in subsequent ones. The woman should, during this time, attend to the evacuation of water frequently ; and if the bowels have not recently been evacuated, it will be well to make use of an injection, so as to remove everything from their lower portion.

Should the hour for the regular meal occur, she should refrain from more than a very small quantity of food—better none at all. During the whole period of labor little or no nourishment should be taken, and that, if any, of the lightest kind. If there is thirst, cold water may be taken freely.

Should the medical attendant fail to arrive at this time, as sometimes happens, the woman should be guided by the following rules:

She should continue to move about, etc., until the pains become so severe that she feels indisposed to move about any longer, or until she feels a disposition to " bear down" during each pain.

This disposition to "bear down" is the distinctive mark of

the ending of the first stage of labor (the complete dilation of the mouth of the uterus, etc.), and the commencement of the second stage (the expulsion of the child.) The first stage is by far the longest usually, the pains being short and far between, becoming longer and more frequent as the stage advances, but unaccompanied by any disposition to *bear down*, and, so long as the pains are not bearing down, the patient may keep about with advantage.

After the bearing-down pains commence, she should keep her bed most, if not all the time. It is quite probable that about this time the mouth of the womb is rapidly becoming fully dilated, so as to admit of the exit of the child's head, causing a considerable degree of nausea, and perhaps vomiting once or twice. When this occurs, the labor is always found to proceed rapidly.

During this time, perchance, she will be importuned by the attendants "to bear down forcibly"—that is, to exert the muscle, under the power of the will, in forcing downward. This is a very bad practice; to do so greatly fatigues the woman, but does not hasten the labor. She will soon be *obliged* to bear down, and then it will be useful.

After the nausea ceases, and the head begins to press upon and to dilate the parts below the womb, the pains will become harder and harder, and more and more frequent. At this time there will probably be felt a disposition to hold the breath and bear down whenever the pains occur; this may be done.

She may also feel a disposition to press with her feet against the foot of the bedstead, and to take hold of the hands of her assistant and pull at the same time; this she may also do.

As the labor draws to a close, the woman may very likely feel that she will never live to see the end. Should such feelings be present, she must not indulge them, but keep up good courage; for they will soon give way to a feeling of strength, and of ability to help herself by bearing down, holding her breath, pushing with her feet, and pulling with her hands.

Up to this time she can lie upon her back or upon either side, as is liked best from time to time ; but now she should lie upon her left side, with the back near the edge of the bed, and retain this position until after the child is born.

In due time a long and hard pain will expel the head of the child from the womb. One of the attendants should now receive the head upon one of her hands, and in this manner support it, so that its weight will be sustained by the neck.

She should also now ascertain whether the umbilical cord is wound round the child's neck, and, if it is so, she should endeavor to loosen it, so as to slip it down over the shoulders ; but this must be done with great care, and without the exertion of much force upon the cord. If it can not be done easily, she should desist from further attempts.

While in this condition, the patient may have a long interval of rest before the recurrence of another pain, and the attendant may be frightened because the child does not breathe ; but she has no occasion to be so, inasmuch as the child has never yet breathed, and the circulation is still carried on through the umbilical cord and placenta.

Soon another pain will expel the remainder of the child. At this time the attendant will very carefully bear the head upon the palm of her right hand, and convey it downward away from the patient, just so fast as is necessary to make room for the advancing body.

(If the membranes have not been ruptured, and the child is born inclosed within them, as is sometimes the case, they should be immediately ruptured, either with a pair of scissors or the fingers, and the child removed from its perilous inclosure.)

She will now place the child's head in a position where it will rest easy, and have no obstruction in the way of its breathing. It will very soon begin to breathe, and perhaps cry. This first cry of the child often has a powerful effect upon the feelings of the now exquisitely happy, overjoyed mother.

When the infant is born, and the function of respiration is well established, the beating of the artery of the *umbilical cord* will cease, when it may be tied.   It should be remembered that *until all pulsation has ceased in the cord*—which can be ascertained by placing the cord between the thumb and finger—*it should not be separated*.   It may be tied in two places—one about an inch from the body, and the other two inches further distant from the child.   This should be done with a small, strong ligature, passed two or three times around it, *tightly drawn*, and tied in a hard knot.   The umbilical cord may then be divided, with a pair of scissors, midway between the two ligatures, carefully avoiding the cutting of a finger, toe, etc., of the infant, who in its struggles is apt to get some of these parts in the way just as the cut is being made.   All this should be done under the bed-clothing.

The child is then to be carefully taken out of the bed, and wrapped up closely in a soft flannel blanket well warmed, but so placed as to allow it the most free respiration of pure air.

In the course of from fifteen to thirty minutes the pains will again commence for the *expulsion of the after-birth*—when the woman may bear down, and probably before long its expulsion will be effected.

There is an impression upon the minds of many women that it is necessary for some one to hold the umbilical cord in their hands all the time, after it has been separated from the child, until the after-birth has been expelled; but there is no occasion for this, if a ligature has been tied around it, as I have directed, to prevent its bleeding.

Sometimes it does not pass off for several hours, unless removed by other means than the contractions of the womb; but it is a delicate matter for a person not well instructed in the business to attempt to remove it, and I would have you decline the services that may be proffered for its removal by any but experienced hands. It will be much better to wait many hours for the efforts of nature to eject it, than to run any risk of injury from its forcible removal by any but a skillful accoucheur.

CHAPTER XX.

MANAGEMENT OF THE MOTHER AND CHILD AFTER DELIVERY.

UPPOSING that the child has been born, the after-birth cast off, and that otherwise the delivery has terminated favorably, what next is to be observed as a requirement to the rapid recovery of the mother.

If the mother has heretofore observed the practice of taking daily baths, the first thing that may be done, after the removal of all soiled bed and other clothes, is to give her a bath. If the precaution is taken of placing a blanket or other extra article under her, this can be done by an attendant, rapidly and effectually, without the woman leaving her bed. This bath will cause in the mother a sense of great comfort by its tonic effects, increasing her strength, soothing her nervous system, and promoting a desire for life-renewing sleep.

Among the many whims and caprices that custom has entailed on society, is the one of bands to support the abdomen immediately after delivery. The healthy woman who follows closely a right line of life will require no such bandage. Yet, when such is desired, a wet one is at all times the most desirable and effective in its action. The principal reason for the almost universal use of the bandage after delivery is that, unless applied, the woman's form will be injured.

" The sum and substance of this whole matter is just this : whatever tends to weaken the constitution in general, and the abdominal muscles in particular, must have a tendency to produce laxity of the fibres, thus rendering the part more pendulous. On the other hand, whatever tends to strengthen the system, and to give tone to its fibres, must have a contrary effect. Now, the dry belly-band, even when it is so arranged as to keep its place—which it generally is not—is apt to become heating, and, of course, a source of debility under such circumstances. For this reason it is plain that a cold, wet girdle is altogether better than a dry one. Nor should this even be left on too long at a time without changing and re-wetting it. This should be done, as a general thing, every three or four hours at farthest, and in warm weather oftener."

If, in place of the wet bandage, a rather large, coarse towel is dipped in cold or cool water, the surplus water wrung out, and then placed on the abdomen, with one end of it brought down between the thighs, a more easy and effective application could not be had. It should be changed as often as is directed in the case of a wet bandage, mentioned above. The immediate effect of the wet bandage or towel is to strengthen the abdominal muscles, and so prevent pendulousness, and to cause the womb to firmly contract and rapidly regain its usual size, and so preventing all danger from hemorrhage, fever, etc.

It may be that this method of applying water to the mother after delivery will cause, in a large class of women, a feeling of horror; but it must be remembered that though not generally practiced, and as a rule looked on with suspicion, it is no new thing. The application of cold water soon after delivery was practiced by the Romans, and to this day is practiced by savage nations. It only requires a trial—with the previous preparation by baths, exercise, etc.—to convince the most skeptical of its wonderful effects in palliating the pains and perils of child-birth.

During the time occupied in changing of clothes, position, baths, etc., after delivery, the mother must in no way exert herself, allowing her attendants to do all that is required in the way of effort.

The soiled clothing having been changed, the body bathed, and the wet bandage or wet towel applied, the woman should be allowed to sleep as long as the desire is present. The danger of hemorrhage and sudden flooding occurring during the sleep is very slight when the delivery is effected under right conditions. The bed-clothes should be light, so as to avoid over-heating of the body. The room should be well lighted and thoroughly ventilated during this whole period of recovery. I urge the observance of this rule, for it is the practice with many to exclude every breath of fresh air, as well as light, from the lying-in chamber, taking every precaution to oblige the inmates to breathe over and over again the same poisoned atmosphere.

Not only should the room be kept at a proper temperature and well ventilated, but it should also, for the first week at least, be kept *entirely free from all visitors.* This advice is most important and should be faithfully observed, for much trouble, and oft-times great danger, is caused by mental excitement after delivery, brought on by the officious, though perhaps well-meant presence of visitors. Says Velpeau :

" Most of the diseases which affect a woman in child-bed may be attributed to the scores of visits of friends, neighbors, or acquaintances, or the ceremony with which she is too often oppressed ; she wishes to keep up the conversation ; her mind becomes excited, the fruit of which is headache and agitation ; the slightest indiscreet word worries her ; the slightest emotions of joy agitate her in the extreme. And I can affirm that among the numerous cases of peritonitis I have met with, there are few whose origin is unconnected with some moral condition."

With regard to food and drink:

"The patient should begin directly with the same kinds which she intends to use during the period of nursing. If she is to eat fruit—which I consider good for her—she should take it from the first. Prudence should, of course, be exercised in regard to *quantity* as well as quality of food under these circumstances.

"One of the greatest and most common errors in regard to the diet soon after labor, is that of partaking of articles which are too fine and concentrated in their nature. The bowels tend naturally to sluggishness for some days after confinement; hence the diet should be of an opening nature—such as brown bread, cracked-wheat mush, good fruit in its season, and good vegetables. It is a poor practice to keep a patient for nine days on tea, superfine bread, toast and butter, and the like articles. It is no wonder that women, dieted in this way, become constipated, nervous, low-spirited and feverish."

The daily bath must be continued after delivery, at the same time of day and under the same conditions as before delivery. The day after delivery the woman should be lifted out of bed, and given a sitz-bath of from fifteen to thirty minutes, in water of a cool or cold temperature. The sitz-bath may be continued for a week or fortnight, until perfect strength is secured. Whenever the sitz-bath is given it should immediately precede the general bath. The daily bath, during this condition, should always be followed by rest, and, if possible, by sleep.

"About the third or fourth day after confinement the breasts will become much distended with milk. They may be hard and painful; but if the milk is drawn out of them frequently, either by the babe or by some other means, and the patient has been careful to refrain from any but a very small quantity of the plainest kind of food, there will probably not be much trouble in this way."

At this time, however, she may expect to have something of a chill, followed by more or less headache and fever—called the *milk fever*—for a day or two, when it will pass off; but from the time labor commences until the fever is past, none but the plainest and lightest food should be taken.

In order to prevent the nipples from becoming sore, the mother should—each time immediately after the child has done nursing, after having with the thumb and finger gently compressed it, so as to empty the capillary vessels that were filled by the suction—with a sponge or soft linen cloth bathe them thoroughly, and, after carefully wiping perfectly dry, they may be dusted over with pulverized starch, fine arrow-root powder, or any other dry substance of a like inert or harmless nature.

If the breasts and nipples are treated as recommended in a former chapter, and the above course be observed, there need be no trouble whatever with either breasts or nipples.

After the birth of the child, or as soon after as is convenient, it should be carefully washed all over in soft water, neither too warm nor too cold, with the addition of a little mild soap. A temperature of about eighty degrees, Fahrenheit, will be found the best. The dress should be loose, and merely sufficient for the purpose of warmth. The child should not in any way be bound with its clothing, nor should a binder or bandage be put about its abdomen, for the reason that it always causes more or less harm—that is, if there is no malformation of parts—and always tends to induce the very difficulty it is desired to prevent—namely, that of rupture.

The child should have a daily bath, given between eleven and twelve o'clock, great care being taken not to hurt and fatigue it by rough handling, and that it be done as quick as possible.

"During this daily process of washing, which should not

be done languidly, but briskly and expeditiously, the mind of the little infant should be amused and excited. In this manner, dressing, instead of being dreaded as a period of daily suffering—instead of being painful, and one continued fit of crying, will become a recreation and amusement.

"In this, treat your infant, even your little infant, as a sensitive and intelligent creature. Let everything which *must* be done be made, not a source of pain, but of pleasure, and it will then become a source of health, and that both of body and mind ; a source of exercise to the one, and of early discipline to the other."

In the dressing of the child, the principal object is to have it *warm, light and loose.* The extremities should be as warmly clad as are the other parts of the body, and *short sleeves* and *low-neck dresses* should be avoided as being no more suitable for children than for adult persons, and at all times being unphysiological and promotive of sickness and premature death.

"These remarks in regard to dress are particularly applicable to the first stages of infancy, for many children suffer severely, and even fatally, for want of proper clothing, whose parents, blinded by fashion, are not aware of it.

"Mothers are apt to forget that their children need *exercise ;* that, even in the earliest days of infancy, they wish to kick with their feet, and perform a thousand other muscular movements, which they will not be able to do with the freedom desirable if their clothing is either too heavy or put on improperly."

The nursery-room, in which the child is to live principally, should be well lighted and well ventilated. If proper ventilation is such an important consideration for mankind, it is much more so for babykind. Says Sturno :

"Warm rooms, in my opinion, principally contribute to the extraordinary mortality of children, who are carried off by convulsions during the first months of their life.

"The practice of keeping nurseries very warm is particularly detrimental to children during the period of teething.

"The custom of feeding children with inappropriate articles almost as soon as they are born is extremely reprehensible. No sooner is the infant washed and dressed, than, in quite too many instances, the nurse is ready—with her spoon in hand, and with her cup of gruel, pulverized cracker, or some other equally injurious preparation—to fill its stomach to the utmost of its capacity. This process of stuffing is often continued with a ruinous degree of diligence and perseverance, placing the new-comer in a most pitiable condition. Being incapable of making known its wants by words, its screams of distress, occasioned by the colic and griping thus induced, are taken either as manifestations of hunger—and, to appease this, the stomach is constantly kept in a state of distension by food—or of griping, to relieve which, and 'to enable the little fellow to throw the wind off from his stomach,' recourse is had to catmint tea, aniseseed tea, Godfrey's cordial, soothing syrup, paregoric, or some other palliative or nostrum, by which another source of gastric derangement and indigestion is brought into operation. Thus, between the two, the helpless babe has no chance of escaping from the torments and ruinous consequences of its unfortunate condition."

As with the adult, so with the child; wrong food, in wrong quantities, at wrong intervals, has much to do with its sickness and premature death. At first affecting the stomach, it causes acidity, flatulency, vomiting, diarrhœa and emaciation. If the over-feeding and wrong feeding is kept up, there usually results, from the irritation thus kept up in the stomach, chronic and unmanageable diarrhœa, slow fever, chronic affection of the liver, epilepsy, dropsy of the brain, convulsions, and other dangerous and fatal maladies.

"It not unfrequently happens that the digestive functions are, in the brief period that intervenes between the birth of the infant and the secretion of the mother's milk, so de-

ranged and impaired, that even the wholesome and congenial fluid furnished by the maternal breasts will not be easily
digested. Nature herself points out the impropriety of this
practice of feeding new-born infants by withholding the
nourishment which she provides until many hours after
birth."

Perhaps I shall not find a more appropriate place than
this to speak of the pernicious practice of feeding children,
when just born, with certain articles (some of which are too
disgusting to be even named) with the view of purging off
the contents of the bowels, which is called *meconium*, and
certain other articles to prevent the red gum or the jaundice,
just as though Nature did not provide for the proper care of
the young. I pray you, suffer nothing of the kind to go
into the mouth of your infant child.

"It is very well, immediately after the child has been
washed and dressed, to feed it with *two or three tea-spoonfuls
of cool water*. This operates to cleanse the mouth and prevent it from becoming sore, as babes' mouths are somewhat
apt to do if this is neglected; and on this account it should
be repeated every morning. In cases where the child seems
hungry, it appears to satisfy it as well as anything that can
be given.

"If this is done, children will most commonly lie quiet for
an hour or two, or at least till the mother has become so far
rested as to be able to have her babe applied to the breast.
This may be done, if it is wakeful and disposed to nurse, as
soon as she feels able; but if the child is disposed to lie
quietly, either sleeping or waking, it may be well to let it
lie in some warm place, as in the nurse's lap, or, better still,
close by its mother's side.

"In the course of a few hours, probably, the child will
manifest some disposition to nurse, and in that case it should
be put to the breast and allowed to draw as much as it
pleases; but in case it lies quietly, and shows no such disposition, you should, by all means, let it lie, and not disturb

it, or be in the least alarmed on this account. I have known lambs to run about and be quite active for two, three, or four of the first days of their lives, without receiving anything into their stomachs; and you may rest assured that, if your child lies quietly by your side, breathing easily, and sleeping or not sleeping, it is doing well, and should not be disturbed till it manifests some uneasiness or a disposition to nurse. If well, it will certainly do so in the course of twenty-four hours.

" Do not let the desire to see his bright eyes lead you to disturb his quiet slumbers, nor your desire to see him manifest his uncommon brightness get the better of your sober judgment. Let him rest. When he wakes nurse him, change any of his clothing that may require it, and let him sleep.

" Babes treated in this way will usually sleep a great part of the time for several of the first weeks of their lives. No fears should be entertained in regard to the health of a new-born babe so long as it rests quietly; and it should not be disturbed, as is too often done through mistaken kindness, or to gratify the curiosity or any other feelings of the mother or others."

It is generally supposed that the child must take something to purge off the contents of the bowels, called *meconium*—a tenacious, semi-fluid substance, of a dark color, which, if not carried off within a few days after birth, may become a source of irritation; but it should be remembered that Nature has provided for this want.

"The fluid secreted in the mother's breasts before the birth of the child, is as different from the milk that is furnished by them afterward, as the contents of the child's bowels are from that found in them after it has begun to nurse, and is exactly fitted for the purpose of purging it off.

" If the child is put to the breasts as soon as he seems disposed to nurse, he will obtain enough of this fluid, which is

17

258 THE SCIENCE OF A NEW LIFE.

technically called *colestrum*, even when the mother supposes there is nothing there. I repeat, even in this case he will, in nine cases out of ten, at least, get enough to meet the necessities of the case, and the meconium will be purged off by the colestrum without occasioning any colic, griping, or other unpleasant symptoms. It will not act like physic, producing a rapid succession of stools ; but more slowly, and in the course of two or three days the work will be done, and done as it should be.

"If the mother is able to nurse her child, nothing should be allowed to enter its mouth, for the first few days at least, except the cool water that I have already spoken of, and what it gets from her."

How often should a child be nursed, is a question of some importance. Some advocate every four hours ; others, again, three hours between the times of nursing. Either will do. It is not so much the observance of a certain number of hours between the periods as in the *regularity* in feeding. To give the child the breast every hour one day in feeding, and then perhaps the next the mother to absent herself for many hours, is certainly not a good practice. By endeavoring to accustom and train the infant, as far as possible, to regular periods for feeding, and all other natural operations, much of the trouble otherwise attendant upon the nursery may be avoided, and its quiet much less frequently disturbed.

Healthy infants can be habituated to sleep through the night without waking to nurse during the whole time. This should be done whenever it is possible, for it is a bad practice to allow the child to take the breasts during the night-time.

"If the infant is encouraged to start up at any time of the day or night and demand the breast, or if the latter is constantly offered to it as a means of soothing its cries, whether it be hungry or not, perpetual restlessness and discontent must be the result; and these once established as a habit, the mother's peace and enjoyment, and the child's health and welfare, are sure to be sacrificed.

" The infant may be quieted for the moment in this way, but it will be at the expense of ten-fold trouble and disappointment at a future time.

" By suitable care, almost any child may be taught to require food only at something like stated intervals, and the danger of over-distension of the stomach may thus in a great measure be avoided.

" Care should be taken to avoid provoking the infant to take the breast, in order to *appease restlessness* that may arise from any cause except hunger. It is surprising how soon, by a neglect of this rule, a morbid appetite is created.

" It is too often the custom of mothers and nurses to take it for granted that because the child cries, that it is hungry, and then to force it to take the breast ; or, when fretful from any cause, to appease it by the same means. In this way a quiet is often produced, through the apoplectic state of the stomach, induced by this over-feeding ; but, as I have already intimated, it is at the expense of the healthy tone of the stomach, and, when often repeated, can not fail to produce a disordered action of the digestive organs, and thus do permanent harm."

Mothers whose desire it is to have children free from sickness, and to grow up to adult life, should avoid and shun all manner of patent nostrums—such as paregoric, cordials, soothing syrups, etc., all of which contain opium, and all of which, in their use, are destructive to the nervous system and digestive organs of the child, and seriously affect the child's future health, well-being, happiness and usefulness through life. And especially should those vile, starchy compounds called pap, panada, and the like, be positively prohibited.

WET-NURSE.—When circumstances are present which prevent the mother from suckling her infant, a wet-nurse is the best substitute, provided she be healthy and have a good supply of milk.

In the selection of a wet-nurse great care should be taken. She should be young, perfectly healthy, of a pleasant, cheerful disposition and even temper, and free from all deformities—such as squinting, stuttering, and the like. She should have two good breasts of milk, and the age of her child should be near that of the one she is to nurse, as the milk changes so during the first month that the milk of a nurse with a child six months old would not be proper food for a child just born.

In the feeding of the child the utmost vigilance should be exercised by the mother, as all sorts of deceptions are practiced by professional wet-nurses.

"At one time the stomach of the child is engorged to its greatest extent, in order that the nurse may have the time to herself, and then all nourishment is withheld for an unreasonable period for the same reason; laudanum and paregoric are administered clandestinely that the child may not disturb her rest, and all sorts of deceptions, which require the constant watchfulness of the mother to detect and prevent.

"The diet of the nurse should be the same as for any person in good health; the food should be plain, abundant, and taken only at the regular hours. It is not a fact that a woman while nursing requires a large amount of rich food, or that she should eat before going to bed; all these irregularities tend to destroy the health, which, of course, injures the milk. There are no women with breasts better filled with milk than the peasant women, who subsist on food of the very simplest kind. The practice of allowing nurses porter, ale, or spirits of any kind, while nursing, is always unnecessary; a *healthy* nurse requires nothing of the kind, and no other should be engaged.

"The nurse should be required to exercise in the open air for some time each day, and to take an entire bath as often as twice during the week."

ARTIFICIAL FEEDING.—Failing a wet-nurse, artificial feeding, or bringing the child up by hand, as it is called, is the last resort.

" The kinds of food recommended for the diets of infants are very numerous, but nothing is better than pure cow's milk; it must be perfectly sweet, and, if possible, always from the same cow. There is a great difference in the milk of different cows, though fed upon the same food, and a mixture of the milk of several cows, or a continual change from one to another, is much less likely to agree with the infant than the milk from the same cow uninterruptedly. It is desirable that the nutriment provided for the infant should approach as near as possible to the natural food, and for the child at birth equal parts of milk and water, with a little white sugar, warmed to the temperature of ninety-eight degrees; this approaches very near to the natural aliment, and is the only food required for the first eight or ten months; the water may be gradually decreased, until the end of the seventh month, at which time the pure milk may be given. In cases where the milk disagrees with the child, cream and water will be found an excellent substitute; cream is lighter than milk, it is easily digested, and being more nutritious, a smaller quantity may be given. In many cases the fault is not so much with the food as in the way in which it is given, and in many cases where it is thought to disagree with the infant, if it were given in smaller quantities, and at longer intervals, with perfect rest for half an hour after eating, the trouble would be done away with.

"The food should be taken into the stomach slowly; and here again we should imitate Nature, and allow the child to suck its nourishment from a bottle, instead of being fed with a spoon. In the act of sucking the food is mixed with the saliva, which is an assistant to digestion, and which the digestive organs are deprived of, to a great extent, if any other mode of feeding be adopted.

" A variety of contrivances have been recommended for

the administration of food to infants; any glass bottle of a convenient shape and size, with a few folds of fine, soft linen pierced with a small hole, and adapted to the mouth in the form of a nipple, will answer every purpose. Particular attention must be paid to keeping the bottle perfectly clean; it should never be filled without being previously subjected to a thorough washing of both bottle and nipple in hot water. It will be well to provide two bottles, that one may always be in a condition for immediate use; the bottle should always be glass, its transparency enabling the mother the more readily to detect any uncleanliness."

The nipple-sheath, made of rubber, as well as rubber toys, should be kept out of the reach of infants, for the reason that in the manufacture of rubber large quantities of white lead are used. In the action of biting or sucking through the rubber toy or nipple, the white lead is in a measure disengaged and absorbed into the child's organism, where it injures the bones, causing curvature of the spine, bad teeth, rickets, etc., and otherwise affecting more or less the general health of the child.

WEANING.—The growth and protrusion of the teeth is a certain index of the development of the child's digestive organs, and indicates with great exactness that a change of food is required, and that the digestive organs are in a condition to dispose of the simple varieties of nutriment upon which the child will now be required to subsist. This usually happens from the tenth to the fourteenth month, and if the child has been accustomed gradually to other nutriment, weaning will in most cases be attended with little or no inconvenience. This change should be very gradual, and commence soon after the protrusion of the two first teeth.

It is generally recommended in books and by physicians to feed the infant, at this time of weaning and after, on preparations of arrowroot, pulverized cracker, corn-starch, etc. —articles that possess little or no nutriment, and if there was no milk given along with such food the child would after a time starve. It has been proven by physiologists that articles of diet made from white flour will not in themselves support life. The experiment has been tried on dogs, one dog being fed exclusively on bread made from superfine white flour, and the other on bread made from the whole grain (Graham flour.) At the end of thirty-five days the first dog was dead, having gradually died of starvation, while the dog fed on unbolted wheat bread was strong and healthy. When it is understood that three out of every five children fail to reach their tenth year, I think a radical change is demanded, not only in the department of diet of infants, but also in clothing, pure air, etc.

As the period of weaning approaches, small portions of pure and fresh milk, thickened with soft-boiled rice, applesauce, slightly sweetened, and fresh cream, or a thin gruel made from finely ground unbolted wheat flour, should be allowed the child two or three times a day.

It is desirable that the gradual increase in the quantity should keep pace with the more or less rapid appearance of the teeth, so that after the first eight teeth have made their exit from the gums, the child shall have been, as it were, insensibly weaned. By this course of management the infant's stomach will be gradually accustomed to a more substantial diet, and will be sufficiently prepared, when the proper time of weaning arrives, to admit of an exclusively artificial aliment, with but little, if any, risk of injurious consequences.

After weaning, the staple article of diet for the child should be made from unbolted, well-cleaned and finely-ground wheat, for this grain contains all the constituents demanded by the system of a growing child for nourishment—the bone, muscle, and nerve-making properties. The best and simplest food made from unbolted flour is Graham pudding, the mode of making which is as follows:

"Stir slowly into fast-boiling water, sprinkled from the

hand, sufficient Graham flour to make a thin pudding. Let it boil five or ten minutes and it is done. If set away from the fire for a few minutes before taking up, it will cleave readily from the kettle, leaving it more easy to be washed. Very much depends on the manner of making, as from the same materials a most delicious dish may be made, or one not fit to eat.

" The pudding left from one meal is allowed to cool in the table pudding-dish, and inverted on a platter of the same form for the next meal. Any of this that may be left can be dissolved in the water in which the next pudding is to be made, and so made over ; or a better way is to brown slices of it on a griddle."

Unfermented Graham bread, corn bread, and dishes made from unbolted wheat, corn and oatmeal, plainly, simply and palatably cooked ; apples, and all other fruit in season, and milk, are the *only* articles from which a diet should be selected for the child, and, for that matter for the adult whose desire is for a pure and healthy life.

Care should be taken that suckling is continued no longer than is consistent with the welfare of either mother or child. Says Dr. Eberle :

" To the mother, the effects of unduly protracted lactation are sometimes extremely pernicious. We not unfrequently see women frail, debilitated, and constantly tormented with dyspeptic and nervous affections, suckling their infants for eighteen or twenty months, without suspecting that their ill health is the result of exhaustion from the constant drain of the nutritious element of the blood, which is kept up by suckling. The mother is not the only sufferer from this habit of protracted lactation. After the proper period for weaning the infant, there is a decided change takes place in the milk; it not only diminishes in quantity, but deteriorates in quality, and becomes more and more unwholesome in its character in proportion as lactation is protracted. Let me say here to those mothers who think to lessen the supposed dangers of the second summer by suckling the child through that period, that they are actually increasing the danger by allowing the infant food from which it derives but little nutriment, and which is decidedly unwholesome. I have been particular to point out the evils of this habit, as it is a very common one in our country."

The best months in the year for weaning are the months of March, April and May, September, October, and November.

CHAPTER XXI.

THE PERIOD OF NURSING INFLUENCE.

ENIUS, to be successfully transmitted to the child, must be conceived in the period of preparation, exercised in the period of gestation, and the exercise continued during the whole period of nursing. In the period of preparation the character of the child, in the rough, is originated; in ante-natal life this character is developed; while during the nursing period its character is perfected and established.

The mother's influence during the time of nursing, therefore, is not one lightly to be estimated; and the following expressed thoughts in regard to its observance should be carefully noted and followed by the mother who has obeyed the previous directions in regard to rearing beautiful, healthy and talented children.

To the mother who, through some physical abnormal quality, cannot nurse her child, or who, through some abnormal mental characteristics, will not nurse her child, this chapter does not, of course, apply.

To the first, who, notwithstanding a just observance of

266

right rules for living and a careful trial of remedial measures, is unable to nurse her child, I have naught to say ; but to the mother who can, but will not, nurse her child, it seems to me that such a woman must have some great abnormal quality of soul that lowers her vastly in the scale of *human* kind. This great duty, this sacred trust, should rest with the mother alone, and she who commits the suckling of her child to another, while her own breasts are ready to furnish an ample supply of milk, does not, cannot, possess the qualities of a mother or Christian.

It is indeed a most extraordinary circumstance that a duty which is so strongly enforced by the commands of Nature, and which is connected with so many delightful and hallowed sentiments of the maternal heart, should ever be voluntarily relinquished ; and it is never done without subjecting both mother and child to great liability to injurious consequences.

There is no period of woman's life in which she has such great enjoyment, such perfect physical health, as when she is nursing the offspring of her own blood.

When a mother, through causes avoidable or unavoidable, allows her child to nurse at the breast of a stranger, she loses the chance of permanently fixing and completing the character of the infant, and in a great measure the child draws from the breast of the strange mother mental and physical characteristics that may be undesirable.

The importance of the mother's influence during the period of nursing is greatly under-estimated, and by very many not even believed in. When it is understood that the food the mother daily uses goes to furnish the food of the infant, and that, in being converted into milk in the mammary glands, is influenced not only by the quality and quantity of the food eaten, but also by the mental state of the mother during and immediately preceding its secretion, and that this influence is carried in the milk directly to the child's organism, and affects in a smaller or greater measure the child's mental and physical character, it must be allowed, by all candid, thinking mothers, that its importance cannot possibly be over-estimated.

I have known an instance in which a mother, after a violent altercation with a neighbor, immediately after gave suck to her infant. The child had not been at the breast but a moment when it went into violent convulsions, and for a time it had every appearance of dying. If it had died, there need have been no great surprise expressed thereat. It is well known that men have died in a passion, and the same greatly unbalanced and disorded state of the nervous system of the mother, acquired during a " fit of passion," through the medium of her milk, transmitted to the delicate organism of the child, would bring on premature death, or greatly help to do so.

So, in a smaller or greater measure, the mother's everyday state of mind and body is carried to and impressed on the mind and body of her infant. If the mother, during the two previous periods of introductory and gestative influence, be of a morose, gloomy, fault-finding disposition, and she continues the exercise of these abnormal characteristics during the period of nursing, she will, without the least doubt of the fact, impress the like undesirable qualities of character on her child, and every day's suckling, up to the time of weaning, will more fully and perfectly establish them.

And so of grief and sorrow, pain and anguish, anxiety and fear, or any other of the passions that in their exercise lower and unbalance the nervous force.

In the same way that the mother's habits of thought affect the child's character, so does the food she eats affect the child's physical growth and health, and, in a close manner, its mental characteristics. Eating indigestible articles of diet will cause in the child a disturbed state of the bowels—colic, griping, intestinal fever, etc. ; or drinking ale, beer, wine, whisky, or that filthy mess called porter—so often advised for nursing mothers, to " strengthen them" (!)—will cause in the child not only a predisposition to disease, but also a tendency to be a drunkard.

The use of spirituous and fermented drinks is at all times improper, but especially so during the nursing period. When given to increase the milk they may do so, but it is always at the expense of its quality. The child may seem to thrive nicely for a time, but eventually it will be in great danger of being severely afflicted with some form of cutaneous disease, or something worse, before it is two years old. Says Dr. Tracy:

" One of the worst cases I ever saw was caused in this way. The mother drank porter and ale, one or both freely, while nursing; the child grew very fast and very fat, but such a sight as it after awhile presented, I never wish to see again."

The mother of advanced ideas, who has faithfully followed the directions to be observed during the periods of preparation and gestation, and whose desire it is to continue faithfully to the end, will, during the period of nursing, closely adhere to the plan of life and habits of thought decided on in the commencement.

To this end, she must be as careful as ever, if not more so, in the food eaten. Only the very plainest and simplest food should be used, and eaten at regular intervals. She should, as she values her own peace and ease, and her child's health and happiness, exercise all due care against evils of this kind, for any momentary gratification of her appetite will be dearly paid for by the distress and, if no more, temporary illness of her babe.

Especially during this period of nursing should the mother exercise the qualities (decided on from the beginning) that in their transmitted action will constitute genius. The nine or twelve months of nursing will be the mother's last chance to directly perfect and establish the character of the child, and in no wise should it be slighted. The main requirements to be observed in this direction are but a repetition of those given in Chapters XIII. and XVI., with the additional rule that they be observed immediately preceding each time the child is given the breast.

After an intense application of the brain-power in the direction required—be it that of mechanic, author, inventor, editor, teacher, singer, etc.—the mother immediately following this application should give her child the breast. And precisely so in every department of thought or action intended for the child's future existence, *immediately following the persistent, active effort in trying, the child should be given the breast.* These efforts of the mother should be so timed as to precede the child's regular time for feeding ; for it is a requirement in the right development of the child, that order in all things—feeding, bathing, sleeping, etc.—be closely observed. The philosophy of this requirement is, that the active mental exercise of any organ or set of organs of the mother, impresses the qualities exercised on the milk globules being secreted in her mammary glands ; for it is with the milk as with the blood from which it is secreted —every globule takes on and represents the character of the mother who manufactured it. These milk globules—having, through the rightly-directed, active mental and physical exercise of the mother, taken on a positive character in harmony with that of the mother—are through suckling carried to the child's organism, where it, of course, cannot possibly do otherwise than *reproduce its like.* In this way the quality desired to be reproduced in the child is *perfected and established*—but *only* perfected and established, for during the periods of preparation and gestation they should be *originated and developed.*

During this period—as during the two former periods— the mother and child should live much in the open air. She should continue to take daily exercise ; never omit the daily sponge, air and sun-bath ; wear comfortable and loose clothing ; exercise daily and hourly the bright, happy and joyous side of her nature ; ever surround herself with pleasant and beautiful associations; breathe pure air; drink *only* pure water; eat principally ripe fruits, fresh vegetables, unleavened bread made from unbolted wheat, etc., and, in company with her husband, cultivate the department of thought that is intended for the child's pursuit in life—especially exercising it in positive earnestness just before the time for giving her child the breast.

During this period—as during the two former periods—she should not use alcoholic liquors of any kind, strength, or quality; tea, coffee, or chocolate; pickles, vinegar, or spices of any kind, and as little salt as is possible to get along with; sweets, pastry, etc.; medicines, patent or otherwise; and, above all, she should not allow her husband to have sexual acquaintance with her. Succeed in carrying out, during these three periods of preparation and influence, a strictly pure, chaste and continent life, *and you will have done more for the future health and welfare of the child's soul and body than could be done in any other way, time or manner.*

During the nursing period of the child's life feed it regularly; keep its extremities warm and comfortable; in clear weather give it all the out-door sunshine that can be had; *let it sleep all it wants to;* bathe it daily; do not, I pray you, give it any cordial, soothing syrup, or any other patented trash; and, when it comes to be weaned, let it be done in a gradual manner.

With the weaning of the child I would fain close this chapter, but am tempted to give a few general but very important directions for the child's future guidance.

Up to the age of ten years—fifteen would be better—no book should be allowed in the child's hands, for during this time the child should be allowed simply to grow—sleep, eat, exercise and grow—no more, no less.

All indications of precocity and "smartness" should be suppressed, and it should be made to exercise only the physical, keeping dormant the mental and spiritual departments of its nature.

Only the plainest and simplest food, free from sugar, spices, candies, etc., should be allowed it.

No drugs or patent medicines of any kind should be given it.

The child should be carefully guarded against associates of a bad or doubtful character.

Girls and boys, during this time, should be dressed precisely alike, and in every way treated alike. The more of a "tom-boy" the girl can grow into, the better for her future health, strength and beauty.

The child should at all times be dressed physiologically. It astonishes me beyond measure to see a little girl having her arms and legs bare, and otherwise gaudily bedecked, on the streets, led by her mother, who, though much more able to withstand atmospheric changes, is dressed from head to foot warmly and comfortably. Societies for the protection of animals against cruelty are good enough in their way, but societies for the protection of babies against cruelty would be much more productive of lasting benefit, at least to ungrown humanity at large. It is not only a shame, it is a great sin, this modern style of half dressing children that is so largely practiced in so-called "good society." Dress your children, at all seasons of the year, from the points of the toes to the tips of the fingers, *equally* warm and comfortable, without band or constriction of any kind, and so allow them to grow into perfect models of manly strength or womanly beauty.

PART THIRD.

WRONGS RIGHTED.

PART THIRD.

WRONG RIGHTED.

CHAPTER XXII.

FŒTICIDE.

UT of the overgrown, abnormally developed and wrongly directed amativeness of the man—out of the social bondage and pitiable slavery of the woman, there have been born such wrongs, such miseries, such sufferings, aye, such murders, as to lead an observing and reflecting mind to wonder why God, in the might of His wrath, does not, by an effort of His omnipotent will, sweep off from the face of this beautiful earth the great multitude of people who, knowingly or ignorantly, break His divine laws.

Out of the licentiousness of the man and bondage of the woman there is developed the ever-present and ever-increasing great wrong and monstrous crime of an undesigned and undesired maternity—a wrong and crime, the perpetrators of which, rather than be thwarted in the exercise of the licentious of their nature, commit without thought of consequences here or hereafter, the crime of fœticide—the killing of the fœtus while in the mother's womb—the murder of the unborn.

That this crime is not only wide-spread on this great continent, but is rapidly on the increase, we have the testimony of physicians, whose investigations have been thorough, and whose social standing and integrity cannot be questioned.

Dr. Nathan Allen, of Lowell, has declared in a paper read before a late meeting of the American Social Science Association, that no where in the history of the world was the practice of abortion so common as in this country; and he gave expression to the opinion that, in New England alone, many thousand abortions are procured annually.

Says Dr. Reamy, of the Ohio State Medical Society:

"From a very large verbal and written correspondence in this and other States, together with personal investigation and facts accumulated * * * that we have become a *nation of murderers.*"

And not to large cities alone is this great crime confined, but from towns, villages and hamlets do the death wails of the murdered innocents go up to God for vengeance.

A noticeable proof that forced abortions are on the increase, or that an almost equally great wrong is done by the prevention of pregnancy, is found in the small size of families. Especially is this observable in the New England States, where the native population is stationary or decreasing.

In the paper already referred to, Dr. Allen says:

"Examining the number of deaths, we find that there are absolutely more deaths than births among the strictly American children, so that, aside from immigration and births of children of foreign parentage, the population of Massachusetts is rapidly decreasing. * * * The birth-rate in the State of New York shows the same fact, that American families do not increase at all, and inspection of the registration in other States shows that the same remark applies to all."

Dr. Allen may well ask: "What then is to be the state of society in New England fifty or a hundred years hence?"

Says the Rev. Dr. Eddy, in a late number of the *Christian Advocate:*

" We could prove that in one little village of one thousand inhabitants, prominent women have been guilty of what we will presently show to be *murder*. And sadder still, half of these are members of Christ's Church. Yet here, and elsewhere, where fifteen per cent. of wives have the criminal hardihood to practice this black art, there is a still large and additional per cent. who indorse and defend it. One of the worst features of the case is the fact that, if a young, pure and inexperienced wife is shocked by revelations made by hardened abortionists, she is straightway ridiculed into silence or argued into acquiescence. The very worst feature, however, is, that young girls, too young to marry, are initiated into these mysteries of massacre, thoroughly imbued with a dislike of children, especially their future own, and are thus prepared to perpetrate this horrid villainy, when their more aged instructors are gone up before God. We protest that it is pitiful. To fortify these statements we have Dr. Stewart's testimony : 'But few of either sex enter the marital relations without full information as to the ways and means of destroying the legitimate results of matrimony. Among married persons, so extensive has this practice become, that people of high repute not only commit this crime, but do not even shun to speak boastingly among their intimates of the deed and the means of accomplishing it.' "

It cannot be possible that the large class of women who commit the crime of fœticide, or that class, still greater in number, who are accessories to such wrongs, can be aware of the full import of what they do. They cannot know that in the sight of God and man the deed they do is *murder*, and that at the Day of Judgment as *murderers* they will stand before the throne of God. Let us hope that in doing these things it is because they know not what they do.

Many, to shield themselves from the imputation of wrong, will deny that the killing of the fœtus before its natural time of birth is murder. This is most easily decided.

First, as to what constitutes murder. The taking away the life of any human being designedly, expresses in a general way the crime of murder. Now a great army of self-justifiers will say that life is not present in the child until "quickening" is noticed by the mother; while others, again, may assert that life is not present until the first cry of the child announces its birth. This is a great fallacy. Says Beck, in his "Medical Jurisprudence:"

"The absurdity of the principle upon which these distinctions are founded is of easy demonstration. The fœtus, previous to the time of quickening, must be either dead or living. Now that it is not the former is most evident from neither putrefaction nor decomposition taking place, which would be the consequence of an extinction of the vital principle. The embyro, therefore, before the crisis, must be in a state different from that of death, and that can be no other than life."

Life is present from the very moment of conception. There must be life at this time, else there could be no conception —that is, there must be a germ-cell and a sperm-cell contained in each life, and the moment these two elements are united, there is born a *being* containing the elements of a *soul.* At no other possible time of pre-natal or ante-natal life can the soul and body of a new being be originated than at its conception; and the forcible removal of this being during its growth in the mother's womb causes its premature death, and therefore its MURDER, and the party or parties who do it, or are accessory to it, are MURDERERS.

Says Dr. Eddy:

"Independent of all laws, human authorities or decisions, the true Christian theory is that the THOUGHT of man in the mind of God embraces the entire period of his earthly relations, between the extreme limits of embryotic existence and old age. Who with sacreligious hand does violence to this chain of sacred relations is a MURDERER."

This brings us to the class or classes of society in which are found those who practice forced abortions.

1. Those in whom, by reason of malformation of body, it is found necessary to produce abortion or bring on premature birth.

2. Those women who, being unmarried, are seduced through misrepresentation by men of licentious natures.

3. Those who, being married, desire no offspring, as interfering with their pleasures.

4. Those who, being married, and maternity being forced on them, desire no offspring, because of poverty or sickness, or otherwise being unprepared to lovingly assume the burden of a desired maternity.

These classes are largely made up of church-members and professing Christians. They belong, as a rule, to the middle and higher classes of society, and are distributed about equally in the cities, towns and villages.

Of the first class—those women who require a forced abortion, owing to some physical malformation—I have nothing to say. When it is required to save the life of the mother by the premature death of the child, it should never be decided on or performed without the presence of at least three able and conscientious physicians. The wrong and sin done by such women consists in their marrying at all, or in marrying men of greatly disproportioned sizes. This class is so rare that it is almost unnecessary to mention them.

Those who belong to the second class come first in number of those who designedly practice pre-natal murder. In proportion to the number of this class, there is not near the number of forced abortions produced as in those who are married. When a woman has been betrayed into relinquishing her virtue, and pregnancy follows, she should allow it to go on to its full term. In doing this she will do infinitely less harm to her organization than if she had killed the fœtus, and will also be free from a guilty conscience. But "let no woman, who would avoid a life of shame and disgrace, trust the promises of any man until legally married, for all experience shows that, aside from the moral pollution, she has a right to expect to be deserted, or at least reluctantly married, without the respect or confidence of her husband, with her own confidence in his honor gone; distrust and unhappiness must inevitably result. If she fails to be married to the man, aside from her own spiritual degradation, and feeling of unworthiness to ever enter the marriage relation with a pure-minded man when occasion offers, her good name, if not destroyed by pregnancy or by some filthy disease, is at the mercy of a base libertine, who will not scruple to throw out to his associates insinuations as to his success and her folly, which will sooner or later destroy her peace. By a single false step she has entered the broad road that leads to destruction, and she will find little peace in any direction."

What can be said of the third class of wrong-doers, who desire no offspring because interfering with the follies and pleasures of their fashionable existence? Not one good word in extenuation of their unholy lives and unlawful crimes. This class of women, of all these classes, is the most to be reprobated, and deserve in full measure the severe pains and penalties attached to their wrong-doings. Low indeed must that woman be sunken in iniquity, sadly blighted must be her soul, who will allow a love of the hollow pleasures and vanities of a "society" life to overcome the instinctive desire for children, and to such a degree as not to hesitate at the murder of her unborn child.

And lastly, we come to the fourth class—a class largely exceeding in number all those already mentioned put together. It is in connection with this class that the unrestrained licentiousness of the man is paramount. Exercising the low and animal of his nature, without any thought of the loving preparation so necessary to the originating a new soul, and against the wishes of the woman, the man forces an undesired and undesigned maternity on his wife.

What is the result? "On discovering the fact, it becomes repulsive to her nature. She is not prepared to bear the cross and endure the crucifixion. Instantly her soul is filled with murderous intent. She resolves to nip and crush the opening bud of life—to procure abortion—that is, to commit the deed of ante-natal child-murder. She does not feel that it is *her* child. She may regard it as *yours*, but she cannot acknowledge it as her own; and though it must receive its gestational development in her organism, she cannot tenderly and lovingly cherish and guard it as bone of her bone, flesh of her flesh, and soul of her soul. It is so *in fact*, but not in her *feelings*. She asked not for it; her soul repels it as an intruder, thrust upon her without her consent, and in contempt, it may be, of her earnest remonstrance—for thus it often is. The child, she feels, has no right to an existence at her expense. An uninvited and hated intruder is exhausting her vital energies, and robbing her of that which no earthly treasures can ever restore or recompense. Through her physical suffering and mental anguish, an unbidden and loathed guest is feeding and thriving on her heart's blood. Desperation and the bitterness of death are in her heart. MURDER fills her soul toward your unconscious and innocent babe.

"Who is responsible? On whom rests the guilt? It is your work. You forced that heavy burden upon her, and compelled her to bear it. You thrust your child, as an intruder, into the sacred domain of her life, to derive existence through her organism and at her expense, knowing that she was not prepared to welcome it, and to bend the forces of her nature to its growth and support; and contrary, it may be, to her earnest entreaties that she might be spared this pain and anguish till she was ready joyfully to welcome them. But you heeded not her prayer; you assumed the right to decide for her when she was prepared to endure these trials, and under what circumstances she should be a mother. You must have your stated gratification; you have abused your manhood and your wife till this indulgence, as you think, has become as essential a want of your life as your daily food—as the drunkard feels that alcohol is as essential as air to his existence and happiness ; and so you impose on her a maternity which her soul abhors. You horribly tax her vital energies '*without her consent.*' Murder is in her heart toward the uninvited and hated intruder you have introduced into the sanctuary of her life.

"What else do you do, when you impose on your wife a maternity unasked and abhorred ? You commit the development and education of your child, during the most important and susceptible period of its existence, to one who assures you she is not prepared for the charge, who entreats you to spare her, and who loathes the very thought of its existence. Every element of her womanly nature, for the time being, recoils from its presence in her system. She pleads that you would spare her this burden, at this time, and until her nature calls for it, and is prepared joyfully to meet the martyrdom maternity must bring to her. Heedless of her prayers, and, it may be, of threats of death to your child, you demand the surrender of her person to your passion. Maternity ensues. Murder enters her heart toward your child at the same time. She tries to ' get rid of it'—to murder it. She succeeds. The young life you had committed to her care is nipped in the bud, as you were assured it would be before you resigned it to her keeping. Where rests the responsibility? On you, primarily and mainly. You murdered your own child—not, indeed, with your own hands—you drove another to do the desperate deed, and that other, your wife, who came to you, with a loving and trusting heart, to save and be saved; and you, to gratify your selfish passion, drove her to the commission of the crime of ante-natal child-murder—a crime that must for ever weigh upon her soul like a mountain of guilt and shame ; a deed, after the doing of which no true woman can ever, in this life, stand proud and stainless, in conscious innocence and dignity, before the tribunal of her womanhood. She has done a deed for which great Nature can find no ex-

cuse but ignorance; but which, even when done in ignorance, she regards as a violation of her just laws, and pun-
ishes as such with appropriate penalties—the loss of self-respect and the consciousness of degradation."

The following letters—giving a plain, unvarnished insight
into the life of women wedded to men who, through over-
developed or misdirected amativeness, bring such sin and
sorrow on what would otherwise be happy and enjoyable
lives—I copy from a work entitled "The Unwelcome Child,"
by Henry C. Wright, to which book I am also indebted for
the above-quoted paragraphs:

"Before we married, I informed him (the husband) of my
dread of having children. I told him I was not yet prepared
to meet the sufferings and responsibilities of maternity. He
entered into an arrangement to prevent it for a specified
time. This agreement was disregarded. After the legal
form was over, and he felt that he could now indulge his
passion without loss of reputation, and under legal and religious sanctions, he insisted on the surrender of my person
to his will. He violated his promise at the beginning of our
united life. That fatal bridal night! It has left a cloud on
my soul and on my home that can never pass away on earth.
I can never forget it. It sealed the doom of our union, as it
does of thousands.

"He was in feeble health; so was I; and both of us mentally depressed. But the sickly germ was implanted, and
conception took place. We were poor and destitute, having
made no preparations for a home for ourselves and child. I
was a stricken woman. In September, 1838, we came to
——, and settled in a new country. In the March following my child developed—under a heart throbbing with dread
and anguish at the thought of its existence, was born. After three months' struggle, I became reconciled to my, at
first, unwelcome child. But the impress of my impatience
and hostility to its existence, previous to its birth, was on
my child, never to be effaced; and to this hour that child is
the victim of an undesired maternity.

" In one year I found I was again to be a mother. I was in a state of frightful despair. My first-born was sickly and very troublesome (how could it be otherwise ?), needing constant care and nursing. My husband chopped wood for our support. Of the injustice of bringing children into the world to such poverty and misery I was then as sensible as now. I was in despair. I felt that death would be preferable to maternity under such circumstances. A desire and determination to get rid of my child entered into my heart. I consulted a lady-friend, and by her persuasion and assistance killed it. Within less than a year, maternity was again imposed upon me, with no better prospect of doing justice to my child. It was a most painful conviction to me ; I felt that I could not have another child at the time. All seemed dark as death. I had begged and prayed to be spared this trial again, till I was prepared to accept it joyfully ; but my husband insisted on his gratification, without regard to my wishes and condition,

" I consulted a physician, and told him of my unhappy state of mind, and my aversion to having another child, for the present. He was ready with his logic, his medicines and instruments, and told me how to destroy it. After experimenting on myself three months, I was successful. I killed my child about five months after conception.

" A few months after this, maternity was again forced upon me, to my grief and anguish. I determined, again, on the child's destruction ; but my courage failed as I came to the practical deed. My health and life were in jeopardy ; for my living child's sake I wished to live. I made up my mind to do the best I could for my unborn babe, whose existence seemed so unnatural and repulsive. I knew its young life would be deeply and lastingly affected by my mental and physical condition. I became, in a measure, reconciled to my dark fate, and was as resigned and happy as I could be under the circumstances. I had just such a child as I had every reason to expect. I could do no justice to it. How could I ?

" Soon after the birth of my child, my husband insisted on his accustomed injustice. Without any wish of my own, maternity was again forced upon me. I dared not attempt to get rid of the child, abortion seemed so cruel, so inhuman, unnatural and repulsive. I resolved again, for my child's sake, to do the best I could for it. Though I could not joyfully welcome, I resolved quietly to endure its existence.

" After the birth of this child, I felt that I could have no more to share our poverty, and to suffer the wrongs and trials of an unwelcome existence. I felt that I had rather die at once, and thus end my life and my power to be a mother together. My husband cast the entire care of the family on me. I had scarcely one hour to devote to my children. My husband still insisted on his gratification. I was the veriest slave alive. Life had lost its charms. The grave seemed my only refuge, and death my only friend.

" In this state, known as it was to my husband, he thrust maternity upon me twice. I employed a doctor to kill my child, and in the destruction of it, in what should have been the vigor of my life, ended my power to be a mother. I was shorn of the brightest jewel of my womanhood. I suffered, as woman alone can suffer, not only in body, but in bitter remorse and anguish of soul.

" All this I passed through under the terrible, withering consciousness that it was all done and suffered solely that the passion of my husband might have a momentary indulgence. Yet, such had been my false religious and social education, that, in submitting my person to his passion, I did it with the honest conviction that, in marriage, my body became the property of my husband. He said so; all women to whom I applied for counsel, said it was my duty to submit; that husbands expected it, had a right to it, and must have this indulgence whenever they were excited, or suffer; and that in this way alone could wives retain the love of their husbands. I had no alternative but silent, suffering submission to his passion, and then procure abortion or leave him, and thus resign my children to the tender mercies of one with whom I could not live myself. Abortion was most repulsive to every feeling of my nature. It seemed degrading, and at times rendered me an object of loathing to myself.

"When my first-born was three months old, I had a desperate struggle for my personal liberty. My husband insisted on his right to subject my person to his passion, before my babe was two months old. I saw his conduct then in all its degrading and loathsome injustice. I pleaded, with tears and anguish, for my own and my child's sake, to be spared; and had it not been for my helpless child, I should then have ended the struggle by bolting my legal bonds. For its sake, I submitted to that outrage, and to my own conscious degradation. For its sake, I concluded to take my chance in the world with other wives and mothers, who, as they assured me, and as I then knew, were, all around me, subjected to like outrages, and driven to the degrading practice of abortion.

"But, even then, I saw and argued the justice of my personal rights in regard to maternity, and the relation that leads to it, as strongly as you do now. I saw it all as clearly as you do. I was then, amid all the degrading influences that crushed me, true and just in my womanly intuitions. I insisted on my right to say when and under what circumstances I would accept of him the office of maternity, and become the mother of his child. I insisted that it was for me to say when and how often I should subject myself to the liability of becoming a mother. But he became angry with me; claimed ownership over me; insisted that I, as a wife, was to submit to my husband '*in all things;*' threatened to leave me and my children, and declared I was not fit to be a wife. Fearing some fatal consequences to my child or to myself—being alone, destitute, and far from helpful friends, in the far West, and fearing that my little one would be left to want—I stifled all expression of my honest convictions, and ever after kept my aversion and painful struggles in my own bosom.

"In every respect, so far as passional relations between myself and husband are concerned, I have ever felt myself to be a miserable and abject woman. I now see and feel it most deeply and painfully. If I was with a child in my arms, I was in constant dread of all personal contact with my husband, lest I should have a new maternity thrust upon me, and be obliged to wean one child before its time to give place to another. In my misery, I have often cried out: ' O God! is there no way out of this loathsome bondage ?'

"It was not want of kindly feelings toward my husband that induced this state of mind, for I could and did endure every privation and want without an unkindly feeling or word, and even cheerfully, for his sake. But every feeling of my soul did then, does now, and ever must, protest against the cruel and loathsome injustice of husbands toward their wives, manifested in imposing on them a maternity uncalled for by their own nature and most repulsive to it, and whose sufferings and responsibilities they are unprepared and unwilling to meet.

"Yours,

"——— ———."

In commenting on this, Mr. Wright says:

"'Strong language!'—'too strong and sweeping epithets!' Can you, as a man, a husband, and a father, read the above extract, and feel or say that my language is too strong? The above is the experience of a living wife and mother, nearly *verbatim* as written by herself. It is a simple, unvarnished, affecting story, but bearing on its face the stamp of truth, and the evidence of a sense of conscious injustice inflicted by the husband, and of a degradation self-inflicted, solely to escape what seemed to her a greater evil. Can such 'loathsome injustice,' on the part of husbands and fathers, toward their wives and unborn children, be reprobated in too strong terms?

" Husbands ! it is your licentiousness that drives your
wives to a deed so abhorrent to their every wifely, womanly
and maternal instinct ; a deed which ruins the health of
their bodies, prostitutes their souls, and makes marriage,
maternity, and womanhood itself degrading and loathsome.
No terms can sufficiently characterize the cruelty, meanness,
and disgusting selfishness and injustice of your conduct,
when you impose on them a maternity so detested as to
drive them to the desperation of killing their unborn children, and often themselves."

The following letter gives the experience of a husband
and wife, and by a mutual friend, who is also a wife and
mother :

" Some fifteen years ago, a man of culture, and engaged
in public life, was united in marriage with an intimate friend
of mine.   With pride and confidence, he selected her from
a large and admiring circle of friends, as one embodying his
ideal of womanly excellence.   My friend was thought a fortunate girl (only seventeen), and many thought him quite as
fortunate.   They were much in society, and she began to
enjoy life intensely.

" She was too much a woman not to desire offspring some
time, but she felt unprepared to have maternity forced upon
her youth and inexperience.   It came at a time when her
husband's calling led him much from home, to mix in the
society she so much enjoyed, and which she felt was con-
tributing to make her what she so much desired to be—her
husband's fitting and equal companion.   It was not without
a severe struggle she resigned these advantages and checked
her aspirations.   However, she submitted, though she keenly felt the sacrifice.

" Though overwhelmed with the greatness of her responsibilities, and an undefined dread of physical suffering, she
was determined not to appear weak, but bravely to meet and
bear the burden imposed upon her.   Her husband was absent
when the trial hour came ; but when he returned, he took

his babe and wife to his bosom with pride and joy, though its gestational development had, apparently, scarcely given him an anxious thought.

"My friend's future looked bright. She did not see or understand the fact, that she was to continue to develop the germs of human beings into life, with little sustaining help from the father, whose caresses generally ended in exhausting her vital powers by passional indulgence. She did not complain, but rather rejoiced, as she saw her other powers of attraction to her husband depart one by one, that she was so organized as to be able to meet what she knew he considered an essential want of his nature.

"Eleven years passed, at which time she gave birth to her sixth child. She was a devoted mother, of a joyous spirit, and possessed of wonderful elasticity. But woman cannot be entirely happy in maternity alone, without the presence and sustaining power of her husband. If she is a true wife, she desires to be more to her husband than merely the mother of his children.

"Her husband made for her a beautiful material home, and seemed happy when with her; but he was much away; he sought other pleasures, social and intellectual, in which she could not participate; she must stay at home, alone, with her children. Little did he know the trials of patience and strength in his wife, in being compelled to bear the responsibility of the health and training of her little ones alone. The world called her a happy wife, and she felt that she ought to be so; but a dark cloud was coming over her once joyous spirit. She began to realize the fact, so fatal to a wife's happiness, that her husband did not feel her to be his equal, and a fitting companion to meet his social and intellectual necessities. When he brought home a friend, she listened to conversations and discussions in which she could not participate. She felt keenly the growing distance between them, and she knew too well how it had come about.

"She quietly made up her mind to have no more children. How did she propose to bring it about? Not by asking her husband to deny himself his accustomed indulgence; no, that, she thought, would be to cut herself off from her strongest hold on his affection and confidence, and to sever the last link of the chain that bound them together. She did not expect that any precaution would enable her to escape conception. She brought herself to do what was most repugnant to her nature, and which, as she felt, would destroy her self-respect, and make her, in her own estimation, a degraded woman—namely, TO PROCURE ABORTION.

"The first shock given to her constitution by this abuse of her nature was comparatively light. But once did not suffice. As a longer interval passed without a new-born babe than ever before, she had begun to take her place by her husband's side in society, earnestly praying that she might be spared maternity evermore. Her husband delighted to have her with him. He felt that he had a right, by law and the customs of society, to his gratification; he persevered in demanding it, and she continued to yield. Several times in four years did she nip the young flower of fœtal life in the bud, and each time told more and more terribly on her constitution, until the power of conception was nearly destroyed, at little more than thirty-five years of age. She was shorn of her womanhood, and became a sickly, broken-down wife and mother, in the very spring-time, as it were, of her life, being driven frequently to perpetrate a degrading outrage upon herself, or endure a maternity abhorrent to her soul; and all to gratify the sensual passion of her husband, thinking thereby to secure his affection and respect. How fatally mistaken! By yielding, she strengthened his *passion*, but not his love.

"Reflecting on her sad experience, in the light of your book on 'Marriage and Parentage,' which I had placed in her hands, she saw clearly where the wrong had been, but for a long time felt powerless to destroy what she regarded as her last hold on her husband. He was absent, and I prevailed on her to write and lay the matter frankly and plainly before him, and send him your book. She was then prostrated in body and soul by the last outrage upon her womanly and maternal nature. She wrote, and, hoping that you may do good with these letters, the husband and wife have granted me the privilege of copying portions of them for you. Here is a part of hers to him:

"'MY DEAR HUSBAND:

"'I feel like lying down and weeping that I have become unworthy, intellectually and spiritually, of mating with you; but *love* is the foundation of true marriage, is it not? and I feel strong in my love-nature. It is high, and deep, and rich, and who shall say, if rightly cultivated, what flowers of intellect and spirituality might not blossom out from its soil?

"'My husband! forgive me if I say that I deeply and sadly feel that my womanhood has been robbed of its most precious charm for *your* sake, through a weak indulgence and subjection to that in you which is lower than the spiritual. My body has been painfully desecrated, perhaps not more by your act than mine. You suffer the loss of that refining and ennobling influence which only an *undefiled* woman can impart to man.

"'In view of our past, words cannot express my remorse and self-condemnation; but, believe me, the bitterest suffering is caused to me by the knowledge that, through this sin and misery, I am rendered incapable of becoming to you a tithe of what I desire to be. How can you do otherwise than shrink from the wreck I am fast becoming? And although I may feel, in my moments of anguish and remorse, that *you* are as much the cause of my mental and physical wreck and imbecility as I am, God grant I may not unjustly murmur or accuse you!

"'It is said: "Men never love complaining women.

Alas! if they treated their wives with half the respect and tender consideration they do other women, there would be less ground for complaint.   I am convinced, *that in proportion as woman yields to the demands of animal passion in her husband, in that same ratio he loses his love and respect for her.*   By bitter and humiliating experience this conviction is forced upon me.

" 'My husband! I love you.   The power lies in you to bless and save me, the power lies in me to bless and save you; but have we not cursed each other instead?   I cry unto you for life—will you give me death?   I would make my womanhood a crown of glory to your life—your manhood to mine.   Shall we allow the very life-essence of our being to be exhausted in sensual indulgence, till we lose the power to feel and appreciate a pure spiritual love?   My heart is reaching out to you for life, at the same time that my body is suffering untold agonies from the outrages perpetrated on my nature to escape the anguish and horror of an unwelcome maternity; outrages which have polluted and humbled my soul, and nearly destroyed my body—all for your sake; that I might retain your love and respect.

" I would rather lay down my life now than live without your love.   Can we not love purely and nobly, without prostituting that love in mere sensual indulgence?   My soul would arise and go to you as an inspiration from God; but I am suffering, and a realization of my present condition, my physical diseases, and mental anguish, and the knowledge that it was all caused by having maternity put upon me when I was not prepared joyfully to meet its trials and responsibilities, and the consciousness of the terrible outrages that I have been driven to perpetrate on myself and your unborn children, harden my soul, and lower me in my own opinion, so that I do now feel, and shall yet more deeply feel, if this function is still to be imposed upon me, that I am unworthy to appear in society.   But for the consciousness that your passion has been, unconsciously and ignorantly, it may be, the primary cause of my misery and conscious degradation, I should scarcely dare to claim the right any more to rest in your bosom as your wife. We have both erred.

" ' You love my person ; you worship the *animal* in me. If you love not my mind, my heart and soul more, and feel not more reverence and worship for the God in me than for the animal—if I am unworthy and unable to meet the wants of your intellectual and spiritual nature, PERISH ALL OUTWARD BONDS ! Tell me, have I no power to hold you by any bonds but the sensualistic ? Has my soul no power over you ? If this be so, let me no longer seek to hold you at all. It crushes me, and overwhelms me with conscious degradation, to feel that I have no power over your intellectual and moral nature ; that you come to me, caress me, and call me WIFE, only that I may administer to your sensual pleasure, and that you have no fond regard and loving adoration for me, except for my mere outward, physical womanhood. I cannot live so, feeling that your presence and caresses are ever to be but a prelude to the surrender of my person to your animal passion.

" ' I know I have powers of soul, which, if suffered to be developed, without this horrible crucifixion, might bless you. I will not yet believe that you will turn a deaf ear to this appeal of your wife, who, as you know, has had and can have no life apart from you. I pray, with tears, that you will spare me from a maternity which my soul repudiates, and whose sufferings I cannot endure. You will not deny me this privilege, which, more than anything else, I ask of you.

" ' Though much guilt is on my soul, through repeated efforts to get rid of the results of your passional relations with me, and save myself from the pain and anguish of a maternity I have felt unable to bear, and of giving birth to children that I do not want, yet I will not despair of salvation reaching me through your love. To live as pure as my aspirations are, and have my life the natural outgrowth of the deep love which I feel and must express or die, would bring us both nearer heaven.

" ' I cannot consent to have the woman, *the real soul-and-spirit woman* in me, obliterated. I cannot believe it is my destiny to have the *woman* expunged from my nature. I want to be a strong, pure woman. I want to be lovely to you. Yet, heretofore, the strongest manifestations of love to you have, usually, had little other effect than to arouse your animal nature, and thus have been so turned as to render me unlovely; for a wife must become unlovely and repulsive to her husband the moment he ceases to reverence her soul, and feels that she is to him but the means of mere sensual gratification.

" ' You will acknowledge that there is a terrible wrong somewhere. May God show us a Moses to lead us out of this wilderness, this Egypt! You have often chided me for feeling unworthy of your love; reminding me how strange it was, since other and worthy men regarded me highly, and that I did not feel myself unworthy *their* regard. Were there no abuse of our sexual nature, your tender and noble love would so elevate and consecrate the functions of my womanhood, that I should no more be tormented with that want of self-respect, which, alone, ever causes me to doubt your love, and feel unworthy of it. I feel, at times, that love would not, could not, thus crush my womanhood; that it would, by intuition, guide you in your passional relations with me, so as never to do a wrong or outrage to my nature, even unwittingly. The feeling which other men's regard awakens in me is not brought down and thus prostituted to sensual gratification, but is awakened only to vitalize and bless soul and body. Help me and save me, by your manly strength, even from myself!

" ' I appeal to you, in behalf of myself, of my husband, and my children. Deep and enduring consciousness of guilt and shame must rest on my soul, in view of the outrages I have perpetrated on myself and my unborn children, whom I was reduced to the necessity (as it then seemed to me) of killing before they were born, or of cursing with an existence loathed and detested even by the mother that bore them.

" 'My husband! you will, for *my* sake, for *your own sake*, for *our children's* sake, reflect on these things, and send me your reflections. You will respond to this appeal from

" 'YOUR LOVING WIFE.'

"THE HUSBAND'S RESPONSE.

" 'MY SUFFERING WIFE:

" 'I have a word to say to you now, such as I never said before. Your letter has revealed you to me as I have never before seen you. It shows me to what utter misery I have brought you—how, for my gratification, you have descended into the lowest hell.

" 'You intimate that I treat other women, personally, more tenderly and reverently than I do you. That is true: to my shame and regret I say it. And yet, why should I do so? Why should I crush and desecrate you, while I have too much respect for other women ever to think of doing the same to them? There is no reason for it. You are my dearest love. I should treat *you* more tenderly than any others; be more careful of your health, and beauty of body and soul. Of all women, the husband should most anxiously watch over the health of his wife, and most shrink from the abuse and desecration of her physical as well as spiritual womanhood.

" 'But I have not been wholly blind to your deep misery. I have seen it, and, at times, feared that I might be the cause. I did not dare ask the cause. Feeling not myself that degradation and misery of which you speak, I did not know how you suffered; but I should have known, had I not been blinded by passion, and by the false idea that man-

had a right to the indulgence of his passional nature whenever he wished it, and that, too, without regard to the feelings of his wife, or the welfare of the child that might
ensue.

" ' True, I, at times, heard your words of remonstrance
and entreaty, but they did not touch my heart ; my passion
made me deaf or indifferent to your appeals to my manhood
to spare you from a maternity which you could not joyfully
welcome. I was lost in my own hell, and tormented. I
was blind ; but now and then glimpses came to me, from
your own keen anguish, of the real truth. But the blur of
selfish, craving passion would come over my sight, and I
would go on my old way, cheating myself always, and sometimes you, into the feeling that it was all right; that man
had a right to that indulgence, whatever might be the condition of the wife, and whatever her feelings in regard to
maternity. At least, I persuaded myself and you *that I
could not help it*, and that my health would suffer unless I
frequently held that relation with you.

" ' Now that blind dominion of passion is at an end. Your
appeal to my manhood has reached its deepest depths. The
gratification of animal passion shall no more guide me in
my relations to you. That it ever has is my shame, as well
as your degradation. I wish you could see my soul as it
now is ; you would see a resolution in it. The deep wail of
your spirit has reached my heart, and I am ready to go up
with you out of the perdition into which my uncontrolled
sensualism has cast us.

" ' You have descended into hell, for my gratification. You
have consented to terrible anguish of body and soul, for no
higher object than my momentary pleasure. You have sacrificed your body and soul, your self-respect, your unborn
children, on the altar of my ungovernable passion. From
this hour, I will seek to repair the wrong I have done you.
I have forced on you, in contempt of your entreaties, a maternity which could not be otherwise than most hateful to

you. I have compelled you to pass through sufferings of body and anguish of mind which you were not ready to meet, and which were all the more severe because they were imposed by one whom you loved, and who should have known better. I have imparted to you the elements of a new life, when your very soul spurned and loathed them. I have filled your heart with deadly hatred toward the young life, my own child, that was being developed beneath it. I have compelled you to a deed of all others the most loathsome and hateful to a pure, refined and noble woman—to the *murder* (it should have no other name) of your children, to the murder of *my* children, ere they were born, to save them from the more fearful and horrible doom of an unwelcome and hated existence.

" ' Talk not to me of *your* guilt, of your unworthiness to stand by my side, and to tread with me the path of life as a true, noble and loving wife. If you are guilty, what am I ? If you feel degraded by the loss of self-respect, what ought I to feel ? The fault is all my own. I should have known better, and had a higher appreciation of the passional relation. Had I consulted your wishes as to maternity, had I counselled with you as to when you could, with safety and exultation, take charge of the germ of my child, and naturally develop it into life—had I never imposed on you a repulsive and abhorred maternity, would the stain of abortion now darken your soul ? Yes, I see it all ; the deep damnation of the deed is my own, and would to God that the penalty might descend on me ; that I could save you, my long-suffering, too lenient and forgiving wife, the pain and anguish.

" ' God help me ! I am very sick at heart. The bitterness of death enters my soul, as I reflect on the unseen and unexpressed pain of body and desperation and anguish of soul to which my ungoverned passion has brought you. Can you forgive me ? Can you again restore me to your loving confidence ? Can you ever again respect my manhood, which has brought upon you all this woe? I will, henceforth, comply with the teachings of the book you sent me, and hold my entire nature in abeyance to your wishes and happiness, and in all my passional relations with you, my object shall be your health and happiness, rather than my own gratification.

" ' Dearest! believe and trust me now, for I mean what I say, and it shall be done. I have written it here, and this shall be my pledge; and if ever I urge on you a relation that will subject you to the liability of maternity, when you do not call for it, lay this pledge before me, and it shall be respected.

" ' We shall yet rejoice together on earth as we never did before. This world may not bring to you entire restoration to health of body, nor peace of mind, nor yet self-abandoned trust in your husband; but the effort to effect this, on my part, shall not be wanting. Believe me, and trust to the love, the faith and energy which your letter, and that experience of Ernest and Nina, have awakened in me. We will together seek the aid of the angel helpers, who never condemn save to restore and bless, and who are even now lifting up and vitalizing the desponding and heart-stricken.

" ' Dear wife! look up, and trust—*trust*—TRUST! and with strong nerve, and in conscious pride and innocence, you shall yet stand by my side, and tread with me the pathway of the future, a proud, loving, trusting, joyous wife. Your soul shall yet shine with deeper lustre on my manhood, to elevate and save your conscience-stricken, but not despairing husband. You shall yet be, in deed and in truth, my savior, and I will be yours.

" ' These are not idle words, but come from the heart of your loving, penitent, yet hopeful and confident

" ' HUSBAND.'

"It will do your heart good to know that that husband has, thus far, been true to his pledge; that that wife is now blooming again in comparative health. Hope and triumph are shining in her face, love quickens the intellect and vitalizes the whole woman. And woman is intuitional, to understand and appreciate a true and noble manhood. You will not wonder, then, that she feels nearer to him, in mind and spirit, than ever before—for now she understands him, and he her. Could they have talked over the subject of passional relations, and understood each other before they entered upon their marriage life, it had saved her years of anguish. May their history be a beacon-light to warn others to shun the rocks and shoals that lie, unseen, in the inner depths of wedded life!

"God speed you in your efforts to vindicate the most sacred and important of all human rights—*the right of woman to say when and under what circumstances she shall assume the office of maternity, and the right of her child to a joyous welcome into life.*

"With fervent prayers for the triumph of truth on this subject, I am

"Your friend,

"———— ————."

Commenting on the foregoing letter, Mr. Wright says:

"My friend, how many wives would thus appeal to their husbands, if they dared? 'Sever the last link of the bond that binds her to her husband!' Mere sensualism 'the last link' in such a union! I do not like to talk of *chains*, *links* and *bonds*, in connection with such a relation. Talk of these in connection with slaveholders and slaves, but let them not sully a relation like this! '*The last link,*' indeed! Yet it is true; it is, often, the first, and last, and only link that binds the husband to the wife, in what is called marriage. Man seeks woman as a legal wife, that he may legally and respectably give indulgence, without restraint, to his passion. If the wife seeks to preserve her soul and body from desecration, he threatens to leave her, and seek his gratification where he can find it. She submits, to keep him with her;

both of them unmindful and regardless of the results to the child. ' Perish all outward bonds' of marriage at once, rather than that the relation should continue in this way !"

Let us look at some of the effects of forced abortions on the body and soul of the mother.

In producing abortion at *any* period of gestation she runs a great risk of losing her life ; death may occur from flooding or subsequent inflammation. Very many women die from this cause, whose acquaintances and even near friends never know the true origin.   It is difficult to get at a nearly right proportion of deaths, but it may be safely stated that one woman in every ten who effect forced abortions die— either at the time from hemorrhage, or shortly after through inflammation, etc.

" It is a mistake to suppose that death must be immediate, and owing only to the causes just mentioned.   The rapidity of death, even when directly the consequence, greatly varies ; though generally taking place almost at once if there be hemorrhage, it may be delayed even for hours where there has been great laceration of the uterus, its surrounding tissues, and even of the intestines ; if metro-peritonitis ensue, the patient may survive for from one to four days— even, indeed, to seven and ten.   But there are other fatal cases, where on autopsy there is revealed no appreciable lesion, death, the penalty of unwarrantable interfering with nature, being occasioned by syncope, by excess of pain, or by moral shock from the thought of the crime."

A score of natural births at the full period, under right conditions, would not entail on the mother a shadow of as much pain and danger as would one forced abortion.

Allowing the woman has been so fortunate as to escape death, there follows in the wake of the crime done such an array of evil results as might well deter any woman from the commission of this great crime.   Diseases of the pelvis— such as vesical and uterine fistula, adhesions of the os or vagina, etc., all of which are often incurable ; uterine displacements, and all their attendant miseries. Sterility sooner or later results, so that when the woman really desires offspring, her desires and prayers bring no echoing response. Should the woman succeed in bearing children, they will likely be puny, unhealthy, deformed and short-lived.

If there is one thing more than another that will destroy beauty it is the one of criminal abortion. Tight dressing, corsets, licentiousness, and, above all, abortion, will in whole or in part very effectually and very quickly destroy the most beautiful face and form a lovely woman ever was endowed with, and hurry her with rapid strides to premature age, with its attendant faded skin, wrinkled face and bent form. The woman who produces abortion destroys the bloom of her ripe womanhood, hardens and deepens the face-lines, angularizes the hitherto rounded contours, the outward loving expression of the soul's interior presence is darkened, the rich maternal love-nature is lost, and premature old age comes on with galloping strides.

When the "turn of life" arrives, there is often present a tendency to that fatal disease, cancer.

And lastly, there is the ever-present remorse of conscience— the ever-present phantom of a great crime—a crime against humanity—a crime against the loving mercy and justice of God, ever asserting the individuality of its thought-nature, ever destroying all peace and happiness of the perpetrator. And well it may; for if murder will not do it, and especially the murder of one's own child, what will do it?—what can do it?

If the result of a forced abortion is so great in its effects on the organism of the mother, would it not be preferable and advisable to allow the child to arrive at its full development, and after birth, by a dose of Prussic acid, or a cord round its neck, put an end to its existence? "This," you may exclaim, "is horrible!" No doubt of it; but it does not differ in the least from the taking life during its existence in the mother's womb—and it has this to recommend it:

that the murder of the child after birth would prevent all the serious after-consequences to the mother that attend its pre-natal murder. Without doubt, the doing this would subject the perpetrator to arrest, imprisonment and trial for murder before a jury of her countrymen, yet this trial and punishment would be but an evanescent and trifling affair in comparison with the trial she will have to encounter at the Bar of Judgment, the throne of God, before the earth's assembled multitudes, and having as witnesses these undeveloped souls that she thoughtlessly and recklessly or knowingly and determinedly deprived of life before even they entered on their post-natal existence. For it should be remembered that the moment conception takes place at that moment a new soul is originated, and that this soul, cut off by a murderer's hand from growing and developing into perfection, wings its flight to another world, there to remain and be a witness against the one who loosed it from its earthly tenement. There is no doubt about this, and all self-argument will avail naught against the great truth that the soul—no matter what its stage of development—never dies.

Says Bishop Coxe, Protestant Episcopal Bishop of Western New York, in concluding a late Pastoral Letter to his people:

"I have heretofore warned my flock against the blood-guiltiness of ante-natal infanticide. If any doubts existed heretofore as to the propriety of my warnings on this subject, they must now disappear before the fact that the world itself is beginning to be horrified by the practical results of the sacrifices to Moloch which defile our land. Again I warn you that they who do such things cannot inherit eternal life. If there be a special damnation for those who 'shed innocent blood,' what must be the portion of those who have no mercy upon their own flesh?"

Should the woman fail in accomplishing her desire, as very often happens, the child will likely be born with fractured limbs, club feet, loss of sight, hydrocephalus, or in some other way will be deformed. But whether it will be deformed or not, it will be born with a disposition quarrelsome, revengeful, and often murderous in its tendencies.

What are the means to be employed to prevent the further growth of this tendency to produce forced abortions? A great number of women who are guilty of this great sin do it through ignorance, and they need but fully realize the enormity of the crime to forever banish all thoughts of murdering their unborn offspring.

It is noticeable that among Roman Catholics fœticide is not practiced. It is prevented through the terrors of the confessional, for it is included in their faith that a child dying *in utero* is unsaved because unbaptized. If this is so, and Protestants continue to practice fœticide to such an extent as is at present done, there is no reasonable doubt why the Roman Catholic Church will not ultimately attain the ascendancy on this continent, and so hold the balance of power in its management—truly not a desirable prospect.

The underlying cause for this great wrong is the overgrown and misdirected quality of amativeness, coupled with love of wealth and display. This may be considered the root of the whole matter; and until women—but especially men—are educated into a right understanding of the use and abuse of amativeness, or, better still, until they are *born* with normal and well-regulated social propensities and governing sentiments, just so long will the crime of fœticide be prevalent in society.

If ministers would learn more of human physiology and phrenology, and less of the dogmas of religion, and preach, practice and teach them, they would do infinitely more for the good of their congregations in particular and humanity in general. All ministers and teachers should be as well learned in the laws that govern the sexual organism, and other departments of human physiology, as they are in the supposed legitimate pursuit of their lives. Every college, academy and school should have a department allotted to the study of physiology, and especially that branch of it so necessary to a right knowledge of life socially and sexually. And until this knowledge is taught and disseminated equally with geography, astronomy, French, etc.—branches that are of infinitely less importance—just so long will there be abroad among the people the sexual and social iniquity that springs from ignorance of the laws of the human organism, which are the laws of God.

The class in which fœticide most largely predominates is the last in the list above enumerated—those who, being married, have, through the licentious needs of the husband, maternity forced on them when they do not desire it, or in no way are prepared for the duties and responsibilities attending it. When such a husband persists in debasing, through the exercise of his animal propensities, not only his own higher nature—if he has such a quality—but also the loving, trusting and pure nature of his wife, I know of no other remedy that would be effectual than that of separation of the wife from her licentious master, the husband. This may involve circumstances that would cost the wife much anxiety, but it cannot—be the consequences never so serious, and the future prospect never so gloomy—cost as much as would her debasing slave-life with her so-called husband.

Prevention in this, as in all other departments of human wrong, is at all times preferable to a cure ; and if, in marrying, the Law of Choice is closely observed, no such social errors can possibly happen.

" Maidens ! a word to you. Never enter into the physical relations of marriage with a man until you have conversed with him freely and fully on maternity, and the relation that leads to it. Learn distinctly his views and feelings, and his expectations, in regard to that purest and most ennobling of all the functions of your nature, and the most sacred of all the intimacies of conjugal life. Your respect, your beauty, your glory, your heaven as a wife, will be more directly involved in his feelings and views and practices, in regard to that relation, than in all other things. As you would not become a weak, a miserable, imbecile, unlovable and degraded wife and mother, in the very prime of your life, come to a perfect understanding with your chosen one, ere you commit your person to his keeping in the sacred intimacies of home. Beware of that man who, under pretence of delicacy, modesty and propriety, shuns conversation with you on this relation, and on the hallowed function of maternity. Concealment and mystery, in him, toward you, on all other subjects pertaining to conjugal union, might be overlooked ; but if he conceals his views here, rest assured it bodes no good to your purity and happiness as a wife and mother. You can have no more certain assurance that you are to be victimized, your soul and body offered up, *slain*, on the altar of his sensualism, than his unwillingness to converse with you on subjects so vital to your happiness. In the relation he seeks with you will he, *practically*, hold his manhood in abeyance to the calls of your nature and to your conditions, and consecrate its passions and its powers to the elevation and happiness of his wife and children ? If not, your maiden soul had better return to God unadorned with the diadem of conjugal and maternal love, than that you should become the wife of such a man, and the mother of his children ?"

In the right observance of the Law of Choice ; the succeeding growth into a true love-marriage—a perfect soul-union ; a faithful conformity to the Law of Continence ; and, when a love-child is desired, the fulfillment of the Law of Genius, is found the only true line of life, and the only real mode of avoiding sexual sin and preventing its attendant miseries.

CHAPTER XXIII.

DISEASES PECULIAR TO WOMAN—THEIR CAUSES, SYMPTOMS AND CURE.

ISEASES peculiar to women are so many in their variety, so serious in their results, and of such frequent occurrence, as to be a source of large revenue to physicians, who otherwise would have to take to a change of occupation to earn a livelihood. And not only does the so-called regular physician reap the benefits derived from woman's heedless observance of the laws that govern her organism, but quacks—with their patented nostrums, and their quack instruments of support, likewise patented, coupled with their indelicate and unnatural quack examinations—almost entirely rely on this class of complaints for the money with which they so sumptuously live and so lavishly advertise.

Out of a hundred women, in any large or medium sized city, there may on examination be found *one* who has a perfect normal play of all the functions of her body—the remaining ninety-nine being troubled with neuralgia, or otherwise "dreadfully nervous," or have some one or other of the many "female complaints."

This state of things will continue to increase, unless women adopt the true mode of life sexually, socially and morally—and especially until they come to understand that in being sick they sin ; and instead of ever bringing to the surface their petty sickness and ailments, they should be ashamed to allow even their near friends know their condition—just as much ashamed as if caught in breaking the eighth or ninth commandments, or any other law or commandment intended for our physical or moral guidance.

This assertion, applying equally to man, may appear severe, but yet it cannot be gainsayed. A man or woman is as responsible to God for laws broken and sins committed physically, as they are responsible for the non-observance of the moral law intended for their spiritual guidance. A man being sick from over-eating, drinking alcoholic liquors, sexual excesses—or a woman from tight dressing, wafer-soled shoes, corsets, or idleness, is as liable to the inevitable punishment consequent on his wrong-doing, as if he had fouled his spiritual nature by lying, swearing, stealing, etc., and in either case should, when possible, in shame hide the effect and endeavor to remedy the cause.

Corsets, constrictions of dress, love of display, idleness, and sexual excesses, are the positive underlying causes for most of the diseases peculiar to women enumerated below ; and to regain health it is only necessary to return to a just and faithful observance of these unbending laws, that govern and direct the delicate machinery of "the house we live in."

Absent menstruation is where the menses never have made their appearance. The time at which menstruation should first appear in women varies so, according to climate, habits, etc., that it is impossible to fix a definite time for its appearance. It usually occurs at about fifteen in the southern part of the continent, and a little later in the northern. Provided the girl is otherwise healthy, the non-appearance of the menses should cause no anxiety, and medicine used for the purpose of bringing them on should be shunned. It is a fact that females may menstruate without any hemorrhagic discharge being visible. When their non-appearance is owing to absence of the ovaries or womb, the sexual characteristics of woman are wanting—the breasts being small and flabby, the body lacking fullness and roundness of outline, and occasionally there is a slight beard on the upper lip. When this state is not indicated in the young woman, but she otherwise embodies a healthy, happy, enjoyable state of being, no means should be employed to force the appearance of the menses, other than a right observance of eating plain food, drinking only pure water, and plenty of out-door exercise. The longer a woman puts off the ripening of the first ovum, by living on plain and unstimulating food, freedom from mental excitement, reading novels, dancing, etc., and the avoidance of all that tends to a "hot-house growth," the longer will she retain her youth and beauty.

When through debility, congestion, and other symptoms, indicating a low state of the vital powers, they do not appear at the proper time, the symptoms noticeable will be: an effort at menstruation every month, marked by shiverings, pain in the small of the back and the lower part of the abdomen, aching down the thighs, with a feeling of weight and fullness of the womb. The general symptoms are pain and throbbing in the head, pain in the side, stomach and bowels, a feeling of great weakness, etc. In the treatment, the first requirement is to remove the general debility, and strengthen the system by a vigorous attention to right dietary rules, baths, exercise, and especially by the breathing at all times pure air, and so give Nature a chance to perform her requirements. Above all, do not use any forcing remedies, for these are not only ineffectual, but oft-times dangerous. The sitz-bath is a valuable agent to assist. It should be taken of a temperature to suit the patient, daily, before going to bed, remaining in it from ten to fifteen minutes. A vaginal syringe injection should be employed at the same time. The daily sponge, air and sun-bath, already mentioned, should never be omitted. The clothing should be warm and loose, and the feet kept dry and warm. Good fruit, coarse bread, corn bread, unseasoned vegetables, etc., should be used as food. Out-door exercise—such as brisk walking, rowing, horseback riding, or any variety of calisthenic exercise—are great aids.

Retained menstruation occurs when the blood, through some impediment—closing of the mouth of the uterus, adhesion of the walls of the vagina, imperforate hymen, etc. —is not expelled. It may be known by a sense of weight or fullness in the pelvic region, which is increased at each menstrual period ; a feeling of weakness and heaviness in the back and loins, aching sensations down the thighs, etc. The treatment required is mainly of a surgical nature, and is unnecessary to give here.

Suppressed menstruation is caused by sudden colds, bodily injuries, debility, mental shocks, inflammation of the ovaries or womb, from exhaustion by amative excesses, etc. When suddenly arrested it constitutes *acute* suppression ; if the suppression be gradual, *chronic* suppression. The symptoms of suppression are sometimes quite violent, while at other times but little disturbance ensues. The treatment does not differ from that in the case of absent menstruation. The patient's general health should be carefully restored. The use of warm hip and foot-baths and the wet bandage should form part of the treatment.

Chronic suppression may result from an acute attack, or it may arise from enfeebled health or some disease of the vital organs, as the lungs, stomach, etc. It should be treated on the same plan recommended in absence of the menses.

Irregular menstruation. The menses without being entirely suppressed, may be irregular in time, in quality, or in quantity, caused by some derangement of the general health. The treatment is similar to that mentioned in absence of the menses.

Painful menstruation is caused by sudden colds at the menstrual period, or soon after delivery, by exhaustion, caused by the luxurious indulgences of civilized life, by unnatural or excessive excitement of the organs. The symptoms present are more or less pain in the pelvis, weakness and distress in the small of the back, tenderness and swelling of the breasts, headache, etc. Clots of blood are formed in the uterus, and sometimes a false membrane is thrown off, either entire or in shreds, which is expelled with violent bearing-down efforts, with intervals of comparative ease, like those of child-birth. These pains, and the expulsion of a membrane, might readily be mistaken for a miscarriage. The attacks last from one to four days, during which time many patients are unable to walk or even stand, and especcially so during the bearing-down contractions of the uterus, while others are obliged to keep their beds. A cure can only be effected by means of proper treatment during the intervals. The bowels should be kept regular by right diet, and, when constipated, should be freed by enemas of tepid water. Vaginal injections of warm water, and warm or hot sitz-baths, and otherwise the treatment as recommended in the case of suppressed menstruation should be commenced in earnest to prevent its recurrence. Every law of health should be observed, and every possible cause of ill health abstained from. A free, happy, unexcited and unexhausting life will greatly help. *During the attack* a cold or hot sitz-bath should be taken, and continued while the pain lasts. The relief is more immediate by the hot bath; but the cold bath, at a temperature of from sixty to seventy-five degrees, is the best. At the same time a hot foot-bath, as well as vaginal injections, may be employed. These baths should be repeated on every return of the pain.

Profuse menstruation. In a perfectly healthy state, the menstrual discharge is light in color, lasts about three days, and does not generally exceed two ounces; yet the quantity of blood discharged varies so much with different females, that any excess over this amount would not be a symptom of excessive menstruation, unless accompanied with a failure of the general health. Natural menstrual fluid does not coagulate or clot, and when clots do appear, they indicate not only that the discharge is unhealthy, but also the presence of excessive menstruation. The causes for this disease are repeated child-bearing, excessive coition, enervating modes of life, mental excitement, hard and exhausting labor, etc.

But the great cause is produced by husbands who, by excessive and sensual indulgence, claim the legal right to destroy and oft-times murder their wives, and in such a way that no coroner can hold an inquest. It is required, during the existence of this disease and its treatment, that a rigidly chaste and continent life be observed. Sexual intercourse should be totally abstained from until the cure is complete and permanent; and when the husband will not allow this, the wife should separate from him, either permanently or for a time, or else make up her mind to a wretched present existence, with no better prospect than a premature death. During the flooding the patient should lie down on a mattress, and remain perfectly quiet until all threatening symptoms have passed off. If this does not check the discharge, sufficiently cold wet cloths should be applied to the abdomen, and frequently changed, and cold water injected into the vagina. Cold water may be drank freely from the beginning. During the intervals, to effect a perfect cure, a close observance of the laws of health should be carried out. Especially should a chaste and continent life be observed.

Vicarious menstruation occurs when there is hemorrhage from any other part of the system than from the uterus—as from the nose, lungs, stomach, bladder, nipples, or some other part of the body—which takes the place of the proper menstrual discharge. The sudden arrest of an accustomed discharge is usually the immediate cause of vicarious menstruation. This disease, not usually a dangerous one, can be cured by restoring to its normal action the obstructed menstruation by the means already given.

Cessation of menstruation, occurring at between the ages of forty-five and fifty, and commonly termed "turn of life" or "time of life," is not to be regarded as morbid in itself, but only where the woman has been or is in ill health, when she will be peculiarly liable to a variety of maladies—as rheumatism, cutaneous eruption, ulcers of the legs, cancer and other affections of the breasts, apoplexy, insanity, etc. This predisposition to disease, on the cessation of the menstrual function, can only be avoided by a close observance of the laws of health ; for if the woman is in sound health, the "turn of life" will cause her no more trouble or suffering than would the cessation of lactation.

Chlorosis, or "green sickness," is generally connected with some one of the various disorders of menstruation. It is more a disease of general debility than of abnormal uterine action. Among the usual causes are the indolent and luxurious habits of life of the wealthy, and excessive labor, insufficient and wrong food, and impure air, etc., of the poor. Amative exhaustion, self-abuse, constipating food, patent medicines, idleness, impure air, tea, coffee, excess of flesh meats, etc., tend alike to enfeeble the body in general and the digestive organs in particular, so that there is not sufficient vital power to establish and carry on menstruation, and "green sickness" is the result. The mind of a chlorotic woman is a prey to fretfulness and gloomy forebodings ; her sleep is broken and disturbed by frightful dreams ; there is singing in the ears; specks before the eyes ; partial loss of sight ; trembling of the limbs ; nervous pains in the face and in various parts of the body. The stomach loathes food, or craves the most disgusting and unwholesome things—as chalk, dirt, ashes, and even insects. The bowels are genererally costive, but sometimes loose, and the urine is pale and generally scant; the face is bloated, the eyes are sad and languishing, the lips pale, and the skin cool, clammy, and often cold, especially about the hands and feet. In the treatment of chlorosis, the great object is to improve and restore the general health. The patient should breathe pure, bracing air; she should exercise as much as her strength will allow; her diet to consist of ripe fruits, laxative vegetables, brown bread, etc., as recommended in a previous chapter. Water is the best and only allowable drink. When any article of food disagrees with the patient its use should be discontinued; for food, when undigested, irritates and weakens, rather than strengthens. The dress should be warm, equally covering the extremities, and loose enough to allow the most perfect freedom of every movement. The daily sponge, air and sun-bath should never be neglected. Some judgment may be required, in extreme cases, in managing the bathing appliances. It is better to commence with water of a warm temperature, slowly reducing the temperature as the circulation improves. The mind should be diverted by innocent amusements, social intercourse, and works of charity and benevolence; and all depressing mental influences, and every thing calculated to work on the feelings and affect the nerves should be studiously avoided. All preparations of iron, chalybeate water, or drugs of any kind, patent or otherwise, should also be carefully shunned. They invariably do harm—never any good.

Inflammation of the ovaries is comparatively rare. When present, it is characterized by deep-seated and severe pain, accompanied with heat and swelling in one or both groins. It is to be treated as would any other inflammation—by the constant application of cloths or bandages dipped in cold water; frequent hip-baths; bowels to be kept open by enemas of tepid water; rest, and a very plain and abstemious diet.

Inflammation of the uterus is common with married

women—rarely affecting the unmarried. It is caused by blows, falls, violent exertions, etc. The symptoms are chilliness, followed by fever; heat and uneasiness in the region of the womb, with occasional sharp pain in the back, darting forward and down the thighs. The pain is much increased by coughing and by hard pressure over the womb. In severe cases the symptoms are much more positive, the whole system being involved in the feverish disturbance.

Chronic inflammation is a much more common disease than the above. It is very insidious, and may make considerable progress before attracting the attention of the patient. When the local symptoms are noticeable, there is a dull pain in the lower part of the abdomen; depression or sinking down of the womb sometimes; and frequently a mucus, or white discharge, which is sometimes tinged with blood, if there is ulceration. Pain in sexual intercourse is perhaps one of the earliest and most common symptoms. Pain or some uneasiness in emptying the bladder and bowels is also a common symptom. In the treatment of acute inflammation of the uterus, when there is much fever, the body should be frequently sponged with cold water, or the cold wet-sheet pack should be employed once a day for an hour. Two or three times a day moderately cool sitz-baths should be taken. A cold wet bandage should be kept on the lower part of the abdomen, and renewed as often as it becomes warm. Frequent injections of cold water into the vagina, and occasional injections of water, either cold or warm, into the rectum, if there is constipation, will be beneficial. The patient should breathe pure air, in a cool, well-ventilated room, and take no food until the violence of the disease is abated, and then it should be as simple as possible. Should the disease be of the chronic form, the above treatment may be adopted, but with a moderation in the temperature of the water and in the number of baths; otherwise the great aim should be to improve the general health.

Ulceration of the uterus is one ot the effects or terminations of inflammation, and is produced principally by the irritation caused by excessive sexual intercourse. Among prostitutes the disease is almost universal. All manner of ememagogues greatly help to produce the disease, as does also habitual constipation and wrong habits generally. The symptoms are nearly similar to those of inflammation. At first there is a mucus discharge, but after a time it may become leucorrhœal, the quantity being usually increased after each menstruation. The treatment consists of the same general plan as that mentioned for inflammation, the first requirement being to regain the general health. For local treatment there is nothing better than repeated vaginal injections of cold water, from fifteen to thirty minutes at a time. The doing this faithfully ten to fifteen times a day, with careful observance of the Plan of Life, and absolute freedom from sexual intercourse, will insure a speedy recovery. A cure can always be effected without caustics, and the patient should never allow their use.

Tumors in the uterus grow either in its walls, in a solid, fleshy body—when they are called *fibrous*—or they are attached to the mouth by a slender stalk or pedicle, in which case they are called *polypous* tumors. The fibrous tumors seldom produce any constitutional effect, and the symptoms are mostly mechanical. These are comparatively rare. Polypous tumors vary in size from a pea to a child's head. When they attain a considerable size there is a bearing-down pain, straining and difficulty in evacuating the bladder and bowels, and sometimes frequent and profuse floodings. When the disease progresses so as to cause paleness, loss of flesh, palpitation of the heart, etc., it should be removed by a skillful physician.

Cancer of the uterus is the most fearful and fatal disease to which the womb is exposed. It rarely attacks young women, and is most common about the "change-of-life" period. The disease is frequently hereditary, and when there is a predisposition and cause likely to excite the womb, cancer may be developed. In the first stage, that of *hardening*, the symptoms are such as arise from pressure ; while in the second stage, or that of *open ulceration*, the pain is severe, acute and darting, or burning. In this stage there is more or less loss of blood, which when discharged is thin, greenish, black, dirty white or brown, and has a very offensive smell. The skin is yellow, or of a yellowish hue, there is slow fever, night sweats, loss of flesh, want of appetite, and, in short, general derangement of all the functions of the body. There is only one possible cure for this disease—the strictest hygienic diet, verging on starvation, the purest and most invigorating life, and a course of the most active purification by a judicious use of baths, air, light, exercise, drinks, food, etc. By the adoption of this course in the early stages a cure is possible, and at *any* stage it is the only hope.

Corroding ulcer and cauliflower excrescence. These are also malignant diseases of the womb. The symptoms very much resemble those of cancer—so much so that the distinction cannot well be made in domestic practice. About the only difference between corroding ulcer and cancer is the absence, in the former, of the filling up and around the diseased part, and the thickening and hardening, which has been described as the first stage of cancer. The most distinctive symptom of cauliflower excrescence is a copious watery shedding at first, which after awhile is streaked with blood, and finally changes to a profuse flooding. The other symptoms are almost identical with cancer, and the treatment should be conducted on the same plan.

Displacements of the uterus. These disorders, so common in women—more, perhaps, than any other disease arising from a local cause—indicate the great extent to which women have departed from a natural life. Especially is this applicable to the "higher classes" of society, although it is to be found in all classes. Few disorders cause more suffering, and few are worse managed.

Prolapsus uteri, or falling of the womb, may be classed

under two different heads—that of *partial*, when it is within the vaginal passage, and that of *complete prolapsus*, when it protrudes externally.

The engraving (Fig. 27) exhibits (A) the uterus in its natural position, from four to six inches from the external opening. In its *partial* descent (B), it ranges from being merely depressed below its normal position to its descent to the bottom of the vaginal canal. Its complete prolapsus is shown in the third drawing (C.)

The local causes for prolapsus are found in the relaxation of the vagina and the muscles of the abdomen, excessive sexual excess, and a constantly constipated rectum, with the daily effort to empty it. The general cause is tight dressing and weight of clothes on the hips, forcing the viscera down on the uterus, and bad habits of life generally —as wrong food, causing constipation, etc., and breathing impure air, sleeping on feather beds, idleness, producing, altogether, debility, and a weak state of the vital power. The exciting cause may be a fall, lifting heavy weights, straining, as in evacuating the bowels, getting up too early after confinement, although this last would never result in falling of the womb, if women would leave off their enervating habits, and

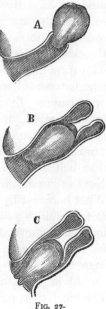

Fig. 27.

live so as to give proper strength and firmness to their muscles.

The symptoms are pain or weakness in the back, with a dragging, bearing-down sensation, as if something were about to come away. These feelings are intensified in standing or walking, and are most troublesome in the evening. There is also, not unfrequently, a whitish discharge, and some straining or difficulty in evacuating the bladder and bowels. There is commonly present a sense of oppression or "goneness" at the pit of the stomach, palpitation of the heart, sadness, low spirits, weakness of the knees, and general exhaustion. The "courses" generally continue regular, there being nothing in the prolapsus to prevent this.

Whatever diminishes vitality in the woman may cause prolapsus uteri, and therefore the acquirement of perfect health must be the first aim in its treatment. Before any mode of local treatment be commenced, the dress must be so made and worn that it will be perfectly loose, and in no manner or form constrict the body. The whole weight of the clothing should rest on the shoulders; with women, as with men, this should be a law. It is useless for any woman who is troubled with falling of the womb to think of curing, or attempting to cure it, until she adopts a short and perfectly loose dress, the weight of which, with the rest of her clothing, should hang entirely from her shoulders. The woman, having decided on the reform in dress, has more than half adopted the plan for a certain and rapid recovery. Next in importance is the adoption of right dietetic habits. What is meant by this has already been so often mentioned as to require no further details. Of course, a life of chastity must be observed. The daily bath, with thorough after-friction and kneading, especially in the region of the abdomen and loins, by the hands of a strong, healthy person, should be had, in the rays of the sun, when it is shining. The local treatment should consist of vaginal injections of cold water, these injections to be repeated several times a day; hip-baths of cool or cold water taken daily, followed by friction; enemas of water thrown up the rectum to keep the bowels in order. Should the womb be partly or entirely out, a stream of cold water from the syringe should be made to play directly on it, after which—the woman lying on her back—it should gently and gradually be pushed up as far as practicable. The woman should retain the horizontal position from half an hour to an hour afterwards. Before rising a temporary support may be employed, by the introduction of a piece of very soft sponge, but it should never be allowed to remain in longer than an hour at a time, as in that case it may do more harm than good.

In the treatment of falling of the womb, if the patient has a desire for a speedy recovery, she will reject the application of caustics, supports, and especially pessaries, for they will do great harm and positively no good. The use of pessaries causes great pain, irritation, leucorrhœa, and often ulceration. Cases are recorded where the pessary has passed into the bowels.

The loose dress, hip and general baths, thorough rubbing and manipulation of the abdominal muscles, cold water vaginal injections, improvement of the general health, and avoidance of constipation by proper food and enemas, will insure a perfect, radical cure of this most frequent and most annoying of complaints.

Retroversion of the uterus. After prolapsus of the womb, this is the most common displacement. In this form, the fundus of the uterus generally tilts backward against the rectum. (Fig. 28, D.) In an extreme case it is called *retroflexion* (A.) It may be caused by congestion of the fundus, rendering the upper part of the womb heavier than in its natural state. It most commonly occurs in the early stages of pregnancy, by suffering the urine to accumulate in

FIG 28.

the bladder.   The symptoms are straining and difficulty in passing the urine and in emptying the bowels; a dull, aching and constant pain in the back, and a sense of weight in the rectum.   The treatment—after first restoring the uterus to its normal position, by bringing the cervix down with the forefinger of one hand, and pushing up the fundus with the other—consists in precisely the same plan as that given for prolapsus.

Anteversion of the uterus.   In *anteversion* (B) the body of the organ inclines forward toward the bladder, and the neck projects backward toward the rectum.   When the fundus and neck are flexed on each other at an acute angle, it is called *anteflexion* (C.)   The causes for the uterus bending forward are weakness of the abdominal muscles, constipation of the bowels, presence of tumors, or violent accidents.   The treatment, after returning the organ to its natural position, is the same as in prolapsus.

Leucorrhœa, or "whites," is the term applied to a colorless, white or yellowish discharge, secreted from either the mucus membrane of the vagina or uterus, or both.   The inflammation may be either acute or chronic, the last being most common.   Among the numerous causes for this disease mentioned by writers are a sedentary life, reading books of fiction, too early marriages, solitary pleasures, sexual excesses, frequent child-bearing, abortion, stimulating and constipating food and drinks, want of cleanliness, ill ventilated rooms, mental emotion, pessaries in the vagina, etc. The symptoms in the early stages, should the inflammation be of an acute character, are heat, soreness about the vagina, with a feeling as if the parts were swollen.   The discharge is at first small in quantity, thin, and of a whitish character, but it gradually becomes more profuse, thicker, and assumes a yellowish or greenish hue.   Generally, these earlier and more acute symptoms are not present, and the disorder is marked more by its effects on the constitution, than by great pain and uneasiness in the parts affected.

When the inflammatory symptoms have continued an uncertain length of time, or when the disease has gradually undermined the constitution without any permanent local symptoms, there is the following train of sympathetic and general disorders resulting from this apparently trivial whitish discharge, which has become so common in civilized life that many women consider it natural to them, and not an evidence of disease resulting from bad habits. Patients afflicted with chronic " whites," beside pains in the back and lower part of the abdomen, and in various parts of the body, suffer from depraved appetite, from sour stomach, headache, hiccough, and, in short, the thousand-and-one symptoms of dyspepsia. They are sensitive to cold, especially about the feet, while the head is unusually hot ; they are troubled with palpitation of the heart and fainting fits, with pains in the breast, etc. ; the face becomes pale, the eyes hollow, and they weep without cause ; they become careless, impatient, and feel a sort of languor and dejection, a sensation of strangling or choking, and an involuntary sadness ; they are apathetic, melancholy, hypochondriacal, etc. The treatment, in a great measure, should be of the same general and local plan as for prolapsus. In the early stages vaginal injections of tepid water, followed by cold water, five or six times a day, should be observed. The hip-bath, repeated twice or thrice a day, from five to ten minutes at a time, followed each time by active friction on the back, hips, and lower part of the abdomen, is one of the main reliances for a speedy cure. Sexual intercourse must be rigidly abstained from. It often happens that husbands having intercourse during the presence of the " whites," contract a disease which may readily be mistaken for that foul and disgusting disorder arising from impure sexual intercourse. When leucorrhœa is symptomatic of displacement of the uterus, as it very often is, the first requirement in a cure is the return of the displaced organ to its natural position. If women would avoid this undesirable disease, they must abandon their present sedentary habits, and take oft-repeated exercise in the open air; they must pay more attention to bathing and cleanliness; they must avoid works of fiction, and shun those places of amusement which tend to excite the sexual organs; they must discontinue the use of highly stimulating food and drinks, and especially tea and coffee; they must lead chaste and continent lives; and, in short, they must remodel all their habits of life.

Vulvitis, or inflammation of the external organs of generation, has as symptoms heat, swelling, redness, and a throbbing pain extending to the groin. When the inflammation extends or is confined to the mucus membrane, there will be a leucorrhoeal discharge, with a disagreeable smarting. In the early stages the disease may be aggravated by the rubbing of the affected part by the patient in her effort to relieve the uneasiness. The cause of this, as in other diseases of a like nature, is to be attributed to the wrong mode of life the person follows. Perfect cleanliness of the parts, bathing and right habits of living, are the requirements necessary to its cure.

Pruritis occurs when, with inflammation of the vulva, there is an intolerable itching of the part affected. The symptoms are an intolerable itching, attended with a burning, smarting, disagreeable and sore feeling. Through sympathy, and through the desire to rub the parts, which is almost irresistible, *nymphomania* is sometimes produced. Says Dr. Churchill:

" In severe cases, when the parts are very tender, there is no sexual desire excited; but in other and slighter cases, where friction does not occasion distress, this is sometimes the case; and that which was at first adopted for the relief of the pruritis, may give rise to other sensations as imperious in their desire of gratification, and which increase by indulgence, so that the patient is reduced to a very melancholy condition; utterly unfit for society, she is injured by solitude, which leaves her to the uncontrolled dominion of her imagination ; her mind, influenced by the excitement of the organs affected, is occupied with lascivious thoughts and impure desires, and her conduct (in defiance of herself, as a patient expressed it) toward the other sex shows the influence of her bodily disorder."

The cause for this disease is somewhat obscure. In its treatment, " the whole mass of blood should be purified of its grossness and irritating humors as rapidly as possible. The wet-sheet pack, and the prolonged tepid half-bath, are usually indicated. Sitz-baths of a mild and soothing temperature—from seventy-five to eighty-five degrees—should be employed with a frequency proportionate to the urgency of the case. The bowels must be thoroughly cleared of all irritating fœcal matter by means of copious enemas of tepid water; and the patient's diet should be extremely abstemious, and restricted to plain brown bread and unsugared fruit, until the local irritation is overcome."

There are other diseases and malformations of the external organs—as adhesion, absence, excessive development, etc., of the labia, enlargement of the clitoris, etc., that might be mentioned here ; but as they are of rare occurrence, and require, in most instances, the presence of a surgeon, I omit them.

CHAPTER XXIV.

DISEASES PECULIAR TO MEN—THEIR CAUSES AND SYMP-
TOMS, WITH DIRECTIONS FOR HOME-TREATMENT AND
CURE.

lVING other than a conti-
nent, chaste, and true life,
man entails on his own constitution, and oft-times on
his children and his children's children, penalties of
such a foul, disgusting and
loathsome nature, as in
their presence and development to warn all who have
doubts as to whether a licentious life—with its great
and ever-present penalties
—or a strictly continent
life — with its attendant
strength, beauty, growth,
and development of the physical and soul-life of the individual—is the most preferable and most desirable for example and precept.

If men whose abnormal desires lead them into the ways
of promiscuous intercourse, could but see some one or more
of the victims to be found at all times in any of the large
hospitals—the foul, loathsome ulcer; the poison eating away

gradually, slowly, but surely, the flesh ; the eyes gone, the nose destroyed, giving the face a most hideous aspect ; the bones of the skull eaten, exposing the brain; the mark of manhood obliterated altogether, a loathsome living death— they would think twice before venturing into the meshes of her whose " feet take hold on hell." The breaking of no other human law entails on the wrong-doer such fearfully prompt, repulsive and incurable penalties as does the un-natural one of miscellaneous intercourse. The *very first* transgression oft-times develops the poison of syphilis, the non-desire for which may be inferred from what one of the most distinguished of French surgeons has said : " I would not have a chancre of the size of a pin's head on my person for all Paris."

But, alas ! notwithstanding such dangers, such possible re-sults, and the express commandments of God, men will do this unclean thing, and in doing it they will suffer the pen-alty attached to the transgression, and how to avoid the full measure of the penalty all such anxiously desire to know.

Gonorrhœa is so named from two Greek words meaning a flow of semen, it being supposed, in the early history of the disease, that the discharge consisted of semen, instead of a mixture of mucus and pus, its true nature.

The symptoms, appearing between the second and fifth day, are at first very slight, there being an uneasy, tickling and smarting sensation at the mouth of the canal, which on examination is found to be more florid than usual, and moist-ened with a small quantity of colorless and viscid fluid, which glues the lips of the meatus together. This moisture, after a time, loses its clear, watery appearance, and assumes a milky hue. These early symptoms are present when the contagion is yet confined to the extreme portion of the urethra. This first stage generally lasts from two to four days, when the symptoms gradually become more intense, until, in about a week after exposure, the second or inflam-matory stage may be said to commence. During this stage the mucus membrane covering the glans has a reddened and angry look, the extremity of the organ is swollen, the discharge—now of a thick, yellowish, creamy color—has become copious, there is intense pain in passing the urine, excited by the irritation produced by the salts contained in the urine, and in consequence of the urethra being contracted and more or less obstructed by the discharge, the stream is forked or otherwise irregular. A person with gonorrhœa is apt to be troubled with nocturnal erections, when it often happens that the penis is bent in the form of an arc, producing *chordee*, caused by the effused lymph on the under surface of the organ rendering it less extensible than the remaining portion. It sometimes happens that sympathetically there is enlargement and tenderness of one or more glands in the groin, producing *buboes*. This second stage lasts from one to three weeks. This is followed by the third or final stage, which is characterized only by the disappearance of the more prominent symptoms, and a gradual return to health, the discharge becoming less and less purulent, and finally completely disappearing. This last stage may last for weeks or months, depending on whether it is treated and the mode of treating it.

The causes of gonorrhœa, in the male, are produced from having intercourse with a woman having this disease, or from a woman having simply inflammation of the uterus, "whites," dysmenorrhœa, or even if intercourse be had during the menstrual period. When produced in this last way, the man and woman—or husband and wife, as sometimes happens—must otherwise lead irregular and unhygienic lives ; but established and reliable authorities have asserted that it may arise from intercourse with women who themselves have not the disease.

Gonorrhœa, in the woman, may occur in the urethra, vulva or vagina—one being affected, the others will be more or less so. For many reasons, it is much less common in women than in men. The symptoms—often obscure—do not differ from the usual early symptoms of inflammation of the other mucus membranes. The discharge, at first transparent, becomes muco-purulent, and, when the disease has attained its height, thoroughly purulent. When secreted from the vagina it is of an acid, creamy, fluent nature. When the vulva is affected, there is an early sensation of heat and itching, the labia and nymphæ swelling to a great degree. This form of gonorrhœa occasions intense suffering in the woman. When the vagina is affected, it rarely fails to extend to the *cervix*, and so produce barrenness.

In the treatment of gonorrhœa, the indications are first to restore the general health; and second to allay the local inflammation. It is a fact that cannot be gainsayed, that the men who acquire such diseases are almost invariably gross, as well as licentious in their habits of living. The first requirement in the direction of a cure (and this will apply with equal force to *all* acute diseases of the sexual organs) is that the patient give up the use of tobacco, alcoholic liquors, milk, flesh, grease, seasoning, and a stimulating diet. He should live on the very plainest of food, such as baked apples and potatoes, thin gruel, unleavened bread, tomatoes, prunes, oranges, etc. During the stage of acute inflammation, but very little of any kind of food should be taken; perfect rest, in bed or on a lounge, should be observed. Next in importance to a right diet is bathing the whole body with tepid water, this to be repeated until the superficial heat is reduced to a normal standard. For the local treatment, sitz-baths of tepid or cool water, varying in time from fifteen minutes to an hour—changing the water, if necessary—will afford decided relief. The sitz-bath should be repeated as often as the inflammatory symptoms are aggravated. When resting, the genital parts should be enveloped in wet cloths.

In women, in addition to the above, vaginal injections of tepid water should be used often.

The adoption of the above mode of treatment will effect

a prompt and permanent cure, when a drug-treatment, with its calomel, sugar of lead, caustic, copaiba, cubebs, turpentine, etc., will not only aggravate the disease, but perhaps produce gleet, buboes or stricture.

Gleet. When an attack of gonorrhœa is badly treated, and not thoroughly cured, there may follow immediately, or perhaps not until after an interval of several weeks or even months, a thin, watery discharge from the urethra, which is termed *gleet.* This discharge may continue for months, and in many cases for years. In most cases of gleet the discharge is the only symptom. In some instances, however, there may be a feeling of uneasiness in the organ or peritoneum, or an itching about the glands, which may either be constant or attendant only upon the passage of the urine. In some cases the discharge is constant, and sufficiently copious to stain the linen, but in the majority it is perceptible only in the morning on rising. It is a well-established fact, that persons infected with gleet will communicate gonorrhœa to healthy subjects, and that by aggravation gleet is readily transformed into gonorrhœa. A hearty meal, alcoholic stimulants, sexual indulgence, violent exercise, exposure to sudden changes of temperature, may bring on a copious purulent discharge, attended by tumefaction of the parts, scalding in urination, and all the symptoms of acute gonorrhœa.

In the treatment of gleet the directions for general treatment in gonorrhœa should be adopted. For the local treatment the sitz-bath is indicated. Commencing with tepid water, which will slightly increase the discharge at first, the temperature should be daily lowered, so that at the end of a week very cold water may be used. This bath may be applied two or three times a day, fifteen to twenty minutes at a time. The case of a gentleman who had gleet at this moment occurs to me. It had been of some two years' duration, the patient having tried the best physicians in vain. Drugs, applications and injections of all kinds had been tried, only to make the discharge seem worse, The patient had the offer of a sea trip on a sailing vessel, which he accepted. The trip lasted for nearly three months, during which time, owing to peculiar circumstances, the food was not only of the plainest in quality, but of the smallest in quantity. The patient landed in better health than he had for a long time experienced, and entirely cured of his gleet. I mention this case simply to show that in this disease, as in almost all others of a sexual nature, if the patient would adopt a line of life involving in it pure air and plenty of it, simple diet and little of it, rest, cleanliness of body, freedom from tobacco, alcoholic liquors, and sexual intercourse, it would absolutely be all that would be required to cure him of his disease and restore him to perfect health.

Phimosis. When the prepuce or skin is in such a condition as to prevent its being drawn behind the glans, the disease is called phimosis. It may be congenital, or result from inflammation or obstruction. When the affection is congenital, the cure is effected by dividing the prepuce, or performing circumcision. When it is caused by an inflammatory engorgement, a prompt reducing of the inflammation, by the application of alternate warm and cold-water dressings, is desirable. The system should be kept free from feverishness by bathing, and the bowels should be moved by copious enemas of tepid water.

Paraphimosis. When the prepuce has been drawn or forced above and behind the glans, and cannot be drawn over it, the disease is called paraphimosis. Persons having phimosis may draw the prepuce violently behind the base of the glans without being able to replace it, thus inducing paraphimosis. After the lapse of a few hours or days, the parts behind and in front of the stricture become swollen, when ulceration or gangrene may follow, and perhaps relieve the stricture, but with an unnecessary loss of tissue. Paraphimosis is sometimes met with in boys, as the result of their first attempt to expose the glands. The first indication in the treatment is to reduce the inflammation as in phimosis, to be followed by an attempt to reduce the strangulation by compressing the glans, and carrying the prepuce over it to its normal position. Failing in this, the last resort is to excise the ring causing the strangulation.

Strictures of the urethra may be classified as *transitory* or *permanent*—transitory when the result of muscular spasm, congestion or inflammation—permanent when through wrong treatment there is produced a permanent thickening and contraction of the urethral canal. *Transitory* stricture of the *inflammatory* form is produced by gonorrhœa and its mal-treatment, and the injudicious use of catheters or bougies. It is known by local heat, pain or swelling, with inability to urinate, unless with extreme pain. When of the *spasmodic* variety, it is usually seated at the neck of the bladder. It may be induced by violent exercise, long retention of the urine, or sexual excesses. *Permanent* stricture may be located in any part of the urethra, but it more frequently occurs in the membraneous and bulbous portions of the canal. It generally comes on slowly and insidiously. The individual first observes a few drops of water remain after the whole seems to have been discharged, then notices a fine spiral or divided stream, and lastly, discharges his urine by drops only, requiring a long time to empty the bladder. It occasionally happens that the patient loses all contrc¹, and the urine dribbles away continually. The usual methods in treating stricture are by the introduction of bougies, the application of caustic, or by incision—all impossible in the home-treatment of the disease. If the patient will but firmly resolve to lead a rigidly plain and simple life—absolute freedom from all stimulating food and drink, tobacco, flesh-meat, etc., eating less of plain food than the system is capable of assimilating, living a strictly continent life, and, along with the every-day general bath, to take twice a day, for half an hour at a time, a cool or cold-water sitz-bath, drinking nothing but pure water, and as much of it as may be desired—he will, in the course of from one to three months, be thoroughly cured of transitory stricture, and in from four to twelve months—depending much on the previous habits of the individual—he will be cured of permanent stricture, and that without any of the dangers or after-results attendant on the introduction of bougies, caustics, etc. The very worst cases of permanent stricture, after long trials and failures with bougies, etc., have in this way been permanently removed and effectually cured.

Swelled testicle is one of the most frequent complications of gonorrhœa of the urethra. Before the commencement of the tenderness and swelling, there is sometimes felt a dull pain in the peritoneum and in the groin. As a rule, swelled testicle may be said to supervene on gonorrhœa after the fourth or fifth week. It always disappears on the effective cure of the gonorrhœa.

Inflammation of the prostate gland is another result of mal-treatment of gonorrhœa. The gland—a small body about the size of a chestnut, situated before the neck of the bladder—is enlarged, causing a frequent desire to urinate; the stream, being generally quite small, is only forced out by prolonged straining, and excites a severe scalding sensation in the deeper portion of the canal. Complete retention of the urine sometimes occurs, requiring the use of the catheter. Tepid and cold hip-baths, with moderate quantities of dry food, along with other hygienic requirements, are all that is necessary to perfect a cure.

Inflammation of the bladder is attributable to the same cause as the preceding. The inflammation is almost always confined to the neck of the bladder, causing difficult urination and a frequent desire to urinate. The treatment is the same as in inflammation of the prostate gland.

Vegetations are papillary growths, identical in their nature with warts, which appear on different parts of the integument, in the neighborhood of the genital organs. They are most frequently met with on the mucus membrane covering the glands and lining of the prepuce, upon the margin of the urethra, upon the vulva in women, and occasionally upon the neck of the uterus. They are in no way connected with venereal disease, though they are most frequently observed in those who have been affected with gonorrhœa or syphilis. The treatment consists in their removal by the knife, caustic or ligature. The best mode of destroying them is by that of caustic, and the best caustic for the purpose is nitric acid.

The chancroid. By the chancroid is meant the "simple," "soft," "non-infecting," or "non-indurated chancre" of various authors. It is a contagious and local ulcer of the genitals. In the comparison of the three poisons of gonorrhœa, the chancroid and syphilis, Bumstead, in his "Venereal Diseases," says :

"The only property common to them all is their communication, for the most part, by contact with the genital organs. The poisons of gonorrhœa and of the chancroid are alike, in that their action is limited and *never extends to the general system;* nor does one attack afford the slightest protection against a second. They differ in that the poison of gonorrhœa may arise spontaneously, while that of the chancroid, so far as we know, never thus originates ; that gonorrhœa chiefly affects the surface—true ulceration being rarely induced—and, in its complications, most frequently attacks parts connected with the original seat of the disease by a continuous *mucus* surface, as the prostate gland, bladder and testicles ; while the chancroid, on the contrary, is an ulcer involving the whole thickness of the integument or mucus membrane, and its complications are seated in the *absorbent* vessels and ganglia. It would also appear that the poisons of these two affections are limited to one common vehicle— namely, pus. This conclusion is sustained by the fact that neither the poison of gonorrhœa nor that of the chancroid ever reaches the general circulation, and it is well known that pus globules are not capable of absorption. When the purulent matter of a chancroid enters the absorbent vessels, as occurs in the formation of a virulent bubo, it is arrested by the first chain of lymphatic ganglia, and goes no further. The syphilitic virus is alone capable of infecting the system at large, and of affording protection by its presence against subsequent attacks. Unlike the poisons of gonorrhœa and the chancroid, it is not limited to purulent matter, but exists in the blood, in the fluids of secondary lesions, in the semen, and probably in other secretions. There is no opposition whatever between these three poisons; they may all co-exist in the same person, who may at the same time have gonorrhœa, a chancroid, and a chancre of the syphilitic lesion."

The chancroid arises only in consequence of contagion from its like. It is most generally found in the vicinity of the genital organs, although it is sometimes found in urethra, vagina and rectum, or wherever there is a mucus surface. It is rarely met on the head or face, where, on the contrary, the initial lesion of syphilis is not uncommon. The vehicle of the chancroid virus is the secretion of the ulcer, which, if it be inserted beneath the epidermis of any other part of the body, a chancroid is equally the result.

The following are the symptoms of a chancroid when fully formed:

" Its outline is circular, unless modified by the shape of the solution of continuity in which it is implanted; it has a punched-out appearance; the edges are jagged, abrupt and sharply cut, and do not adhere closely to the subadjacent tissues; the fluid secretion is copious and purulent, and it is surrounded by an areola which varies in width and depth of color with the degree of inflammation present. They are more frequently multiple than single; but when one chancroid appears at the outset as the immediate result of contagion, others are apt to spring up around it from successive inoculation, since the original ulcer pours out an abundant secretion, and its presence confers immunity against others."

In the treatment of chancroid, prompt attention to the general health of the individual is almost all that is required, for the disease being a self-limited one, it will get well in the absence of all treatment, other than that of perfect cleanliness of the parts. But when not promptly attended to, by the adoption of a strict diet of plain food and bathing, it is apt to be followed by a bubo. If the pustule is noticed the second or third day after contagion, it can be destroyed by burning with nitrate of silver; but after this time—say, within from three to six days—nitrate of silver will be too feeble, and it will require the application of a much more powerful caustic, as nitric or sulphuric acid, applied by means of a glass rod with a rounded extremity, although a simple piece of wood—as an ordinary lucifer match—will do. On the acid first touching the ulcer, the pain for an instant will be very severe, but it becomes much less acute on subsequent applications, of which there should be several to render the destruction complete. Great care must be taken to prevent the acid from touching the neighboring surfaces, which should be protected by dry lint or other material. When it is too late to apply the acid, cloths wet in water should be kept on the parts affected, and often changed. When the application of acid has produced suppuration, the wet (linen) cloths should also be employed. This, with the perfect cleanliness of the parts, and perfect cleanliness of the cloths used, and careful attention to the general health, will always result in a cure.

Chancroids may occur upon the integuments of the penis, in the urethra, near the meatus, on the female generative organs, and on the anus and rectum. The treatment, except where they cannot be got at, is similar to that recommended above.

Buboes. This is an affection of the lymphatic ganglion, dependent, in the great majority of cases, upon the presence of a chancroid, although they may be caused by gonorrhœa or sexual excess. A bubo, with a primary syphilitic sore, or chancre, which is accompanied by induration of the ganglia, which never suppurate unless under the influence of some additional exciting cause. The occurrence of buboes is favored by a scrofulous constitution, by wrongly-treated chancroids, by mechanical violence, undue exercise, excesses in diet, and by sexual intercourse during the existence of a chancroid or gonorrhœa.

Bumstead divides buboes into three classes : first, the *simple, inflammatory bubo*, the symptoms of which are a swelling in the groin, attended with tenderness on pressure and pain, which is aggravated by pressure or the standing posture. The gland is felt to be somewhat enlarged, but is still movable beneath the integument, which preserves its normal color. This condition may last for an indefinite period—during the continuation of the ulcer, or even after its cicatrization, and yet finally disappear without suppuration. In simple inflammatory bubo, most frequently, only one gland is affected ; if others are involved, they are commonly so to a less degree. In less fortunate cases, the inflammatory symptoms increase in severity ; the tumor acquires larger dimensions, and becomes adherent to the skin and underlying fascia, so that it is no longer movable ; the pain and tenderness are increased ; motion is difficult ; the skin becomes reddened ; suppuration is ushered in with a chill ; the presence of matter is indicated by a soft spot in the midst of the general hardness, and soon after by distinct fluctuation ; and although resolution is still possible, yet commonly the contents of the abscess are discharged through an opening in the integument formed by the process of ulceration.

Second, the *virulent bubo*, which receives its name from the fact that the pus which it contains is contagious, and will upon artificial inoculation give rise to a chancroid. A virulent bubo is due to the absorption of virus from the surface of a chancroid, and its conveyance, by means of the lymphatics, to the ganglion. It is usually situated on the same side as the chancroid, but sometimes upon the opposite side, and sometimes both groins are affected, especially when the ulcer is upon any part in the median line. Prior to its spontaneous or artificial opening, the course of a virulent bubo is that of a simple bubo, and the patient should understand that the early symptoms of the two are identical; though the distinction between them is fully justified by the inevitable suppuration and specific properties of the one, and the possible resolution and simple character of the other.

Third, the *indolent bubo*, the inflammation of which is of a subacute character, closely resembling the well-known scrofulous inflammation of the glands of the neck in children. There may be a moderate amount of pain, tenderness on pressure, and difficulty of motion, although these are rarely severe or of long continuance. The tumor very slowly enlarges, perhaps to the size of a hen's egg; the skin covering it becomes thin, and of a livid red color, and fluctuation can be detected without being ushered in by chills and fevers, as in the case of inflammatory bubo. After a time several openings form spontaneously, and there escapes a thin, flaky, watery-looking fluid.

The object to be aimed at in the treatment of buboes is to subdue inflammation and avert suppuration, if possible. To this end, perfect rest and a low diet of plain, simple food is of the first importance. In the early stages, cold wet cloths, frequently renewed, should be constantly kept on the swelling. Three or four times a day the parts may be fomented for fifteen or twenty minutes at a time, and then immediately after covered with cold wet cloths, over which dry ones should be placed. Twice a day a sitz-bath, moderately cool, may be employed. The close observance of these rules in the early stages will certainly prevent suppuration; but should the bubo indicate by its tenseness and throbbing pain the commencement of suppuration, warm wet cloths should be constantly employed until matter forms, when, if the abscess does not open spontaneously, it should be cut with a lancet.

Syphilis. This disease is propagated in various ways, but in most cases it depends principally upon sexual intercourse. Being an infectious disease, the presence of the virus, when brought in contact with surfaces covered with thin epidermis, or when denuded of its cuticle, it is transmitted from one individual to another.

After contagion, there follows what is called the *period of incubation.* This period continues until the first indication of a sore—the future chancre—and lasts from ten to twenty days. The first noticeable symptoms after infection are a sense of heat and tenderness of the urethra, slight inflammatory condition of the head of the organ, smarting sensation after urinating, and after a time the appearance of a minute red and hard pimple—the chancre. When the chancre is on the internal surface of 'the prepuce, and so protected from the air and friction, "it has a circular but sometimes irregular outline. Its surface is smooth, often looking as if polished, destitute of the consistent and adherent exudation of the chancroid, and of a red or grayish color. Its secretion is a clear serum—free from pus globules, unless the sore has been irritated—which may often be seen issuing from minute pores, after the previous moisture has been wiped away. It has no surrounding areola, and leaves no cicatrix to mark its site. When situated upon the external integument, as the sheath of the organ—where most venereal ulcers are chancres—and exposed to the air, it becomes covered with scabs, which give it the appearance of a pustule of ecthyma, or a patch of scaly eruption, and which may readily lead to an error in diagnosis."

In the primary indications of venereal disease—involving as much as they often do of the character and future health of the individual—great care is required in deciding the true nature of the existing ulcer. The chancroid is apt to be taken for the chancre of syphilis, and *vice versa.* This can be avoided by a close comparison of the character of both. The following table, by Dr. Bumstead, gives the diagnostic

22

characters of the chancroid and chancre in a manner that is clear and easily understood :

DIAGNOSTIC CHARACTERS OF THE CHANCROID AND CHANCRE.

THE CHANCROID.	THE CHANCRE.
ORIGIN.	ORIGIN.
Always derived from a chancroid or vlrulent bubo.	Always derived from a chancre or syphilitic lesion.
Has no period of incubation.	Has a period of incubation.
ANATOMICAL CHARACTERS.	ANATOMICAL CHARACTERS.
Generally multiple, either from the first or by successive inoculation.	Generally single; multiple, if at all, from the first; rarely, if ever, by successive inoculation.
An excavated ulcer, perforating the whole thickness of the skin or mucus membrane.	Frequently a superficial erosion; not involving the whole thickness of the skin or mucus membrane, of a red color, and nearly on a level with the surrounding surface. Sometimes an ulcer, when its
Edges abrupt and well-defined, as if cut with a punch, not adhering closely to subjacent tissues.	Edges are sloping, hard, often elevated, and adhere closely to subjacent tissues.
Surface flat but uneven, "worm eaten," wholly covered with grayish secretion.	Surface hollowed or scooped out, smooth, sometimes grayish at centre.
No induration of base, unless caused by caustic or other irritant, or by simple inflammation, in which case the engorgement is not circumscribed, shades off into surrounding tissues, and is of temporary duration.	Induration firm, cartilaginous, circumscribed, movable upon tissues beneath. Sometimes resembles a layer of parchment lining the sore. Generally persistent for a long period.
PATHOLOGICAL TENDENCIES.	PATHOLOGICAL TENDENCIES.
Secretion copious and purulent, auto-inoculable.	Secretion scanty, chiefly serous; inoculable with great difficulty, if at all, upon the patient, or upon any person under the syphilitic diathesis.
Slow in healing. Often spreads and takes on phagedenic action.	Less indolent than the chancroid. Phagedena rarely supervenes and is generally limited.
May affect the same person an indefinite number of times.	One attack affords complete or partial protection against a second.
CHARACTERISTIC GLAND AFFECTION.	CHARACTERISTIC GLAND AFFECTION.
Ganglionic reaction absent in the majority of cases. When present, one gland acutely inflamed and generally suppurates. Pus often inoculable, producing a chancroid.	All the superficial inguinal ganglia, on one or both sides, enlarged and indurated; distinct from each other, freely movable; painless, and rarely suppurate. Pus never inoculable.
PROGNOSIS.	PROGNOSIS.
Always a local affection, and cannot infect the system.	A constitutional affection. Secondary symptoms, unless prevented or retarded by treatment, declare themselves in about six weeks from the appearance of the sore. and very rarely delay longer than six months.

During the first week—and invariably within the first three weeks—of the ulcer, induration of the glands of the groin takes place, forming buboes, and so insidiously that the patient may be entirely ignorant of them. When firm pressure is made on them, there is a feeling of slight tenderness, but not of severe pain. After the chancre has disappeared, the induration of the glands will remain for months, and while it lasts is an indication of the previous existence of a chancre. A syphilitic bubo differs from a chancroid bubo in that it seldom or ever suppurates.

The *constitutional symptoms* show themselves in from three to five months, when, if the patient has went without treatment, or been badly treated, there will be noticed a general lassitude, accompanied by headache and fleeting pains in various parts of the body ; slight itching and tenderness of the scalp ; an eruption of blotches or pimples upon the skin; pustules upon the hairy scalp ; eating away of the cartilages of the nose, throat, etc.

In the treatment of syphilis, the " regular" way has been by mercury and iodide of potassium, which has and ever will result in harm to the patient. In the first stages, immediately the nature of the sore has been decided to be a chancre, the patient should look to the conditions that regulate his general system. If he uses tobacco and alcoholic liquors, he must discard them completely. He should avoid all gross and stimulating food, and all manner of spices and condiments, as well as tea, coffee and chocolate. He should confine his diet to the smallest possible quantity of ripe fruits, bread made from unbolted wheat flour, cracked corn, cracked wheat, etc., and pure water. This may seem a rigid and severe initial requirement in the treatment, but as it is the only possible way of assisting Nature to throw off the poison, the patient must adopt it in full measure, if a radical cure is earnestly desired. Next in importance to diet is bathing. Upon rising in the morning the patient should take a sitz-bath, and at the same time a foot-bath. The water in the sitz-bath should be, at the commencement, of a tepid temperature, and gradually lowered until it is cold— as cold as the patient can comfortably bear it. The water of the foot-bath should be warm, and increased in temperature until it becomes hot. At the close of the bath it should never be neglected to dash cold water on the feet, or dip them for a moment into cold water. This sitz and foot-bath should last from fifteen to thirty minutes. Between ten and eleven o'clock, A.M., this hip and footh-bath should be repeated, followed by a general bath of the whole body, given thoroughly, effectually and rapidly. After drying, thorough friction of the whole body by the hand, from five to fifteen minutes, by the patient, and, if convenient, assisted by an assistant; this should on no account be neglected. Should the sun shine, allow its rays to fall directly on the patient's nude body during the time of friction. Before going to bed, which should be at an early hour in the evening, the sitz-bath should be repeated, with the addition that, before it is taken, cloths wet in hot water should be wrapped around the loins, half way down the thighs, and including the generative organs. These should be kept on until there is decided redness of the skin after taking them off, to be immediately followed by the sitz-bath, the water of which should be, as already mentioned, of a tepid temperature, and gradually increased during the bath to as low a temperature as the patient can bear and readily react after.

If the bowels are costive they must be kept open by enemas of water. The head should be kept cool by the application of cold wet cloths. The mind should be kept free from all irritating thoughts, and the surroundings should be pleasant and enjoyable.

If these directions are promptly begun and faithfully observed, the constitutional indications of the disease will be prevented; and the continuance of this plan of treatment for months, and if necessary for years, will effectually eradicate the disease from the system.

But with many, owing to the fact that the superficial chancre—the form which most generally precedes syphilis—is so indolent and so insignificant a sore that it may readily pass unnoticed, or, if seen, be mistaken for a mere abrasion, the constitutional symptoms—heralded in by headache, giddiness, diminished mental vigor, uneasiness about the neck, pains in the joints, and weakness of the legs—often present themselves before the patient is aware that the poison of syphilis has taken hold of his entire body.

When this has occurred, the treatment requires a closer observance of hygienic laws, and a very much longer time to effect a radical cure. The remarks as to diet and habits of life in the primary indications, apply with four-fold force when the disease is constitutional. Patients who acquire syphilis have almost invariably heretofore led wrong lives—eating too much and wrong kinds of food, drinking alcoholic liquors, using tobacco, and in many other ways being irregular in their habits. If a cure is desired—and who with syphilis does not desire a cure?—a prompt and radical change must be adopted. Tobacco and all manner of stimulating drinks and foods must be shunned ; gluttony must be avoided, making it a rule to eat *only* to live ; general habits of life must be reconstructed, and a plan of life marked out, the close observance of which will allow the *vis medicatrix naturæ* of the body to assert its all-healing presence.

The baths should consist of a wet-sheet pack lasting from fifteen to sixty minutes, according to the feelings of the patient, taken daily between the hours of eight and nine in the morning. At between eleven and twelve o'clock the daily towel or sponge-bath should be taken, followed by friction and the air and sun-bath ; and three times a week, an hour or so before going to bed, a sitz-bath, together with the hot water foot-bath.

Abundant exercise—when possible, in the open air—should always be had.

Great care must be employed in keeping surface-sores perfectly clean, and all cloths, water, etc., used about them should be handled with great care, as the exuding virulent matter, even when diluted, is capable, when brought into contact with any abraded surface, of propagating the disease.

To free the system entirely of the disease, it may be necessary to follow up this line of treatment for years. Day after day, month after month, and year after year, the patient should never neglect to closely follow all the requirements necessary to the regaining of a clean, sweet, healthy body, free from the faintest syphilitic taint.

It is the opinion of many that a few doses of mercury, in some one of its many forms, will cure syphilis. This is a great error. Mercury or no other drug ever has or ever will cure syphilis—or, for that matter, any other disease. The use of mercury in this disease, instead of curing it, simply for a time prevents its outward manifestation, and when the peculiar effect of the mercurial poison has weakened, the syphilitic poison—more virulent and more destructive than ever—again appears, making it more difficult than ever for the life-force of the individual to get rid of it. Allowing two persons to have syphilis, one of them to be treated with mercury, and the other without mercury or any treatment whatever, I would in the end much rather be the possessor of the constitution of the individual who had used no mercury or other treatment, than that of the one who had used mercury.

It is sometimes asked, in the case of persons who have had syphilis, how soon they could marry, without the chance of entailing the disease on their offspring, and it is a question rather difficult to decide. If the disease has not yet passed into the constitutional stage, and the reform plan of treatment here given be adopted and faithfully observed for two years, I think the system of a naturally strong person would in this time be entirely free from the taint of syphilis.

If the disease has passed into the constitutional stage, and has in a measure destroyed parts of the body by ulceration, it may require for its total extinction the close and faithful observance of hygienic and reform remedial measures for from five to eight years, and even then there might be doubts of its non-transmissibility.

Involuntary nocturnal emissions. This disorder, so widespread, occurs generally at night during sleep, when there is an involuntary erection of the organ, followed by a general genital excitement and a discharge of semen. It is the general prevailing opinion that if these involuntary emissions do not occur oftener than once in two or three weeks, no harm to the individual is done, the emissions acting as Nature's safety-valve. Notwithstanding all that physicians and others may say to support this assertion, it is a great error —an error that entails on the individual, sooner or later, serious constitutional effects. Should the emissions occur oftener than this the symptoms of impairment of the health are more pronounced. The morning after the emission the first noticeable symptoms of the harm done the body are a pain above the eyes, or on the top or back of the head; eyes sensible to light; ringing in the ears; tenderness of the spine; weakness of the back; pain in the legs, from the knees to the ankles, and coldness of hands and feet. He gradually grows into vascillating habits of thought and action, weakening his will-power; continually possessed with doubts and fears as to the future; irritable in temper, and unhappy in all his social relations.

There is another class of men—those possessing a preponderance of the vital temperament—in which seminal emissions develop a different train of symptoms, such as dyspepsia, constipation, torpid liver, and diseased state of the skin, as shown by the eruption on the face. This class of patients are much easier to cure than the first mentioned, whose nervous system is primarily involved. A noticeable difference in the symptoms between these two types is in the loss of memory—the first scarcely ever showing a loss of memory until the disease has progressed almost beyond hopes of recovery ; while in the last, dullness of perception and loss of memory is one of the first indications of impairment of the constitution.

The causes for seminal emissions are self-abuse at some time of life, and sexual excesses at any time of life, or it may be of a hereditary nature. The disease may be developed in a person who has committed sexual excesses, and who never has practiced masturbation. The prime cause is the practice of self-abuse at some time of life. There are many married men who, although they get what they demand sexually, will yet have seminal emissions while occupying the same bed with their wives.

Just here I must protest against the often-advised remedy for involuntary emissions and spermatorrhœa—namely, that of marriage. A man having these diseases, and following out this advice, will soon sorely repent of the deed, and be tempted to curse his adviser. Marrying, as a supposed help to a cure, implies that through sexual excess or legalized prostitution, the disease, or rather the involuntary emissions, will, through voluntary action, be diverted into a possibly legitimate channel. This is not only a great error, it is a great sin—a sin and wrong done the man's own body, done the woman he marries, and the children he generates. If he have children, they will not only be predisposed to the disease, but will very likely, when they arrive at a marriageable age, be either impotent or sterile. No man having seminal emissions, gonorrhœa, consumption, or any other disease, should marry, or even in the remotest way think of it, until he recovers fully from the disease. It is a help to a cure, in the man having this disease, to court the society of females, enjoying their companionship, living purely and chastely in their presence—but *no further*, until he can lay claim to a perfect manhood.

In the cure of this disease, that so insidiously destroys the intellect, strength, and very manhood of the individual, the first great requirement in its successful treatment is to lead a *perfectly continent life*. If he be married or not, and co-habits little or much, he must stop it at once. If he practices self-abuse, he must also stop it at once. The next requirement is to follow out as closely as possible the Plan of Life laid down in a former chapter. One of the items of this plan is the constant exercise of the will-power in every required direction necessary to a cure—a most important adjunct, and one that can be used with much effect in the permanent prevention of emissions.

" In waking moments, every man who has not debased and enervated his will is perfectly able to keep his thoughts entirely pure. It is of his own free will that he sins. Hardly less is his power of keeping his dreaming thoughts pure, if he goes the right way to work. Not at all less is it his duty and his true profit to endeavor to do so. Patients assert that they *cannot* control their dreams. This is not true. Those who have studied the connection between thoughts during waking hours and dreams during sleep, know that they are closely connected. The *character* is the same sleeping or waking. It is not surprising that, if a man has allowed his thoughts during the day to rest upon libidinous subjects, he finds his mind at night full of lascivious dreams —the one is a consequence of the other, and the nocturnal pollution is a natural consequence, particularly when diurnal indulgence has produced an irritability of the generative organs. A will which in our waking hours we have not exercised in repressing sexual desires, will not, when we fall asleep, preserve us from carrying the sleeping echo of our waking thoughts further than we dared to do in the daytime. An Italian gentleman, of high station and character, was troubled with frequent emissions, which totally unnerved him. He determined, resolutely, that the first time any libidinous idea presented itself to his imagination *he would awake ;* and, to insure his doing so, dwelt in his thoughts on his resolution for a long time before going to sleep. The remedy, applied by a vigorous will, had the most happy results. The idea, the remembrance of its being a *danger*, and the determination to awake, was never dissociated even in sleep, and he awoke in time; and this reiterated precaution, repeated during some evenings, absolutely cured the complaint."

The patient should never eat a late meal. If he can conform to two meals a day—the last one at two or three o'clock in the afternoon—so much the better; it will do a great deal toward helping him to a cure. His bowels should be freed every night just before going to bed; when this cannot be done naturally, the bowels should be moved by the injection of tepid water. The bladder should be evacuated once or twice during the night. The mind should be kept employed during the day, and free from any reading or conversation that would have a tendency to excite the amatory feelings. Daily physical exercise should never be neglected. The bed or pillows should not be of feathers. Early to bed should be the rule, and to rise immediately on waking should never be omitted. To prevent lying on the back during sleep, tying a towel round the waist, so as to bring a hard knot opposite the spine, will be serviceable, and of itself will often prevent emissions. The close observance of these rules, and especially the close observance of the Plan of Life already referred to, will enable a man who is troubled with nocturnal seminal pollution to cure himself, and regain his perfect manhood. It is a fact that should impress itself on the mind of the man having this disease— that as long as he has seminal emissions, whether they occur frequently or at comparatively long intervals, just so long is he losing from the fountain-head of his system the etherial requisites that go to make up the sum of his growth toward perfect manhood and physical perfection. A man living a pure, chaste and continent life, exercising his sexual nature *only* for the purpose of reproduction; abstaining from all the gross, filthy and debasing that attaches itself to the thought, the breath, and the nourishment of modern civilization, will, can, *does* live a life the span of which may stretch over a period of fifty, seventy or a hundred years, and not have one single nocturnal emission. This is as Nature intended it, as God ordained it, and anything differing from this, even in the smallest measure, entails on the doer the penalty attached to all violated laws.

Diurnal emissions include any emission of semen, voluntary or involuntary, occurring during the waking hours, and not necessarily preceded by erection——the immediate exciting cause being sexual excitement, defecation or micturition. This condition is rare, and indicates a very weak state of the sexual organism. The treatment is the same as in nocturnal emissions. Great care must be taken in noticing the nature of the discharge, and not to confound semen with the secretion of the prostate and other glands. It is just at this point that quack doctors frighten nervous individuals into the belief that the fluid they occasionally secrete in this way is the true semen, and so extort money from their patients, and, if they use their medicines, ultimately completely undermine their health.

Spermatorrhœa. When involuntary seminal emissions—especially if connected with self-abuse or sexual excesses—have continued for some time, there is produced in the individual a state of enervation, a weakening of the life-force, characterized as spermatorrhœa. The ancients evidently knew something of this disease, for Hippocrates, in describing a disease which he calls *tabes dorsalis*, says :

" *Tabes dorsalis* proceeds from the spinal cord. It is frequently met with among newly-married people and libertines. There is no fever, the appetite is preserved, but the body falls away. If you interrogate the patients, they will tell you that they feel as if ants were crawling down the spine. In making water or going to stool, they pass much semen. If they have connection, the congress is fruitless.

They lose semen in bed, whether they are troubled with lascivious dreams or not; they lose it on horseback or in walking. To epitomize: they find their breathing become difficult, they fall into a state of feebleness, and suffer from weight in the head and singing in the ears."

The symptoms of spermatorrhœa are well described by many authors, and may be summed up in the following fearful catalogue:

"Weakness; emaciation; listlessness and languor; dimness of vision; mental indolence or stupidity; loss of memory; a wandering or dreamy state of the mental powers, with inability to concentrate the mind on any particular object or pursuit; aversion to society, especially that of females; melancholy; indifference to ordinary sports and social pleasures; palpitations of the heart; shortness of breath; coldness of the extremities; flushed face; cadaverous appearance of the skin, often accompanied with a peculiar and very disagreeable odor; irritation, uneasiness, or a creeping sensation in the spinal marrow; gnawing at the stomach; voracious appetite; soft and flabby flesh; vacant expression of the countenance, etc.

"Some of the above symptoms may be absent in a given case, but the majority are usually noticeable. In some cases the patient will be timid and confused; easily agitated; discouraged about trifles,; annoyed with constant apprehension of indefinable calamities; especially weak in the loins, back and legs; absent-minded, querulous, etc.

"Impotence, loss of sexual power or passion, or the opposite extreme—constant and insatiable desire, convulsive and epileptic affections, paralysis, confirmed dyspepsia, marasmus, consumption, mania and idiocy, are among the final and fatal consequences.

"In a great number of individuals, both young and adult, an enervated state of the body exists, which the profession, as well as patients, characterize by this somewhat vague term of spermatorrhœa, which is as peculiar and as certainly to be distinguished by its own symptoms as fever, or any other general disease. Of course, many a man has believed himself laboring under the complaint when he was not. This is the case with various other diseases. There is, however, as regards this particular ailment, an additional reason for the existence of much hypochondriacal fancy about it. From the painful stigma which its existence casts on the past life of the patient, and the secrecy he would naturally desire, as well as from the somewhat doubtful nature of the symptoms to an experienced eye, this disease has been and is used by unprincipled practitioners as a means of imposition to a very great extent. Every disease or fancied ailment which their unfortunate victim can be persuaded into believing spermatorrhœa, is called spermatorrhœa forthwith; and, in the agony and terror of humiliation, the wretched and often innocent patient becomes a fit subject for the wickedest cruelty, and, I need hardly add, the most extravagant extortion."

In the treatment of spermatorrhœa, much discrimination is required in applying rules adapted to the circumstances of each individual case. The directions given for the cure of nocturnal seminal emissions are applicable here. In addition to the morning towel or sponge-bath on rising, followed by friction, at noon, between eleven and twelve o'clock, a sitz-bath of from ten to twenty minutes, in cool or cold water, should be taken daily. It should be followed by friction and the sun and air-bath. When there is a tendency to coldness of feet or great heat of head, the hot foot-bath, followed by dipping the feet for a moment into cold water, should be employed daily at bed-time. A faithful and persistent observance of the Plan of Life, and the directions mentioned in connection with involuntary seminal emissions, and the above simple baths, will, unless the disease has made very great progress, effect a rapid and permanent cure.

Miscellaneous disorders affecting erection, emission and the semen. There are morbid states, affecting the perfect fulfillment of reproductive requirements, that occasionally happen and give rise to much trouble. I will briefly enumerate some of them.

Slow erection is more frequently a peculiarity arising from temperament than a disorder. Men of a lymphatic temperament experience this symptom, just as a person possessing a highly nervous organization experiences the reverse. Stimulants of any nature, intended to hasten the act, will do great harm, and should never be employed. When it arises from temperament, no interference is required. *Non-erection*, when not caused by self-abuse or spermatorrhœa, may be the result of intense mental application; and, when so caused, simply refraining from brain-work will remedy the trouble. *Imperfect erection* is understood when erection may occur, but not to its proper extent; or, when it does take place, it lasts so short a time that intromission of the male organ is impossible. Premature excitement and perversion of energy is one cause, while a previous habit of masturbation is very often the underlying cause. A careful treatment of the cause will easily cure the disorder. *Irregular erections* occur when, through violence or some other cause, inflammation of the spongy portion of the urethra takes place, followed by a deposit of plastic lymph, preventing the natural distension of the part, and so causing a curved appearance of the organ on erection, producing great pain while it lasts. This disorder but rarely happens. *Priapism or permanent erection*—erection, instead of being absent or imperfect, may be only too perfect and too persistent, remaining erect either permanently or during long periods. This disorder is caused by some peculiar condition of the spinal cord and brain. It may also be caused by uncleanliness of the parts; sitz-baths will almost always effect a cure. The parts underneath and around the prepuce should always be kept clean. In a man whose desire it is to lead a continent life, the daily morning and evening washing of this part should never be neglected. *Satyriasis.*—" Erection, again, may be not only morbidly frequent and persistent, but connected with maniacal sensuality that is one of the most awful visitations to which humanity can be subject. Continual erections, immoderate desire for connection, and erotic delirium, have been given as the definition of satyriasis. The probable explanation of such aberration is, that the brain or medulla oblongata has received some injury from excessive indulgence that seems irreparable. A low animal organization, with a strong hereditary disposition to lust, has been overtaxed by the enormous license the victim has permitted himself, or some undetected lesion has taken place, which puts the man at once beyond his own control, almost out of the category of rational or moral agents, and leaves him in a condition in which there seems, indeed, little hope of any restoration."

Premature ejaculation is one of the most common sexual complaints met with. "Patients complain that semen is emitted so readily that if they even converse with women, or if they ride on horseback, it will come away; that the friction of the trowsers will often be sufficient to produce emission, and that ejaculation is attended with scarcely any spasm. In other instances, erection is hardly complete before emission follows, and then, as the erection immediately ceases, the intended intercourse fails." The causes for this disorder, primarily, are that the parts are weakened by self-abuse or sexual excess—while nervousness, want of will-power, or natural impetuosity may be the immediate cause; uncleanliness of the glands, and the accumulation of smegma under the prepuce are also prolific causes. The remedy is to restore and strengthen the parts by the means already given, and the living of a continent life.

Non-emission. A man may be able to have connection, with perfect erection, but having no emission following, and no feeling of pleasurable sensation.

"Among the causes of this, the most frequent, perhaps, is stricture, often of old standing. In such a case the mechanical obstruction prevents the passage of the semen, and it is only when erection has passed away that the fluid oozes out.   In very severe cases, I believe, the semen, if emitted, passes back into the bladder, instead of forward, and may be noticed in the urine in the form of a thick, viscous substance.   But I would here warn the reader against mistaking for semen all deposits observed in the urine.   These are of the most miscellaneous and varying composition.   Mucus from the bladder, the lithates, the phosphates, produced by a variety of causes which this is not the place to inquire into, and which only a medical man can diagnose.   True semen is very rarely found in any perceptible quantity deposited in the urine."   Non-emission may also be caused by a want of consentaneous action between emission and erection, or by complete obstruction of the vasa deferentia. This disorder, as a rule, requires surgical treatment.

CHAPTER XXV.

MASTURBATION—ITS CAUSE, RESULTS AND CURE.

OOKS and pamphlets on this subject, in great numbers, for scores of years past, have been printed and widely disseminated; and yet, if we are to believe those physicians and educators whose paths lie across the records of deeds done in secret, masturbation is as prevalent—and perhaps more so—in our day as in days gone by. In schools and out of schools—females as well as males—married as well as single—are to be found those bearing the imprint of the great wrong done their souls by this low, debasing, unmanly, cowardly practice of self-abuse.

The extent of this vice cannot be ascertained—its nature prevents it; but that it is, in connection with sexual excess, lowering and undermining the health, strength and ability of thousands of the young—who otherwise would make their mark in this world—is palpable to all who possess the skill to rightly judge from plainly visible effects back to legitimate causes.

The practice of this vice, so common among boys, and not very uncommon among girls, is one of the great reasons why they never attain distinction in their educational endeavors, or attain high positions in the world's department of work.

Let us glance at some of the results of masturbation, as affecting the health and character of the individual; the array is altogether an undesirable one: headache, dyspepsia, costiveness, spinal disease, epilepsy, impaired eyesight, palpitations of the heart, pain in the side, incontinence of urine, hysteria, paralysis, involuntary seminal emissions, impotency, consumption, insanity, etc. It must not be understood that these diseases are *always* caused by this degrading vice; but that they are often so caused, abundant evidence will show. Affecting so markedly the physical part of the individual, it affects in as marked a manner the moral department of the masturbater.

"He lays down his nobleness, dignity, honor and manhood, and is no longer bold, resolute, determined, aspiring, dignified, but becomes depreciated, irresolute, undermined, undetermined, tamed, and conscious of his degradation. No longer comprehensive in planning, efficient in executing, correct in judgment, full of thought, strong in intellect, courteous in manner, noble in mien, and gallant to woman; but he becomes disheartened, uncertain in his plans, and inefficient in their execution, and a drone to himself and society. So, too, the female, diseased here, loses proportionably the amiableness and gracefulness of her sex, her sweetness of voice, disposition and manner, her native enthusiasm, her beauty of face and form, her gracefulness and elegance of carriage, her looks of love and interest in man and to him, and becomes merged into a mongrel, neither male nor female, but marred by the defects of both, without possessing the virtues of either."

Thousands of sick ones are treated for diseases that neither physician or friends know the real cause and nature of.

Consumption—or a wasting fever resembling it—carries off its thousands yearly. Insane asylums, whether the keepers allow it to be so or not, are more than half filled by the victims of this degrading vice. Says Dr. Workman, in his Annual Report of the Toronto Lunatic Asylum :

"There is one cause, of a physical form, which I fear is very widely extended, but which I almost dread to mention, which all over this continent appears to be peopling our asylums with a loathsome, abject, and hopeless multitude of inmates. Its victims are not intemperate ; nay, indeed, not unfrequently very temperate as to indulgence in alcoholic beverages ; these are very modest, very shy, very (dare I say it ?) pious—as such, at least, they often are sent here, with sufficient credentials ; very studious, very nervous, very everything save what they really are. * * * * I have recently made a careful scrutiny of the character of the cases of insane men on behalf of whom applications have been made, and from whose friends and physicians details, in our circular form, have been received. The result has been frightful. I hesitate to state the proportion in which—I feel fully assured or morally certain—secret vice is present. * * * * In hardly any instance is it found that parents have any suspicion of its existence, when they place the victims in the asylum ; indeed, very many of them appear to be totally ignorant of the very existence of such a habit; and nothing can be more painful and embarrassing to an asylum physician than correspondence by letter with such persons, when the conviction is established in our minds that the insanity of their beloved one is associated with the destructive habit, and that in all probability it has been produced by it. The very frequent, indeed almost invariable observance, that the habit of secret indulgence is encountered, not in persons of rough manners and what are called coarse morals, but in those of an opposite character ; not in the grossly ignorant, nor even in the profane, but in the better informed and passingly religious ; not in the lover of manly sports and invigorating enjoyments, but in the ostensible economizers of constitutional power, and the shunners of youthful frivolities; not in those who, in language or in acts, are regarded as overstepping the limits of modesty or chastity, but among those who evince no wish to mingle with the other sex, or sometimes, indeed, evince an utter aversion to it; the observance of these and many other related facts, has constrained me to the belief that modern society, modern training, and modern exaction, are all too severe upon youth."

To refute the argument that love and religion are the prime causes for insanity, Dr. Workman says:

"The skillful physician, who measures the feeble, paltry, accelerated, yet lazy pulse—who feels the clammy, cool, somewhat repulsive skin—who notes the pallid countenance, the waxy features, and frequently foul breath—who tries to gain one steady, confiding, open look from his patient, and whose questions in a certain suspected direction are met with hesitation, equivocation, or affected mortification, well knows how much truth there is in the charge against love; and he will, in similar cases, acquit religion.

"I have in strong remembrance a case apparently chargeable to religion. The patient, before entering here, did hardly anything but attend prayer-meetings and preachings; he was away from one church, and off to another, as fast as opened doors permitted him. In the climax of this fervor he was sent to the asylum. *We* know how much religion had to do with his insanity—not more than smoke has in kindling the fire from which it proceeds."

Dr. Workman well asks:

"What is to be done to check the progress of the evil?— for that it is progressing and accumulating is beyond doubt. Surely the right course cannot be to avoid all notice of it, or to do all we can to ignore its very existence; much less to manifest disapproval of those who proclaim the evil. Yet this is exactly what many do. It is unnecessary to speak more pointedly; those who have so done will be able to apply these remarks—it is to be hoped profitably—and will see that they have erred in believing that their mistaken delicacy is to be regarded as the equivalent of their neglect of duty. The first rational step toward the removal of an evil is the recognition of its existence and the ascertainment of its magnitude. Can it be right that, through a fastidious delicacy on the part of those possessed of information, the youth of our country should be permitted to fall into the traps and pitfalls with which their paths are studded? Of all the hidden dangers besetting them, assuredly none is of a more hideous or more destructive character than that here alluded to."

What are some of the causes for the adoption and practice of masturbation by boys and girls, and its continuance, in very many cases, to manhood and womanhood? The great underlying cause, that of perverted amativeness, is undoubtedly transmitted by the parents to the child. As already explained in a former chapter, the husband and wife, in their life of lust and licentiousness, especially during the ante-natal life of the child, endow in full measure the quality of abnormal and perverted amative desires in the nature of the child. The child, on arriving at five, eight, or ten years of age, adopts, as naturally as it would the observance of any other transmitted quality, the exercise of its perverted amativeness, by the only means known to it—that of self-abuse. Especially will it be prompt in adopting this foul and sickening habit, if its father—in connection with the exercise of licentiousness during the child's ante-natal life— has at any time of *his* life practiced self-abuse. A father, having been at any time of his life a masturbater, and leading other than a perfectly chaste and continent life during the child's growth in the mother's womb, will, as surely as night succeeds day, have a child that will likewise masturbate. There is no doubt about this. A man and woman, perfectly healthy, closely observing the Law of Genius in

358 of a NEW LIFE.

the development of a new being, will have a child that will grow up to perfect manhood or womanhood without even the thought of masturbation entering his or her head; and if, on attaining a reasoning age, they are advised and instructed in the right object and use of the sexual department of their system, they cannot, by example or otherwise, be made to do this unclean thing.

It being decided that transmitted abnormal amativeness is the underlying cause for masturbation in children, let us glance at some of the immediate exciting and predisposing causes.

One of the most effective of the exciting causes is wrong dietetic habits. That a child—as thousands are—can be fed on highly seasoned and gross food—lard, eggs, pastry, animal food, pepper, salt, candies, pickles, tea, coffee, etc., and, as very many are, on some form or other of alcoholic liquors —and not have amative desires, is utterly impossible. Feeding with food, gravies, pies, tea and coffee, to a five or ten-year old angel from heaven, would produce in it a tendency to self-abuse, avoiding all mention of a child of the earth, born with an inherited tendency.

Uncleanliness of the body, sleeping on feather beds and feather pillows, sleeping with bedfellows, unventilated sleeping rooms, confinement in doors, constipation, worms in the intestines, retention of urine, late suppers, tobacco and alcoholic liquors, are a few of the many exciting causes inducing this habit.

Example is often a strong and ruling cause, as is also the practice that very many nursery-maids have in producing friction of the genital organs of the child to keep it quiet. The foolish practice that many parents have—a reflex of their own perverted natures—of talking to children about "sweethearts" and "lovers," will start a train of thought in the child's mind that will lead to an early adoption of the habit, if not already practiced.

Before giving the means necessary to effect a cure of this

disorder, it would be desirable to notice some of the signs indicating the presence of the habit in the individual. Says Dr. J. C. Jackson:

" Of the signs whereby masturbation is almost infallibly indicated, impairment of nutrition, accompanied by capriciousness of appetite, stands prominent. Proverbially true is it, that all masturbating boys and girls, whether of younger or older ages, are voracious eaters, though exceedingly capricious in their appetites, and are not satisfied with any food unless it is so highly seasoned or highly flavored as to answer for the present their apparent demands. I have never seen a person who was a habitual indulger in this vicious practice who could be satisfied, on any occasion, with the presentation to him or her of nutrient food, simply yet healthfully and relishably cooked. One of the signs, therefore, whereby I am led to decide whether or not persons are in the habit of masturbating, is the particular disgust or dislike which they show for food, which they are otherwise accustomed to eat, if it is simply cooked. I could give a list of articles which masturbaters have a great liking for, and for which but very few other persons care, unless they are in the same relative condition of health, caused by sexual excesses. I never knew a girl to eat lime off the wall, or to chew up her slate-pencils, who was not to a greater or less extent a victim of this practice. I never knew a boy who was accustomed to eat lumps of salt without anything with it, and in fact I might say who was a very inordinate eater of salt upon his food, who was not, or had not been at some period of his life, a masturbater. I do not believe that there is a boy fourteen years old to be found in the United States, who uses tobacco habitually in any form, who is not a masturbater ; and I am sure that the same may be said with truth of both boys and girls who are in the daily habitual use of stimulating drinks, whether they be of liquors that are distilled or those that are fermented ; also those who have a *passion*, as we term it, for eating spices and condiments ; boys and girls who have a *hankering* after cloves, cinnamon, carraway, mace, and the like, are surely habitually associated with this practice.

"Of girls, there is more liability to be deceived, in endeavoring to find out the causes for their apparent ill-health than there is of boys ; because neither parents nor members of the family, nor in fact physicians, are at liberty, under the laws regulating the social relations of the sexes, to exercise as frank, free and full inspection and examination into all the causes that produce disease among females as they are among males. Owing to this, masturbation is practiced with much more unsuspiciousness among girls than among boys, especially at or about the time of puberty. If, at that period, the girl shows any infirmity, feebleness, lack of vigor, or anything of that sort, the mother has all her attention directed toward the development of the menstrual function. She is afraid that the child who is " getting to be a woman" is likely to fail in the upspringing of this new activity, and to have, in consequence, "a sick time ;" she is apt, therefore, to draw a foregone conclusion about it, and to proceed to "doctor" her daughter. In a large number of cases, what are supposed to be the derangements of the menstrual function, consequent upon a girl's arrival at puberty, as shown in her illness or perhaps severe sickness, should be attributed to a habit of rousing up, by artificial means, her sexual organism to unnatural excitement, the reactionary effects of which are seen in her morbid states of body, and about which her parents and friends are so often alarmed. Let it be borne in mind, then, by parents, whenever any such particular, unnatural, or unaccountable conditions of appetite show themselves as I have alluded to—in fact, when any strange, out-of-the-way alimentive caprice, is exhibited by a boy or girl, for which there is not the most obviously plain interpretation at hand—the exposition of it is to be had only by and through the acknowledgment of the fact that the party is a masturbater.

"Another sign of masturbation upon which I have accustomed myself to place great reliance, and which I have seldom known to be incorrect, is the particular gait which masturbating girls and boys show when the habit has become ripe in them. One used to close and specific observation in this direction can detect a boy who is educated to this vice, by the peculiarity of the motion which is discernable at the junction of the locomotive organs with the body. Such a victim, though he may be young, quite young, or though he may be in his teens, walks, when you see him posteriorly, as if he were stiffened. He does not show the peculiarity so much when walking slowly, or when running very fast, as he does when *walking* fast; then he impresses the looker-on that he is rheumatic, and suffering from stiffness in the small of his back. As far as you can see such a boy, when he is in rapid walking-motion, you can tell him.

"A masturbating girl who is past the age of puberty *may* be known by her gait, notwithstanding the difficulties in the way growing out of her style of dress, although it is by no means as easy to settle the matter as in the case of the other sex. Girls who have followed masturbating habits, from the age of ten years up to that of seventeen or eighteen, show, usually, strong indications of it in the failure of their glandular development. Such persons are apt to be flat-breasted, or, as we term it, flat-chested—the breasts not filling as they would do under better and healthier states of the nutritive and secretory systems. They become round-shouldered; their heads seem to be dropping forward all the time, and their shoulders are drawn forward, as if forced in that direction and kept there by mechanical appliances. They fall in and become hollow at the pit of the stomach; and they uniformly, as masturbating boys do, sit crookedly. They are particularly subject to a sideling gait, going one side at a time, as it were, as though there were a spirit of antagonism set up between their organs of locomotion, one leg being impelled to motion, while the other is as strongly impelled to rest; and so alternations of activity and repose become manifested more in opposition than in co-operation. This gait or style of motion, therefore, may be characterized as a wiggle rather than a walk, which peculiarity by such persons is sometimes made more positive than is necessary in order to conceal so much of it as is inevitable."

Lallemand observes:

"When a child, after having proofs of memory and intelligence, experiences daily more and more difficulty in retaining and understanding what is taught him, we may be sure that it is not only from unwillingness or from idleness, as is commonly supposed. Beside the slow and progressive derangement of his or her health, the diminished energy of application, the languid movement, the stooping gait, the desertion of social games, the solitary walk, late rising, livid and sunken eye, and many other symptoms, will fix the attention of every intelligent and competent guardian of youth."

O. S. Fowler gives the following summary of the signs of masturbation:

"The private sensualist may be further known by his pallid, bloodless countenance, and hollow, sunken, and half-ghastly eyes, the lids of which will frequently be tinged with red; while, if his indulgence has been carried very far, he will have black and blue semi-circles under his eyes, and also look as if worn out, almost dead from want of sleep, yet unable to get it, etc. He will also have a half wild, or half lascivious, half foolish smile, especially when he sees a female. He will also have a certain quickness yet indecision of manner; will begin to do this thing, then stop and essay to do that, and then do what he first intended; and in such utterly insignificant matters as putting his hat here and there, etc. The same incoherence will characterize his expressions, and the same want of promptness mark all he does. Little things will agitate and fluster him, nor will he be prompt, or resolute, or bold, or forcible; but timid, afraid of his own shadow, uncertain, waiting to see what is best, and always in a hurry, yet hardly knows what he is doing, or wants to do. Nor will he walk erect, or dignified, as if conscious of his manhood, and lofty in his aspirations, but will walk and move with a diminutive, cringing, sycophantic, inferior, mean, self-debased manner, as if depreciated and degraded in his own eyes; thus telling you perpetually by his shamed looks and sheepish manner that he has been doing something low, contemptible and vulgar. This secret practice has impaired both his physical and mental manhood, and thereby effaced the nobleness and efficiency of the masculine, and deteriorated his soul, beside having ruined his body.

" He will, moreover, be dull of comprehension, incorrect, forgetful, heedless, full of blunders of all sorts; crude and inappropriate in his jokes, slow to take the hint, listless, inattentive, absent-minded, sad, melancholy, easily frightened, easily discouraged, wanting in clearness and point of idea, less bright than formerly, and altogether depreciated in looks and talents compared with what he would have been, if he had never contracted this soul and body ruining practice."

In the adoption of a plan for restoration to perfect manhood, it is required as a preliminary that the habit be at once abstained from. Few persons will defile themselves in this unnatural way, when they learn the consequences such acts will entail on their physical and moral natures. Total abstinence being decided on, the next requirement is found in right dietetic habits. Nothing but the very plainest and simplest food should be used, and late suppers, or, what is better, suppers of any kind, should be avoided. All kinds of animal food, milk, eggs, spices, etc., should be shunned. Ripe fruits, in their natural state or plainly cooked, brown bread, wheaten grits, hominy, and vegetables plainly cooked, are the best articles of diet for persons in this condition. If patients have the courage to adopt, as near as they can, a starvation diet, though it will cause depressed feelings at first, their recovery to perfect health will be much more rapid. The bed or pillows should not be of feathers or of down, but otherwise of material that will make it as hard as can be endured without discomfort. The bed-covering should be very light, even in cold weather; the bedroom should be thoroughly ventilated both night and day. "Early to bed and early to rise" should be an invariable rule. No second morning nap should be allowed, but as soon as the person first awakes he should leap immediately out of bed. When possible, sleeping on the back should be avoided. On arising, the towel-bath, with thorough after-friction, should be taken daily, followed by a brisk walk out into the fresh morning air, returning in time for breakfast. A sitz-bath of cool or cold water, lasting for about fifteen minutes, may be taken daily, at any hour most convenient.

The mind of the person must be directed in legitimate channels. All thoughts that bear the impress of impurity must be promptly dethroned, and the mind directed to the subjects of his daily employment, and on plans and operations that look far outward into the future; the past to be as a dream, and, if possible, to remain as such; the future to contain some high aim, and the endeavor required to reach such will carry with it a return to perfect health, perfect manhood and perfect happiness. No man (or woman) is born into this world without having, in a smaller or greater measure, some predominant quality necessary to success in life, the just exercise of which will not only benefit his fellow-beings, but will, or should, perfect his own soul-life, in this world, in preparation for the next. Let the patient find out what particular department in life's workshop he is able by his talents to fill, and, when decided on, let him with the whole earnestness of his nature, the enthusiasm of a new-found life, and the ardor of an earnest soul, follow out by untiring application the attainment of his plans and desires.

"Nothing serves so well to strengthen and sustain the young person who has resolved to attempt self-reformation, as a lively interest in the various reforms of the day; and in becoming a laborer in the cause of temperance reform, health reform, moral reform, etc., he finds himself surrounded by an influence which seems to buoy him up, and give him energy and fortitude to accomplish his own particular renovation of habits. His reading, and studies, and reflections, should be carefully directed to practical and not to speculative subjects. I do not mean that he should become a leader among men in any sense, nor go forward as a champion in any cause; this requires all the vigor of body and energy of mind that we find in those who have never wasted any portion of their vitality; but that he seek such persons as associates, and try to identify himself with and interest his feelings in the principles which they advocate."

The patient should so regulate his every-day employment and exercise as to be tired, at least physically, if not mentally, when he retires to bed.

It requires nothing more than total abstinence from the habit, and a close observance of the Plan of Life, to effect a thorough and radical reformation.

Should seminal emissions result, as is often the case, the plan of treatment given in the last chapter is to be adopted. Marriage is sometimes recommended as a remedy for this habit, especially when it has so grown on the individual as to be difficult of treatment. The remarks made on page 344, in reference to marrying as a cure for seminal emissions, are equally applicable here. The remedy, in its exercise, is much worse than the disease, beside involving in filthy and lustful associations the pure and clean nature of the new-made wife. The man practicing self-abuse, and lacking the force of will to adopt proper remedial measures, and daring to give his enervated, shrunken, almost lifeless soul to the purity, strength and beauty of a ripe womanhood, should, if God would exercise a special indication of His displeasure, be stricken from the crown of his head to the soles of his feet with palsy, and so make of him a living, yet a dead example to all whose thoughts lead them in the desire to marry as a remedy for this filthy and soul-debasing practice.

In girls or women who practice masturbation, in addition to the rules above mentioned, they must avoid all constriction of dress. The wearing of corsets—whether worn tight or not—or constrictions of any kind around the body, prevent a free circulation of the blood, and also operate against its purification, confining it in abnormal quantities in the pelvic portion of the body, and so irritating and creating a desire in the sexual department of the woman that must be allayed in some way—either by an early marriage to the first man offering, and the resulting sexual excess, by clandestine and unlawful excess, or by self-abuse. This fact, having for its basis physiological laws that cannot be gainsayed, is an important one, in the easy treatment of young girls or women for self-abuse. The fashionable women, or the imitators of such, who wear corsets, long dresses, and a pile of false or natural hair, covering that part of the brain in which amativeness is located, will take as naturally to a life of sexual excess—legitimate or otherwise—as would a whisky-steeped, tobacco-flavored male sensualist. Such a woman cannot possibly lead a continent life, and it is almost impossible, in the nature of things, that she should lead other than a life of sexual excess.

In young children, who have been led into the practice by their nurses, it is only necessary to closely watch them, and with right food, bathing, pure air, and exercise, they will rapidly recover.

The requirements necessary for the prevention of masturbation must, of course, commence before the generating of the child, and continue during its ante-natal life. If parents would only adopt the rules and suggestions given in Chapters IX., XII., and XIII., the habit of perverted sexual desires in children would never exist.

Next in importance, as a preventive, is the instructing and enlightening of children in the true use of their sexual organism. In a frank, kind, loving way, the parents should instruct their boys and girls as to the nature, objects and requirements of this great power for good or evil. They should warn them against the danger resulting from abusing it; and if, by accident, they should personally see or be asked to join in the practice, they should be instructed to refuse, and in future to avoid such company. If parents, through ignorance of the subject, or through false delicacy, decline to do this, they should purchase popular works on physiology, and place them in the hands of their children. Parents who allow children to grow up without in any way or at any time instructing or advising with them in the use and abuse of the sexual department of their systems, do them a very great and lasting wrong.

CHAPTER XXVI.

STERILITY AND IMPOTENCE—THEIR CAUSES, TREATMENT AND CURE.

ONE of the first laws promulgated by the Almighty, in the peopling of this earth, was the command: "Be ye fruitful and multiply"—a command that embodies in its natural and legitimate observance incomparable happiness—a happiness that is above and beyond all else, and supreme among the requirements intended for man's growth and perfection. When, through causes avoidable or non-avoidable, this divine law cannot be observed, and no children appear to bless and perfect the love-union of the husband and wife, then there follows, oft-times, great and life-long unhappiness and misery. For the benefit of this last class—a very large one—is this and the succeeding chapter written.

Apart from transmitted physical causes, sterility in most cases is susceptible of removal under certain conditions; yet most women, believing themselves in perfect health, at least not imagining they have any local disease which might be the cause of their condition, think it a dispensation of the Almighty that they should have no children, and therefore take no further thought on the matter; whereas, if they had consulted a reliable physician, the difficulty would have been explained to them, and perhaps removed, and a fruitful and happy life secured.

Sterility in women. Sterility, as occurring in women, may be divided into two classes—the married woman who never has had children, and the woman who, having had one or two, has nevertheless been sterile for many years.

There are two requisites necessary in a woman who is capable of being fecundated. The first is that she has arrived at a mature age; and the second, that she has not passed the term after which conception is possible.

Those causes for sterility depending on violated physiological laws will be first mentioned. Of these, the one that meets us on the very threshold—that of the unlimited sexual excess of the newly married, stands prominent and paramount. If the newly married, before entering into the "bonds," would but learn and know the laws that govern their sexual organism, they would certainly avoid the path that has led so many strong men and blooming women into conditions that involve weakness, sickness, *sterility*, and premature death. Obeying no law, exercising blindly only the animal of their natures, impregnation may result again and again; but, through the repetition and intensity of the act, *they destroy what they produce.* After a time, should this unnatural excess be continued, inflammation is set up in the uterus, which inflammation soon becomes chronic, and, of course, when this results, though impregnation may take place, *conception* cannot, and sterility results—sterility that will be likely to last for years. This result in those newly married explains the cause why so many of this class are married three, four or five years before they have offspring.

A large proportion of the newly married have no desire

for children, interfering as they would with their so-called pleasures ; and, by causes above mentioned, they, without knowing it, are generally successful in the fulfillment of their wishes. But when, after a time, the desire is present—as it always is, sometime or other, in married people who are human—it will be found that sterility in the woman or impotence in the man asserts itself as a just punishment for laws transgressed.

Again, notwithstanding sexual excess, impregnation and conception may ensue and sterility not appear until after the birth of one or two children. This is sometimes the result of lacerations of the neck or lips of the uterus in the first confinement. When such is the case, the accompanying symptoms are those of painful menstruation, profuse leucorrhœa, etc.

Sterility may also result through inability of the uterus to retain the impregnated ovum, in consequence of weakness and relaxation of its fibres, caused by tight lacing, impure air, want of exercise, etc.

When leucorrhœa is present, as it almost always is in the above state, conception cannot take place.

Ulceration of the os cervix, or mouth of the uterus—one of the most ordinary forms of uterine complaints in women of leisure—is a frequent cause of sterility.

When, through long-continued self-abuse, the woman has greatly lowered her supply of vital force, and especially when she arrives at the stage where self-gratification is preferred to natural intercourse with her husband, barenness almost always ensues.

Again, through the almost ever-present and universal debility in women, produced by such utter disregard of all laws—physical, mental or moral—the uterus, from local weakness or other causes, may be so displaced as to prevent the entrance of the spermatic fluid into its cavity. This condition will be easily understood by reference to figure 28, on page 319. The flexion of the womb in the direction of the rectum (A and D), or in the direction of the bladder (B and C), so doubles the organ as to close at its neck the entrance to it, and thus preventing the semen entering its cavity. An almost always present symptom of this condition is painful menstruation.

"In these cases, the menstrual fluid being secreted within, is discharged with more or less pain, often with very great accompanying suffering, by means of the muscular uterine force. No such force is exerted, or can be, to force *in* the seminal fluid, which consequently rarely reaches within the uterus. I am convinced that this obliquity is the present cause not only of sterility, but also of dysmenorrhœa, in very many cases, from the number of such instances which have, within a short time, fallen under my observation."

A prolapsed condition of the uterus will also favor sterility.

The treatment and cure for sterility caused as above, by sexual excess, general weakness, and lack of life-force, produced in any way, are found in the close observance of the laws and suggestions to be found in Chapters IX., XI., and XIII. Most sterile women believe themselves in perfect health—at least they do not imagine that they have any local disease which might be the cause of their condition.

When there is displacement of the uterus present, the organ must be returned to its natural position, and retained there by the means stated in Chapter XXIII.

If, through any of the above causes, sterility is present, it is only required that a return be made to a strictly chaste and continent life, until such time as the wife and husband are restored to vigorous and perfect health, when, if the directions heretofore given for the generating of a new life be observed, conception will surely follow.

The hymen, usually a thin and easily lacerated membrane, may be so thick and strong as to prevent an entrance into the vagina. When this is the case, there is usually a small opening through which the menstrual discharge escapes, causing some pain.   But there are cases on record when no such opening existed, and the menses had been retained until the quantity was immense.   The treatment required for imperforated hymen is its division by the scalpel, and requires the aid of a surgeon.   Its division causes absolutely no pain, and not even bleeding, and therefore no hesitation need be entertained as to its removal.

Through ignorance of the parties on sexual subjects, even a comparatively normal hymen may prevent the consummation of the act.   Says Acton :

" So common is this ignorance, that it is far from seldom that I have met with cases in which the hymen has never been ruptured.   I have no doubt that there are many husbands and wives living together, who believe that everything usual has taken place, although the marriage has never been actually consummated, and that this is far from the least frequent cause of infertility."

Through the effects of disease or accident, followed by adhesive inflammation, there may result such a contraction or stricture of the vagina as to prevent the consummation of the act, and so prevent impregnation.   Sterility caused in this way can only be removed by very gradual dilitation by means of prepared sponge, etc., and requires a long time and much patience.   When the stricture is caused by injuries, the difficulty of treatment is greatly increased.

The presence of tumors or other abnormal growths in the vagina, or in the neck or mouth of the uterus, will also prevent conception.   When they are located in the neck of the uterus, they may be so insignificant as not to be easily noticeable, and yet large enough to fill the passage and prevent the ingress of the seminal fluid into the cavity of the organ. It usually requires, in the treatment of sterility caused by intra-vaginal or intra-uterine tumors, that they be removed by means that requires the presence of a physician ; although, when of small growth, a rigid attention to hygienic laws, and local and general baths, will often result in their disappearance.

Stricture of the canal of the neck of the uterus often results after the subsidence of chronic leucorrhœa, and, until removed, will prevent impregnation.

The Fallopian tubes may be ruptured or obliterated. This occurs generally at the fimbriated extremity. Stricture may also be present in the tube, as may also disease, deformity, or misplacement of its fimbriated extremity.

The ovaries, through chronic congestion or inflammation, may lose their power to develop the germ-cell, and having no service to perform, gradually wither and become atrophied. Tumors or dropsy may also destroy the ovaries, or interfere with the fimbriated extremity of the Fallopian tube in grasping the ripe ovum.

Congenital shortness of the vagina, preventing perfect coition, is an incurable cause, although it may not be accompanied by sterility. A woman of short stature will have a vagina also short, and if she marry a tall man, as very many such women do, there always results great, and often intense pain, when the sexual act is performed, and very frequently sterility results.

The uterus itself may be absent. A married lady who recently came under my notice, on examination for an entirely different object, was discovered to have no uterus, the vagina, about two inches long, ending in a cul de sac. This very rarely occurs.

The ovaries are sometimes feebly developed, and occasionally are entirely absent.

Impotence in man. "Impotence is the term given to all those morbid conditions in man or woman which are opposed to the physiological union of the two sexes—that is to say, coition ; or, in less accurate language, it may be said to be general inability to consummate marriage. Sterility is the term reserved for all those morbid states which, either in the one or the other sex, prevent the reproduction of the species. When, however, the term sterility is mentioned, it more especially applies to the female, and is synonymous with what is generally known as barrenness—impotency being usually applied to the man.

" The forms that impotence assumes are various, though the result is the same in all cases—namely, inability to perform the sexual act. Thus, a man may be entirely impotent, whether he has or has not erection attendant on desire. Again, there may be only a partial erection, lasting an insufficient length of time for penetration ; or the erection may be so weak, or the emission so quick, as practically to render the man impotent ; or a man may be impotent from no emission at all taking place ; or emission may not take place until some time after connection has been attempted."

In the man, as in the woman, continued sexual excess will so lower the vital force of the body, and as a sequence destroy the life-generating power of the seminal fluid, as to make him, at least for a time, impotent. When this is the case, it is only required that the person adopt for a season a continent life, to regain, in a measure, his power to reproduce.

Excess in early married life is almost always certain to produce impotence late in life.

A temporary impotency is sometimes produced by intense and continued mental effort, but is always removed when the drain on the nervous fluid ceases, and the body regains its normal condition.

Masturbation, when practiced for some time, always results in impotency. The very nature of the habit tends in that direction. Lallemand says :

" This solitary vice has a tendency to separate those practicing it from women. At first, of course, it is on the sex that their thoughts dwell, and they embellish an ideal being with all the charms of imaginary perfection; the habit, however, which enslaves them little by little, changes and depraves the nature of their ideas, and at last leaves nothing but indifference for the very reality of which the image has been so constantly evoked to aid their criminal indulgence."

Says Acton : " This strange phenomenon, of self-abuse affording greater gratification than does intercourse with the other sex, the idea of whom, after all, creates the excitement, is more common than generally supposed, and more in accordance with what we should expect than at first sight appears. The masturbater, as Rousseau has described, has to picture in his imagination all the female charms that can exist, so as to be able to rouse his flagging sexual desires. But when he attempts for the first time, or at long intervals, to accomplish sexual intercourse, he finds much difficulty and very little pleasure."

The cure for masturbation, and restoration to perfect manhood, has been fully given in Chapter XXV.

Want of sexual feeling in the man, and a dislike or disgust for the wife, are also given as occasional causes for impotency.

" Want of sympathy or want of feeling, on the woman's part, is not an infrequent cause of apathy, coldness, indifference, or frigidity on the part of the husband. A first failure will so annihilate a man's sexual feeling, that he is never able or anxious to attempt connection the second time. Again, there are cases of amiable men who carry the consideration for the woman they love to such an extent, as to render themselves practically impotent, for very dread of inflicting pain."

Non-descent of the testes is a cause of partial impotence, and almost always attended by sterility. There may be exceptions to this rule, but they are rare.

The presence of hernia, with the required use of trusses, seriously interferes with the reproductive powers ; especially is this noticeable when a double truss is worn. Relief, in most cases, can be secured by the careful and judicious alteration in the size, shape, point of pressure, and method of attachment of the truss.

The enlargement of the veins of the cord—varicocele—is another disorder that, in its severe forms, aggravates, if it does not produce impotency. A suspensory bag, right bathing, and careful attention to diet will generally remedy the disorder.

One of the most common causes of impotence in the man is produced by stricture of the urethra. When the stricture is of a serious nature, after connection the semen will either dribble away, or be thrown back into the bladder. The proper treatment for stricture has been given in a previous chapter.

Obesity is another cause for impotency. "That impotency in males frequently depends upon fat, may be considered an established fact. There is every reason to believe that the same cause occasionally induces sterility in females."

The cure for sterility or impotence, when produced by the cause last named, is the careful avoidance of food containing the fat-producing principle; by a very abstemious diet; by bathing and thorough friction of the skin; by active daily exercise; and last, but by no means least, a life of strict continence.

I will here embrace the opportunity to remark, that a plain, abstemious and simple life is always favorable to fecundity. Let the husband and wife determine to live on the plainest kinds of food, and in as near its natural condition as possible, and bearing in constant remembrance that they should eat only to live; take daily a reasonable amount of healthful exercise, and live, as much as they can, in the open air and sunshine; bathe frequently, accompanying it with friction of the entire body, thus keeping the skin always clean and bright; avoid feather beds and pillows; keep regular hours; live a chaste, continent and lovable life, and the command to "increase and multiply" will be easy of attainment.

Impotency may also result from abnormal conditions of the erectile tissue, as manifested in slow erection, non-erection, imperfect or irregular erection; or it may be caused by

non-emission of the semen, as mentioned above ; by obliter-
ation of the canal of the urethra, from stricture or other
causes ; by a natural phimosis, confining the gland in such a
manner as to prevent the emission of semen ; by retraction
of the organ, from stone in the bladder or some other uri-
nary disease ; and lastly, constitutional syphilis or chronic
gleet may destroy, by its admixture, the vitality of the seminal emission.

Temperament as a cause.—Similarity of temperament in
the husband and wife has been advanced, by some latter-
day physiologists, as being one of the causes of sterility ;
and when children have resulted from such a union, their
early deaths are always predicted.   No more foolish doctrine has ever been promulgated.   The assertion that a
man and woman of well balanced and precisely similar temperaments, in perfect health when marrying, will, because of
this similarity, be sterile, or, if they have children, they will
die prematurely, has no foundation in fact or fiction.   The
union of a man and woman, both of whom are in perfect
health—I care not what their temperaments be, whether
they are precisely alike or totally dissimilar—cannot be otherwise than fruitful, and they cannot have other than healthy
children.   When a husband and wife who, through supposed
temperamental conditions, are sterile, let them adopt a continent life, and follow it out until they both, under conditions mentioned in the Plan of Life, regain in full measure
their health of body and mind, and then let them proceed to
generate a new life under conditions given in these pages,
and I will stake my existence on an unequivocally desirable
result—healthy, beautiful, intellectual children, and many of
them.

CHAPTER XXVII.

SUBJECTS OF WHICH MORE MIGHT BE SAID.

WOMAN'S RIGHTS.

 NWARD, with steady tread, does progression, the great active and vital principle of this, as of all other worlds, develop all that is required in the growth, toward the perfection of laws, required in the social and moral governments of the human race; and in no way is this so palpable as in the emancipation of woman from the slavery and thraldom of past ages. Hitherto looked on in the light of property, and, as property, subject to the whim and caprice of her owner — abused, maltreated victimized, used for the exercise of his lust, his passion, his vanity; bartered and sold—she is now in a fair way of securing what she is and was entitled to from the days of Adam—equality in freedom of thought and action, and right in person and property equally with man.

The non-progressives of society—the drags upon the

wheels of human progress—assert that women not only do not desire this freedom, but that, should they receive it, it would in a measure unsex them, and render them unfit for the peculiar sphere allotted to them. No more absurd doctrine was ever promulgated, for in proportion as women desire, receive and act out the freedom that rightly belongs to the lowest as well as the greatest of God's representatives on earth, just in that proportion will they be enabled to attain perfection and enjoy happiness, and, as a sequence, be able to fill their sphere, be it in the quiet walk of home or in the excitement of legislative debate; be it in the rearing of a family, or in governing the destinies of a nation ; be it in educating the youthful mind, or in preaching Christ's Gospel of salvation.

Out of slavery comes superstition, imbecility, weakness, degradation, and a lapse backward into the shadowy depths of hell. Out of freedom come liberty of thought and action, strength of mind, firmness of will, perfection of body and soul, and a sure and steady growth into the glorious light, joy and happiness of heaven.

Women who are inert, or who oppose this movement for equal rights with men in property and self, know not what they do. If such women have men's adulation and approbation, they think that naught else is requisite, forgetting— in the fullness of their vain, frivolous, egotistical lives—that they, separately and individually, will have to answer in the day that is coming for the use or abuse of the talents placed in their keeping, and that their natures—the unawakened capabilities, undeveloped love-power, and untrained soul-life —can only grow into a resemblance and counterpart of that of the great Master, by the privilege of the most perfect freedom of thought and action, and the fullest rights in both person and property consonant with the rule of rules—the Golden Rule.

If men could but understand and realize that the keeping of woman in her old sphere of serfdom prevents their own growth into a more perfect manhood, they would, without the delay of an hour, not only grant her all the freedom which they now possess, but also would educate her into the great and glorious advantages resulting from the acquirement of that freedom.

As are the women of a nation, so are the men of a nation; as are the women of a family, so are the men of a family. Keep a woman—a mother—in bondage, and the low conditions that spring from a life of bondage will develop themselves in her sons—the future men of the nation. Allow a woman—a mother—freedom, and the noble and radiant conditions that are born of freedom will develop themselves in her children—the future men and women of the nation. These vital facts cannot be misunderstood or controverted by any one who has carefully read and fully understood the chapter in a former part of this work on the Law of Genius, and the immense and almost unbounded influence of the mother on the destiny of the child during its pre-natal influence. Endow a woman with the right of suffrage, the right to her own person, and the right to her own property—rights that are as much of a necessity to every one of God's children as the right to live—and, if she be a mother, the influence appertaining to the exercise of these rights will, in the life of the child, develop all that tends to make man and woman true, pure, charitable, and Christ-like citizens of this present world, and God-like citizens of the next.

To be more explicit: the rights that women should strive for, obtain, and exercise, are:

1. The right of suffrage.

2. The right to own, possess, and manage property.

3. The right to a share in the management of the government of the country—local and general.

4. The right to adopt any employment in life for which her capabilities adapt her—with equal pay for equal work.

5. The right, equally with man, to all the advantages ap-

pertaining to the various educational institutions throughout the land.

6—and last, but certainly not the least—*the right to her own person.*

The violation of this last "right" by the man and husband, whose existence centres in the animal, and the sensual pleasures that come of perverted amativeness, has done more for woman's debasement, degradation and misery, than has the violation of all the other "rights" enumerated. This fact will be more fully understood and appreciated by those who have read Chapters IX. and XI., but especially Chapter XXII.

Let unprogressive men object and oppose ; let inert women despise and decry ; the time must come—is even here—when, notwithstanding the galling servitude of ages, all womankind will secure in full measure liberty and equality equally with man, and the perfection and happiness that comes of its exercise.

All honor to the noble women and brave men, the advanced apostles in the cause of universal emancipation—the perfect freedom of the whole human race, irrespective of color, sex, or nationality—for in doing this, the work of their lives, they have advanced, with mighty strides, the kingdom of God on earth. Their reward in the next life will be great and enduring.

WOMAN'S WORK.

An ever-recurring question to mothers is : "What shall we do with our daughters ?"—and the almost constant solution is : "Get them married." So the plan of life for the daughter is arranged. She is put to school, where she acquires the accomplishments necessary to the securing of the condition aimed at—these accomplishments tending, as a rule, to make her life more than ever a superficial and deceitful one. Her "education" finished, she lives in a condition of comparative idleness and dependence until the hoped-for event is reached.

Even allowing this to be the true mode of life to be adopted for girls and young women—which it certainly is not—one-quarter to one-half of these women cannot become wives. In England and Wales there are from four to five thousand women who are obliged to remain single in consequence of the excess in numbers. In Massachusetts, in the year 1860, the women outnumbered the men by thirty thousand; and in the State of New York there are nearly forty thousand more women than men, between the ages of fifteen and twenty, and the same relation holds good with nearly all the older States. This large number of women, who have no hopeful chance of getting married, must do either of two things—live a life of dependence, or work, and the question presents itself: "What can they do?" Heretofore, unmarried women have been restricted to service, sewing, teaching, or writing—occupations of a necessity that are crowded, making the pay for labor done very small. The remedy—a simple one—is to throw open to her every avocation for which she possesses a decided talent. Equally with boys, she should be started in life with the purpose of acquiring and cultivating the qualities necessary to the trade or profession she is to adopt. She should not only be born with a talent or genius for the department of life which she is intended to fill, but she should be reared and educated to it; and, on attaining majority, she should keep the object in view with a singleness of aim and steadiness of purpose that will preclude the dreaming and castle-building appertaining to marrying and marriage. In doing this, should the offer of marriage present itself, and it consort with the Law of Choice, good and well. Should the offer not present, or if presented be undesirable, still good and well; for a woman, young or old, having in her, by transmission or thorough cultivation, the talents which when exercised, make her independent, she can enjoy the pleasure of life much more intensely, whether married or unmarried, and much more so unmarried than when married and not mated.

"We do not see why women should not do light work on the farm, keep books, become tellers in the banks, agents for insurance companies, engage in various kinds of businesses, enter the professions. At present her education unfits her for many of these, but training comes from experience. No one can learn how to swim until he goes into the water. When we enter upon this experiment, then women will learn from practice to do many things for which both she and the community now think her unfitted.

"When a young man becomes of age, he is expected to take care of himself, and this stimulates him to exertion. In the few cases of rich men's sons, who rely upon their fathers, we see what the effect of dependence is. Generally it robs the young man of energy, and begets habits of idleness and indulgence. Can our girls be trained to dependence without like results?

"We do not advocate a plan of life, or system of education, which ignores the generic differences of sex. What we maintain is, that woman should be trained to do the work for which she is fitted, and should do this just as men do theirs.

"What can she do? This must be determined by trial, and not be prejudiced by false theories. The changes that have already been made have improved her industrial and social position. It is comparatively within a short period that woman's work was limited to domestic service, sewing and teaching.

"Let woman be trained to the employments which require skill, and you at once raise her wages. Open new avenues of work, and she will not be obliged to stitch her own death-shroud. At once she becomes more independent, and rises in intelligence. When young, the girl will not be simply fondled as a doll, or treated as a toy, but be educated in the invaluable habits of self-reliance and independence.

Her character will be strengthened, and her faculties en larged.

"But we are told that if you educate the daughter for a distinct vocation or profession, you unfit her for domestic duties. This is not true, as experience testifies.

" In fact, we maintain that the training which comes from these varied vocations is a much better preparation for the duties of a wife or mother than the girl gets at our fashionable boarding-school, or in a life of ease at home—alternating between idleness and parties. We have vastly more hope of the future generation, when our mothers early in life are trained to some industrial employment or profession, than now, when in so very many cases that period is wasted."

Much encouragement, and much good, sound, practical advice is contained in a late letter from Florence Nightingale, who says :

" I have worked hard—very hard—that is all—and I have never refused God anything ; though, being naturally a very shy person, most of my life has been distasteful to me. I have no peculiar gifts. And I can honestly assure any young lady, if she will but try to walk, she will soon be able to run the 'appointed course.' But then she must learn to walk, and so when she runs she must run with patience. (Most people don't even try to walk.)

" 1. But I would also say to all young ladies who are called to any peculiar vocation, qualify yourselves for it as a man does for his work. Don't think you can undertake it otherwise. No one should attempt to teach the Greek language until he is master of the language ; and this he can become only by hard study. And,

" 2. If you are called to man's work, do not exact a woman's privileges—the privilege of inaccuracy, of weakness, ye muddleheads. Submit yourselves to the rules of business, as men do, by which alone you can make God's business succeed ; for He has never said that He will give

His success and His blessing to inefficiency—to sketching and unfinished work.

" 3. It has happened to me more than once to be told by women : ' Yes, but you had personal freedom.' Nothing can well be further from the truth. I question whether God has ever brought any one through more difficulties and contradictions than I have had.

"4. But to women I would say, look upon your work, whether it be an accustomed or an unaccustomed work, as upon a trust confided to you. This will keep you alike from discouragement and from presumption, from idleness and from overtaxing yourself. Where God leads the way, He has bound Himself to help you to go the way.

" If I could really give the lessons of my life to my countrywomen and yours (indeed, I fain look upon us as all one nation)—the lessons of my mistakes as well as of the rest— I would ; but for this there is no time. I would only say work—work in silence at first, in silence for years—it will not be time wasted. Perhaps in all your life it will be the time you will afterward find to have been best spent ; and it is very certain that without it you will be no worker. You will not produce one ' perfect work,' but only a botch in the service of God."

As far as women become self-supporting, they will be emancipated from the bondage of dependence, and be more free in respect to marriage. This relation will not be entered upon to secure a support, as is so often done now, but more from the promptings of affection. The home will not be less sacred and hallowed, but will rest on a more secure basis.

This movement in favor of woman's emancipation finds a cordiality in the spirit and influence of Christianity. Every step made in improving her condition has been stimulated by the teachings of Christ. As we carry on this work, religion will be the gainer, society reap the benefit, and home be made more effective.

DIVORCES.

Marriage, as God intended it should be, differs widely from the institution concerning which ministers, in its performance, say : "What God has joined together let no man put asunder." I do not believe that in thousands of these so-called marriages God or His divine laws have anything to do with them, for to imagine so would be to assert that He is fallible. The great aim and object of existence in this world is to perfect each one themselves, to help others to do so, and to enjoy the happiness that comes of well-doing. As a necessity to the attainment of this highest state of perfection and happiness, the divine institution of marriage was originated coeval with Adam and Eve on earth.

That marriage, in our age, fails in this its divine purpose is lamentably the case ; yet, in so failing, is it right that the union should be continued, or a separation take place, or a divorce be granted. The question, I think, is not difficult of solution ? If a man and woman enter the state of matrimony, and after a time discover that through deceit, hypocrisy, intrigue or force, one or the other develops qualities that tend to debase, degrade, and make miserable a human life—instead of elevating, ennobling, and making happy and perfect two human lives—then it is naught but right that a divorce be granted, or at least a separation take place. I hold that anything that is an obstacle to the individual's attainment of perfection and happiness, in this life, should be avoided or removed when it does not conflict with the right of others ; and that therefore a wife who, although doing all that her best nature can do to make her married existence one of enjoyment and perfection, is nevertheless abused, maltreated, or wronged in any of the many ways that sordid, licentious, brutal, or covetous husbands may demonstrate, is perfectly justified by the laws of Nature, if not by the laws of man, in separating or being divorced from such a husband. The same argument applies with equal force to the man when the wife is the transgressor.

Yet, though I hold divorce to be a necessity under these circumstances, I *do not allow that it is right for either the divorced or separated man or woman to again marry.* It savors too much of uncleanliness, adultery and fornication. It runs contra to all that is pure, clean and chaste, that a separated or divorced man or woman should again marry. Beside, such men and women are apt to make precisely the same mistakes in forming new unions, and repeating the same *role* of mis-mated miseries, separation and divorce, making the institution that should be divine in its nature and observance a mockery and a farce.

The subject is too deep and too broad to here enter largely into details; but let us look briefly at some of the causes for this great proportion of mis-mated misery and the subsequent separation and divorce.

Primarily stands out boldly the selfishness and lustfulness (coupled with ignorance of physiological laws) of humankind in the choice of life-companions. When any of these traits are in danger of being exercised, or physical laws broken, the State or Government, as guardians of their people's welfare, should step in and prevent the consummation of what would be known by those better educated as certain to terminate disastrously.

This is lamentably not the case; for, " while one-half the clergy spend their time and energies in denouncing divorces, the other half seem equally busy in preparing the way for them. We have already mentioned the case of an Episcopal clergyman in this city, who recently married a schoolgirl of sixteen to a young fellow who applied to him to perform the ceremony, and cases of this kind are of constant occurrence. A St. Louis paper states that a clergyman there, after marrying one couple, wanted to know, in that playful spirit so becoming to the clerical character, if there were any other parties who desired to be married, when a couple of young people, deeming it a good joke, stepped up and were married also.   They were greatly surprised to learn that the ceremony was no joke, but that they were actually made one, and compelled to live together, for better or worse, till death.   Yet these same clergymen will insist that marriage is a divine institution—that the parties to it have been 'joined together by God,' and that they must not be 'put asunder by man.'   There is nothing more impious than such pretensions, and nothing more prolific of divorces than marriages thus performed."

Now, if ministers of God's Word—teachers of the people in the way of life—act in this loose and careless manner in the performance of what should be a divine institution, what can be expected of the selfish, licentious and heedless multitude, who hurriedly crowd into the doing of all that is wrong in life?

As a preventive to mis-mated marriages, laws should be enacted that would reduce the number of persons authorized to perform the marriage ceremony.   These authorized persons, before being allowed to unite persons applying, should require sworn proof: 1. That the man and woman have arrived at proper ages (which proper ages are recorded in a previous chapter); 2. That they are mutually willing to be married; 3. That they furnish evidence of good character and good health; 4. That they produce evidence that they have never been heretofore married, and subsequently separated or divorced; 5. The consent of the parents or guardians might or might not be deemed necessary, depending on whether the laws allowed children to marry; and that the violation of any of these requirements be promptly followed by a penalty, and that some one be appointed to enforce such laws and penalties.

If the above precautions were adopted, and good faith fully observed, coupled with the education of the masses in the true laws of living, and the elevation of woman to an equality with man, much if not all the misery, separations and divorces that appertain to married life would disappear, giving place to marriages that would embody what God intended they should—ineffable peace, holy joy, intense happiness, and the daily growth into a love so strong, so pure, so radiant, as to imply fellowship with Jesus the Christ.

BATHS—HOW TO TAKE THEM.

Scattered through these pages are allusions to the taking of different kinds of baths. To enable the reader, or patient, as the case may be, to more fully comprehend their nature, mode of employing, etc., is the object of their insertion here.

Towel or sponge-bath. Rubbing the whole surface of the body rapidly with a coarse, wet towel or sponge, followed by a dry towel and after-friction with the hands, constitutes this process. This bath may be taken daily, and is absolutely required in all those whose desire is for clearness of skin and purity of body.

The sun and air-bath can be enjoyed only on a clear and bright day, when, with the body entirely nude, lying on a mattress or lounge, the direct and unobstructed rays of the sun are allowed to fall on the body. Persons unused to this bath should at first not remain in it longer than five or ten minutes, gradually extending the time to thirty minutes. The life-giving qualities of this bath, to be understood and appreciated, require only an occasional trial.

Hip or sitz-bath. A small-sized wash-tub will do for this, although tubs constructed with a straight back, and raised four or five inches from the floor, are much the most agreeable. The water should just cover the hips and lower part of the abdomen. A blanket should be thrown around the patient, who will find it also useful to rub or knead the abdomen with the hands or fingers during the bath. This bath may be continued from fifteen to thirty minutes.

Wet-sheet packing. On a bed or mattress two or three

comfortables or bed-quilts are spread ; over them a pair of
flannel blankets, and a wet sheet (rather coarse linen is best)
wrung out lightly. The patient, undressed, lies down flat
on the back, and is quickly enveloped in the sheet, blanket,
and other bedding. The head must be well raised with pillows, and care must be taken to have the feet well wrapped.
If the feet do not warm with the rest of the body, a jug of
hot water should be applied ; and if there is tendency to
headache, several folds of a cold wet cloth should be laid
over the forehead. The usual time for remaining in the
pack is from forty to sixty minutes. It may be followed by
a towel or sponge-bath.

The wet girdle. Three or four yards of crash toweling
makes a good one. One half of it is wet and applied round
the abdomen, followed by the dry half to cover it. It
should be wet as often as it becomes dry.

Injections.—These are warm or tepid, cool or cold. The
former are used to allay pain and produce free discharges ;
the latter to check excessive evacuations and strengthen the
bowels. For the former purpose a large quantity should be
used, and for the latter purpose only a small quantity.

General bathing rules. Never bathe soon after eating, but
only when the stomach is empty, or nearly so. The water
should be soft, and the room of a comfortable temperature.
No bath should be taken when a feeling of fatigue is present. Between eleven and twelve o'clock in the forenoon is
the best time for bathing. After a bath is taken, and the
skin thoroughly dried, the surface of the body should be
briskly rubbed for five minutes with the dry hands. And
remember, that without proper and careful attention to diet,
exercise, rest, and pure air, bathing in itself will not amount
to much as a health restorative.

QUACKS, DRUGS, AND PATENT MEDICINES.

Patients who may be afflicted with any disease mentioned

in Chapters XXIII. and XXIV., must, if they desire a quick recovery, avoid, in any shape or any form, or under any conditions, the leeches who, through ingeniously devised advertisements, circulars, or yellow-covered pamphlets, propose, for a consideration *in advance*, secretly and confidentially to cure them of their trouble. These quack doctors are a curse to civilization. They never get a victim within their cunningly contrived coils, but that they rob him not only of money, but of health—and often in such a measure that they never recover it. In the testimonials of cure they flourish, they lie ; in the assertion that they studied in London or Paris, they lie ; in the declaration that they are regularly graduated M.D.'s, they very often lie ; and in their promise to cure, they lie—knowingly and understandingly lie. The lives of these men—or rather charlatans—are made up of brazen-faced hypocrisy, low cunning, theft and lying—hypocritical in their assertions, cunning in their expressions, thieving in their extortions, and lying in all they do or say. When a man has transgressed and suffers the penalty, let him, if he be a young man, confide in his parents or the family physician, instead of writing to some far distant, or personally applying to some near by quack. The parents will advise and suggest, and the family physician, or any other physician or surgeon of good repute, will help him to a cure, and both will do so without the smallest breach of trust. It is through fear of exposure that many patients are led to consult with quacks, but such patients should understand that no physician living in their immediate neighborhood, having a just regard for his own character and reputation, will allow the slightest hint to escape concerning the maladies of any of his patients. Therefore, avoid all manner of quack doctors, for, no matter in what form they present themselves, they carry in their wake deceit, robbery, and disease aggravated and intensified.

If one could, by some sleight-of-hand endeavor, convert a small portion of every drug and patent medicine into the embodiment of a quack doctor, they would represent and re-quire for their exposition precisely the same words as have been applied to these self-same quacks, with the additional result that premature death much sooner overtakes the vic-tims. Drugs, no matter in what form, under what condi-tions, in what quantity, under what name, patented or oth-erwise, have been, are, and will continue to be, in proportion to their use, a great and positive curse to God's human family.

This great and almost universal delusion—namely, that by the taking of drugs or patent medicines a sick person can be restored to health, is shown in all its absurdity, in the suppo-sition that what will make a well person sick will make a sick person well. This is a great fallacy, as is sadly shown by the millions that have passed off from the earth's surface, be-fore half their days were spent. Since the creation of the world—or since the days of Hippocrates, if you will—*drugs never have cured one single person having disease of any na-ture.* When it is asserted they have done so, it will be found on close examination and argument that the person has re-covered comparative health *in spite of the drugs*, and *not* through their influence.

CHAPTER XXVIII.

A HAPPY MARRIED LIFE—HOW SECURED.

UPPOSING the husband and wife to have been united under the conditions mentioned in a former part of this book, it would hardly be necessary to say much concerning the heading of this chapter, for they would—in fact could not well help—living, an enjoyable, harmonious, and lovable married life.

But, unfortunately, where one couple are united under physiological principles, there are a hundred thousand that are not, and, as an almost certain result, there follows unhappiness in some one or other of its many developments. Now, if these "married but not mated" parties would notice and follow a few plain, generally applicable, and easily observed rules, they would do much toward mitigating the many trials that appertain to married life as exemplified in this nineteenth century.

In the choosing of husbands and wives, it is patent to all observing minds that the selfish and secretive faculties largely predominate with the vast majority of human-kind. After a few days of wedded life—after the glamour that attaches itself to the exercise of the lustful that is in them is exhausted—idiosyncrasies of habit and character that neither admire or desire show themselves in each other; and it may be, and often does happen, that in due time a separation or divorce is secured on account of "incompatibility." It is a noticeable thing that these same parties who have rushed out of an unhappy union on account of "incompatibility," are just as ready to rush into another marriage, seemingly quite as injudicious as the one they have escaped from.

The first great requirement necessary in those whose desire is for a happy and lovable married life, is that the husband and wife come to a definite and conclusive understanding as regards the Law of Continence. The faithful observance of this law I consider one of the fundamental requirements in a successful married life. A life of chastity is preeminently a true and lovable life, while a life of lust leads very far from the growth of two souls into one. It should be allowed by the husband that with the wife should rest the question as to the time when she wished to accept the sacred trust of maternity. What a great, dark, heavy cloud would be swept off from the hearts of womankind—married womankind—if this law, the right of woman to her own person—the right to deny all approaches, save and only when she desired maternity—was universally respected. But ah! the millennium is yet a very great way off, and although reform writers and speakers are doing much toward the desired end, yet will women have to suffer, endure and wait.

If it can be agreed upon between the husband and wife that they will endeavor, by the best efforts of their nature, to live a pure, chaste and continent life, they will have made a very long step in the direction of growth toward a perfect unity of souls

A great assistance to a just observance of this Law of Continence between the husband and wife is the occupying of different beds; for that matter, no two or more persons should make a practice of habitually sleeping together, for the reason that, by contact, the weaker in vital force will absorb from the stronger, and so produce in the stronger a loss of power in the nervous system, as indicated by peevishness, fretfulness, fault-finding, etc. For this reason, children should not be allowed to sleep together or with grown-up persons; men should not sleep with men, women with women, or should husbands and wives who desire to lead a true, pure, and lovable married life habitually sleep together.

Especially should wives, when they imagine their husbands have slighted or ill used them, avoid recounting their troubles to some " very dear friend," who, in nine cases out of ten, will so argue the subject as to make the wife really begin to feel that she is sadly abused, and in a dreamy way to think of separation. The only proper plan is to go to the husband, and in a quiet way recount to him her supposed grievances. It may be, and is often the fact, that the husband may be entirely ignorant of the pain or trouble he carelessly is inflicting, and only requires his attention drawn to the fact to prevent a repetition.

Perfection, in the very far off future, may appear on earth, but just now the human race lacks the elements necessary to this end. To look for perfection in a husband or wife is simply an absurdity. We all have our faults, failings, and backslidings. Some of these are infinitessimal in their proportions, and capable of being remedied by earnest endeavor; while some of them are so glaring and positive in their character as to be a deformity in the soul of the individual. Of the small faults—the disputes, the differences, the sudden angers, etc.—the explosives of imperfect human souls, these would I most urgently advise the husband and wife to strive earnestly to avoid. It is astonishing how, with the vast majority of mankind, and especially womankind, little trifles, little troubles, and little pains will cut so much deeper and last longer than would any great wrong. When anything has occurred that appears in the remotest way to disturb the harmony of married life, *immediately* should the party who has done the wrong make a full and open confession. It is hard for some to do this—especially is it so for the majority of men—but it is the only true way of reparation; confess, and promise to try not to repeat the deed done. Our Saviour has said : " Offences will come," and at the same time He gave the remedy, good for all time : " Go and tell it between thee and him alone." The neglect of this simple rule has been not only a cause of estrangement between husbands and wives, but between relatives, friends and neighbors.

Says Alger, in his "Friendships of Women :"

" Let a husband be the pure and true guardian of his family, laboring always to adorn himself with the god-like gems of wisdom, virtue, and honor ; let him bear himself in relation to his wife with gracious kindness toward her faults, with grateful recognition of her merits, with steady sympathy for her trials, with hearty aid for her better aspirations, and she must be of a vile stock if she does not revere him and minister unto him with all the grace and sweetness of her nature.

" Let a wife, in her whole intercourse with her husband, try the efficacy of gentleness, purity, sincerity, scrupulous truth, meek and patient forbearance, an invariable tone and manner of deference, and if he is not a brute he cannot help respecting her and treating her kindly, and in nearly all instances he will end by loving her and living happily with her.

" But if he is vulgar and vicious, despotic and reckless, so as to have no devotion for the august prizes and incorruptible pleasures of existence; if she is an unappeasable termagant or a petty worrier, so taken up with trifling annoyances that wherever she looks ' the blue rotunda of the universe sinks into a housewifery room ;' if the presence of each acts as a morbid irritant on the nerves of the other, to the destruction of comfort and the lowering of self-respect, their companionship must infallibly be a companionship in wretchedness and loss.

" The banes of domestic life are littleness, falsity, vulgar-
ity, harshness, scolding, vociferation, an incessant issuing of
superfluous prohibitions and orders, which are regarded as
impertinent interferences with the general liberty and repose,
and are provocative of rankling or exploded resentments.
The blessed antidotes that sweeten and enrich domestic life
are refinement, high aims, great interests, soft voices, quiet
and gentle manners, magnanimous tempers, forbearance from
all unnecessary commands or dictation, and generous allow-
ances of mutual freedom. Love makes obedience lighter
than liberty. Man wears a noble allegiance, not as a collar,
but as a garland. The Graces are never so lovely as when
seen waiting on the Virtues ; and, where they thus dwell together, they make a heavenly home."

Closely allied to a man's disposition or " temper," as also
the woman's, is the food they eat and the stomach they put
it into. I have no doubt that in thousands of cases, from
the baby up to the father, these " offences" of disposition in
the members of a family are caused by indigestion, badly
cooked and unhygienic food, placed in a stomach for solution and digestion that is irritable, feverish, worn out, and
incapable of promptly converting the mess sent down into
blood without many and positive expostulations, which expostulations are sent by nerve-telegraph to the individual's
brain, producing in his soul that state of feeling best adapted
to be at war with all mankind, his family, and himself. There
is no doubt about it, that many a person feels irritable, peevish, fretful, fault-finding, cross, etc., who only requires to
live on plain, unstimulating diet and two meals a day to regain their normal and natural beauty and harmony of mind
and disposition.

Another requirement, in those who desire a pleasurable
married life is employment. It is a necessity to our existence on this earth that we work—so that work, rest and
recreation will greatly assist to the end we are all striving
for : happiness and growth toward perfection. Now, if a

wife be of the kind termed "lazy," and especially if she be of the fashionably lazy variety, family quarrels, with their attendant miseries, and perhaps eventually separation, are as sure to follow as day follows night. Show me a man who lives and does not work, and I will show you a rascal. And if a man or woman have not sufficient mental or physical work to keep them employed during the day, you can assert with a certainty that mischief, either of a physical or moral nature, will result. These facts apply with full force in the direction of all husbands and wives who desire to live united lives.

In the doing of work, great care must be taken not to overlook its legitimate object. Work, as a road to wealth, a fortune and retirement, runs contra to all divine laws ; and yet—

"The great aim of the mass of mankind is, to get money enough ahead to make them 'comfortable ;' and yet a moment's reflection will convince us that money will never purchase ' comfort,' only the means of it. A man may be 'comfortable' without a dollar ; but to be so he must have the right disposition—that is, a heart and a head in the right place. There are some persons who are lively, and cheerful, and good-natured, kind and forbearing in a state of poverty, which leans upon the toil of to-day for to-night's supper and the morning's breakfast. Such a disposition would exhibit the same loving qualities in a palace or on a throne.

" Every day we meet with persons who in their families are cross, ill-natured, dissatisfied, finding fault with everybody and everything—whose first greeting in the breakfast room is a complaint, whose conversation seldom fails to end in an enumeration of difficulties and hardships, and whose last word at night is an angry growl. If you can get such persons to reason on the subject, they will acknowledge that there is some 'want' at the bottom of it ; the 'want' of a better house, a finer dress, a more handsome equipage, a more dutiful child, a more provident husband, a more cleanly

or systematic or domestic wife. At one time it is a 'wretched cook,' which stands between them and the sun ; or a lazy
house-servant, or an impertinent carriage-driver. The 'want'
of more money than Providence has thought proper to be-
stow, will be found to embrace all these things. Such persons may feel assured that people who cannot make themselves really comfortable in any one set of ordinary circumstances, would not be so under any other. A man who has
a canker eating out his heart, will carry it with him wherever he goes ; and if it be a spiritual canker, whether of envy,
habitual discontent, unbridled ill-nature, it would go with
the gold, and rust out all its brightness. Whatever a man is
to-day with a last dollar, he will be, radically and essentialiy,
to-morrow with a million, unless the heart is changed. Stop,
reader, that is not the whole truth, for the whole truth has
something of the terrible in it. Whatever of an undesirable disposition a man has to-day without money, he will
have to-morrow to an exaggerated extent, unless the heart
be changed—the miser will become more miserly; the drunkard more drunken; the debauchee more debauched; the
fretful still more complaining. Hence, the striking wisdom
of the Scripture injunction that all our ambitions should begin with this : 'Seek first the kingdom of God and His
righteousness—that is to say, that if you are not comfortable, not happy now, under the circumstances which surround you, and wish to be more comfortable, more happy,
your first step should be to seek a change of heart, of disposition, and then the other things will follow—*without the
greater wealth !*"

The wife, equally with the husband, should guard with
jealous care, all secrets of home-life. Many wives have the
faculty of going around among their neighbors, and exposing—often in a greatly magnified form—every little event
that transpires between the inmates of her household—a
most reprehensible practice. Consider, I pray you, all the
troubles, differences and irritations, be they great or small,

400 THE SCIENCE OF A NEW LIFE.

as inviolate secrets, known only to your husband, yourself, and your God.

To a couple that are newly married, I think it is a necessity to their happiness that they, in commencing a home-life, exclude therefrom everybody—mothers, brothers, fathers, aunts, etc., who should not be allowed to help make up the new household. The presence of any one or more of these relatives prevents, in a thousand ways, the growth into the aims involved in a true married life. Mothers-in-law, especially, have an established reputation for starting little troubles and differences between husband and wife. Of course, there are mothers who are noble exceptions to this rule, but alas! they are rare.

Zchokke, in one of his tales, gives the following excellent advice :

"In the first solitary hour after the ceremony, take the bridegroom and demand a solemn vow of him, and give a vow in return. Promise each other sacredly, never—not even in jest—to wrangle with each other, never to bandy words or indulge in the least ill-humor. Never—I say, never! Wrangling in jest, putting on an air of ill-humor merely to tease, becomes earnest by practice. Mark that! Next, promise each other, sincerely and solemnly, never to keep a secret from each other, under whatever pretext, and whatever excuse it might be. You must continually, and every moment, see clearly into each other's bosom. Even when one of you has committed a fault, wait not an instant, but confess it. And as you keep nothing from each other, so, on the contrary, preserve the privacies of your house, marriage state, and heart, from father, mother, brother, sister, aunt, and from all the world. You two, with God's help, build your own quiet world. Every third or fourth one you draw into it with you will form a party, and stand between you two. That should never be. Promise this to each other. Remember the vow at each temptation. You will find your account in it. Your souls will grow, as it were, to each other, and at last will become as one. Ah, if many a pair had, on their marriage-day, known the secret, how many a marriage were happier than, alas, they are !"

When a married couple are really desirous of living a true, pure, and harmonious life, the object to be aimed at, to secure such a result, is the daily growth into unity of thought, of purpose, and of mind. This approach to similarity of souls constitutes the great secret of a perfect union. I am acquainted with a gentleman who is eighty years of age, and also with his wife, who is seventy-five. You would imagine, on first seeing them, that they were brother and sister, so closely do they resemble each other; and not only in the face is this similarity noticeable, but also in their talk, expressions, and actions. Now this couple began married life as country people usually do, and, of course, had their little differences of character when first married ; but fifty years of married life—a simple, earnest, Christian married life—has resulted in the perfect union of two souls—a union that will be continued, and grow stronger, purer, and more Christlike in the next world. In these days of unhappy marriages, separations and divorces, it does one an infinity of good to meet such a perfect married couple. Incidentally I may mention that they have reared eleven children, every one of them being alive and healthy ; and I may also mention another fact—namely, that the husband, every night of his life, with his family gathered around him, reads a chapter in the Bible, followed by prayer. Now it is just as easy for the great majority of married people to emulate this couple as it is for them to do the reverse. All that is required is unbounded patience with each other, while each is trying to wear smooth the jarring angularities that appertain to all individualities. Smoothness and similarity come after a time, and eventually growth into a perfect love-union results.

Does it ever happen, once in a hundred thousand times, that a newly-married wife and husband, especially during the so-called "honeymoon," ever bend their knees in prayer before the throne of God, asking for His assistance, His guidance, His love, in their new sphere of life? I think not. I may be mistaken in the proportion; but certainly, in the great majority of newly married lives, instead of thoughts of Christ and purity, will be found the works of lust and the Devil.

Now I record it as an incontrovertible fact, that in no married circle can true peace, love, purity, chastity and happiness be found in which is not present the spirit of Christ, and the daily and hourly striving after loving obedience to His divine commands, and especially the nightly prayer for blessings received or desires unfulfilled.

Let the married adopt and follow these hints; let them exercise common sense, sympathy, sensibility and benevolence toward each other; let them wear the garb of modesty and delicacy, cheerfulness and contentment; let them grow into a love of domestic life; let them have children and love them; let them ever exercise the spirit of self-denial, never omitting mutual concessions and forbearance; let them ever observe order and system, neatness and industry, economy and frugality; let them ever exercise the true and pure that is in them, and nightly let their united souls join in prayer to the Father of us all; let them grow into the best part of their natures, and grow out of the bad that is in them, and with hearts, heads and destinies united, they will go up into the Mount of Transfiguration, and bring to earth the Kingdom of Heaven.

INDEX.

AUTHOR'S NOTE.

The subjects of Pre-natal Influence, Law of Continence, Law of Sex, etc., as contained in this work, are of such manifest importance, and so intimately affect the welfare of the human race, as to merit much more inquiry and investigation than has heretofore been bestowed on them. If any reader, in the fulness of a practical, observing mind, has noticed any particular facts, or can make any suggestions, the Author would be pleased to have such person communicate with him. No theories or fancies are desired ; only facts—practical, demonstrable facts. Letters to be addressed to care of Publishers

A FEW EXTRACTS

FROM NOTICES RECEIVED IN RELATION TO

THE SCIENCE OF A NEW LIFE

By JOHN COWAN, M. D.

———

These notices were entirely unsolicited. They are the free untrammelled expressions of papers of acknowledged authority and power; of persons of recognized merit and reputation; and of readers, who on paying for and studying the book, felt impressed to send their meed of praise. Of the many extracts from readers letters, those given here are but a moiety of the hundreds on file at the office of the publishers.

No other book yet published on the subject on which this one treats, has met with so universal an approval for the unexceptionable manner in which it advances rules and suggestion for the elevation and happiness of man and womankind.

————

[*From the Christian Union, Henry Ward Beecher, Editor.*]

A new Edition of "The Science of a New Life" gives us the opportunity of saying that it seems to us to be one of the wisest and purest and most helpful of those books which have been written in recent years with the intention of teaching men and women the truths about their bodies which are of peculiar importance to the morals of society. It will be understood that we here refer to treatises on sexual physiology. No one can begin to imagine the misery that has come upon the human family solely through ignorance upon this subject. Of course, only a man who is more than learned, who is wise and good also, can safely be entrusted with the duty of writing such a book. The spirit in which Dr. Cowan has written is apparently that of earnest devotion to the welfare of mankind.

On a careful examination of Dr. Cowan's "Science of a New Life" I am prepared to give it my very cordial approval, and to wish that it might be in the possession of the two large classes for whose guidance and happiness it was written, namely, "all who are married, and particularly those who contemplate marriage," not excepting those who do not intend or are not likely to marry, but who cannot fail to be enlightened and aided by its teaching. It deserves to be in every family, and read and pondered, as closely relating to the highest moral and physical well-being of all its members. With here and there an opinion or a rule that may be questionable, it is nevertheless a volume admirable for the purity of its tone and purpose, unquestionably sound in its hygienic directions and physiological averments, and extremely valuable in the lessons it inculcates. "The people perish for lack of knowledge" is an ancient declaration, almost as applicable now as it was when first uttered; and it is largely owing to a profound ignorance of the law of birth and parentage, and the laws of our physical organization generally, that "the lusts of the flesh" have gained such widespread ascendancy that millions of the human race are suffering both bodily and mental depravation, that the marriage relation has been so fearfully violated, and that licentiousness and foul disease are inflicting the very life-blood of the people. The essential remedy for these great evils is to be found in Dr. Cowan's work; therefore, may it be circulated far and wide.

Yours, for suffering humanity,   WM. LLOYD GARRISON.

The dedication of Dr. Cowan's book—"To all the Married, but particularly to those who contemplate Marriage"—sufficiently indicates its scope and purpose. It is an earnest plea for temperance in all things, for the subjection of the senses to the spirit, for the rule of purity and continence, especially in that relation of life which most people seem to enter only to find a pretext for discarding both. Without subscribing fully to all of Doctor Cowan's views, which are marked by a strictness approaching austerity it is impossible not to admire and applaud the entire delicacy of manner and the loftiness of aim with which he treats a nice and difficult subject. In an age given over to sensuality, it is pleasant to find one man lifting up his voice in behalf of a pure morality; and we are disposed to condone, if not forgive, an error on the side of severity. The chapters entitled "*The Law of Continence*", "*The Prevention of Conception*" (wherein the author takes the true Christian ground that the only legitimate prevention is abstinence) *Children—their Desirability*, and *Feticide*, might be read with especial profit by that class of the community for whom the book is intended. What they say can scarcely be said to often, and is seldom said at all outside of medical text books, or in a way to make it suitable or useful to the general reader. Dr. Cowan's views about the transmission of genius and the determination of offspring are curious, and not without plausibility, and his medical principles are simple, and for the most part sound. Regularity, frugality, temperance in diet, personal cleanliness, daily baths, not alone of water but of sun and air, a proper amount of sleep; and a moderate degree of exercise—a strict observance, in short, of natural laws, will insure health and go far to insure happiness. If only for the earnestness with which it denounces and condemns the atrocious practice of ante-natal infanticide, or the scarcely less revolting indecencies of prevention, the legal prostitution of all sorts for which modern marriage is made the flimsy veil, this book would be worthy of the praise of every pure-minded man and woman; but it calls for even higher approbation by its recognition and emphatic assertion of what to-day is so rarely recognized or admitted —the essential nobleness, purity, and holiness of the martial state.

2

3

[*From Rev. Octavius B. Frothingham of New York.*]

I have read with care "The Science of a New Life". If a million of the married and unmarried would do the same, they would learn many things of deepest import to their welfare.

Not that I am prepared to give it my unqualified praise; but the substance of the book is excellent, its purpose high, its counsel noble, its spirit earnest, humane, and pure. I trust it will have a very wide circulation.

Sincerely yours,   O. B. FROTHINGHAM.

[*From the Christian at Work.*]

This book is remarkable for the fund of physiological information contained between its covers, nowhere else attainable within so small a compass, and not to be had in its entirely except by those familiar with the French books on physiology.

[*From Judge J. W. Edmonds, Ex-chief Justice of the Supreme Court, New York.*]

I have read the work "Science of a New Life" by Dr. John Cowan and I ought not to withhold from you the expression of my approbation of it. I would have given a good deal for the knowledge it contains in my boy days—some 60 years ago, and I rejoice greatly that it has at length been put in a form to be accessible to all. Not being a physician I do not feel myself competent to express an opinion as to the manner in which the work has been done. It has however been so well done, that I easily understand it and two educated intelligent married woman, who have read it, say to me, on returning it "it is in many respects most excellent and the tendency is to elevate."   J. W. EDMONDS.

[*From the Index, Francis E. Abbot, Editor.*]

Dr. John Cowan's "Science of a New Life" is a work devoted to all that relates to marriage and written in a style and spirit that command our unqualified approbation. It is plain, direct, and practical—yet permeated with so deep a reverence for the marriage relation, and so utter an abhorrence of what we are ashamed to call fashionable abominations, that pruriency will be rebuked, and the love of purity heightened by its perusal. There can be no question that physiological knowledge of this character is sorely needed by thousands and thousands of people, whose innocent offspring must pay the penalty of their parents' ignorance or vice. To those who would put a really unexceptionable book on these subjects in the hands of young persons approaching maturity, we can conscientiously recommend this as one that will enlighten without debasing.

[*From the Pittsburg Dispatch.*]

This is the title of a volume just issued from the press, the author being Dr. John Cowan an eminent physician, and who, judging from the tone of his book, must likewise be a true Christian philanthrophist. It takes up the theory that if ever the reformation of the world is to be accomplished, it can only come through the medium of rightly directed observance of ante-natal laws. Dr. Cowan holds to this belief firmly and supports it by illustrations and arguments whose force will appeal to every intelligent reader. * * * * Desire for physiological knowledge is daily spreading and when taught through such an excellent and correct medium as this, its results cannot be other than valuable.

4

"If ever the reformation of the world is to be accomplished—if ever the millenium of purity, chastity, and intense happiness reaches this earth, it can only do so through rightly-directed pre-natal laws." Such is the sentiment upon which this book is built up—a sentiment not admirably expressed, but admirable in its meaning. To a correct understanding of the laws pre-natal and post-natal, as also to a more thorough comprehension of what marriage should be, and what it should accomplish for mutual happiness, these four hundred and five octavo pages by Dr. Cowan must greatly conduce. They are devoted to topics concerning which no person arrived at years of thoughtfulness should be ignorant. They treat of these topics in a plain, sensible manner, in language that none but a prude can object to, and are apparently written in no spirit of quackery, but for a worthy purpose. Could the book be placed in the hands of every young person contemplating matrimony, it would assuredly do much good.

This excellent work is so superior in style and matter to the numerous worthless books, with which the country is flooded that we are not willing to let it pass without commending it to the thoughtful consideration of our readers. Treating of those important topics that refer to the health and purity of mind and body, ignorance of which, at this enlightened day, is inexcusable; in a manner, earnest and forcible, but chaste and elegant, it is a reliable hygenic and moral guide. Parents often make a terrible mistake, in not speaking freely to their children of physiological laws, and of the social and moral evils, that may beset them in life, and too frequently they acquire dangerous information and fatal habits from corrupt associations. On all the subjects in which men and women are most deeply interested this book is a sound teacher, and to married persons its lessons are invaluable.

It is a difficult as well as a delicate task to discuss in a proper manner the subject of reproduction of a new human life. This the author of this work has undertaken, going into details of facts and philosophy, with constantly applied suggestions of a physiological, sanitary and moral character. The method and execution of the work are quite unexceptionable, and many of its practical suggestions are certainly valuable.

This work is very different from the works that are usually published on this subject. It is a plain but chaste book, dealing with the physical problems which most concern all human beings in the spirit of science and humanity. What we all, as society, need is a better understanding of physiology and the laws of health, so that men and women, knowing these laws and their own constitutions, can live properly, in such physical estate as shall produce the best mental state. This book is a very valuable contribution to that end. There is a lamentable ignorance and shame-facedness about some of the most important offices of life. We have no doubt that with the dissipation of this ignorance there will be a truer modesty, less disease and a happier and purer society.

This work is one of the best of its kind that has been issued from the press during many years.

5

This work is a clear, comprehensive, and yet concise treatment of laws which regulate human life, as well as those which pertain to the married relation. It is an evidently candid attempt to popularize information on one of the most important subjects which come within the range of human thought. The book is worthy an extended sale.

We can conscientiously commend "The Science of a New Life" to all married persons and those contemplating marriage, for whom it is designed. Its purpose is to thoroughly acquaint the people with the laws, that most intimately effect their being, in such a way as to promote chastity and a pure life. If husbands will heed it wives will bless them. Plainness of speech is used; but the requirements of delicacy, nevertheless, are strictly followed. We are quite sure the work will meet the approval of the medical profession. There is no question upon which there is more ignorance; none on which we need more thorough knowledge. And of all the abuses of men, there are none more disasterous than those which this healthy volume seeks to correct.

The title of this work suggests the idea of another life on this earth-plane of existence—higher, holier, and purer in its aims, aspirations, and desires, and yet it does not suggest, or even intimate, to the prospective reader the true character and nature of the volume in its mission before the world. To the actual reader the title is truly significant and appropriate—as the writer so beautifully unfolds the Laws of Reproduction, by and through the observance of which the highest and purest type of humanity may be and is produced. The regeneration of the race, through the laws of physiological and psychological reproduction, is the leading and perhaps the grandest thought of Dr. Cowan's work. If in the reproduction of offspring, all parents would faithfully and persistently observe the laws so fully elucidated by Dr. Cowan in his chapter on "The Land of Genius" the aggregate virtue, mentality developed in four generations would forever redeem the world from the lost blight and curse of sin. If it were within our power, we would put a copy of Dr. Cowan's work into every household of the nation fully confident that the truth therein contained would do more towards regenerating the race than all the pulpits of the land are doing-while the masses are groping in heathenish darkness and ignorance of the Laws of Re-production, by and through which human beings are or may be created spirits of light or spirits of darkness, at the bidding of the human will. This work is written in pure, chaste language, free from all medical technicalities. Of all the works extant on "Re-production" or the "Social Question" now agitating the public mind, we cheerfully concede to it the preference.

This is a scientific work in the true sense. Science being defined to be an aggregation of truths and facts properly related to each other from which valuable deductions may be drawn. Dr. Cowan is a reformer of the radical type, who believes in going to the root of an evil and correcting it there, and we can truly say he goes to the root of the social and physical evils now so deeply afflicting society. Having no faith in negative virtue, or ignorant innocence, he adopts for his motto "knowledge must precede virtue". We commend this work to the careful perusal of the earnest and thoughtful of both sexes.

It is, in our opinion, a mistaken idea on the part of parents and others to allow children to acquire the knowledge of the sexual relations from chance sources, for these sources are always impure. The sexual instinct is implanted in everybody, and makes itself known as surely as the body ripens. And as imagination forms a very large portion of life, we think it far better to have the subjects treated of plainly and publicly rather than to have them restrained to secret companions and to the debased imagination. We, therefore, welcome such a book as this, as one greatly needed. The chapter on "The Law of Continence", "The Prevention of Conception" and "Fœticide" are especially profitable for reading at the present time.

We welcome a publication of this sort with undisguised sincerity, thankful that the time at last has come when fundamental and radical physiological truths may be told to the people plainly. Had such books been placed in the hands of our younger men two and three generations ago, their effect would have been visible enough in the physical character and habits of the men of to-day. All the miseries and happiness of married life are sketched with the hand of one who is perfectly familiar with his theme, and a master. Could men, and women, too, become familiar with such plain and controlling truths as Dr. Cowan here sets forth with such religious seriousness, and form the resolutions forthwith to lead such lives as the following of his simple precepts would render essential, there would, in time, be a visible diminution of a large part of the unhappiness, unquiet, aimlessness and positive misery that afflict society, and a brightening and looking up of faculties now clouded and buried in the thick folds of a needless ignorance. The great specific for health and happiness is Continence. No one ever suffered from that, while the ranks of the wretched, from its opposite, are being continually recruited from all classes of society alike.

I never can tell how thankful I am that God put it in my way in the morning of life. I never had seen the standards of purity lifted so high before, but my heart responded to them the first time I read them. I said *this* is the *truth* and though I have never seen or heard it before, by *that* will I require my life.

"The Science of a New Life" by John Cowan, M. D., is a hygienic and social guide which many men, whether married or single, will be the better for carefully perusing. * * * It is written in a scientific spirit by one who is evidently capable of giving good advice. It is not strictly speaking a medical work, although it treats of the science of the human body and deals to a considerable extent with matters that fall within the province of the physician. But it gives rules for the practice of good and health promoting habits which may be read with profit, especially by young men. It has much to say about the married state and the choice of husbands and wives, with a view to the welfare of their children, but it discusses these and kindred subjects in a refined and Christian spirit, and with much good sense. It devotes a large space to matters more or less physiological in their character, and in so doing treads upon somewhat delicate ground; yet we have failed to detect anything which might be regarded as inadmissible in a book intended for the instruction and to promote the well-being of those into whose hands it may fall.

7

[*From the Albany Evening Journal.*]

The title of this book does not clearly indicate the matter of which it treats, and yet its appropriateness is seen as soon as the reader comprehends the Authors high purpose. The book relates to the fundamental laws regulating intercourse between the sexes. The mass of such books are disgusting catchpennies, cheaply printed, and, if not directly obscene, are without any higher purpose on the part of the writers than to minister profitably to a depraved curiosity. Of Dr. Cowan we do not know except what insight his book gives us. It is evidently written for a conscientious purpose—that of doing good. The subject is one of extraordinary delicacy, but there is no lack of courage in meeting it, and no want of that refinement of language which alone can commend such a work to the good and the virtuous. As an aid in imparting knowledge on various delicate subjects and in exposing the evils connected with the abuse of the system, we can earnestly commend this book. Those who sin through ignorance will be enlightened; those who wish to be purer, and can be influenced by a high minded appeal, will be strengthened; and neither the impure nor the innocent will be made the worse by it. The influence of Christianity is recognized and made the basis for the reform advocated. The general subject is one of such immense importance that any books which conscientiously supplies information without minisering to depraved passions should be welcomed. There can be no indelicacy in popularizing the knowledge of evils into which tens of thousands rush blindly, and in making men and women acquainted with the responsibilities they assume and the dangers they incure when they enter into the marriage relation.

[*From the Utica Herald and Gazette.*]

This work is a treatise on matters relating mainly to the physical welfare of the race. It is a timely warning against the many evils which arise from an abuse or ignorance of the laws which govern the relation of the sexes. As such it is a medical book. It rises, however, above the mere details of anatomy and discusses conscientiously the effects which are in various ways produced upon the character and life. It is outspoken against that sensousness which is to often made to crush out the higher thoughts and aims which should characterise the life union. The matters which fill its chapters are to little understood by those who should know them well. There has been no lack of quack publications called marriage guides, but a plain, truthful treaties, from one whose name is a surety of value, has a good work to perform. Such a book is the publication before us. A portion of its pages is devoted to a denunciation of the apparently increasing crime of child-murder. As a source of information upon matters of vital importance to the classes for whom it is intended Dr. Cowan's treaties can hardly fail to be of great value and utility.

[*From the Scottish American, N. Y.*]

Books of this character can not be multiplied too rapidly, nor can the influence of such works as this, in releasing men and women from the strong bonds of ignorance, vice, and crime, be too highly estimated. The human race, we know, needs something stronger and more powerful than the influence of a single volume, however good, to remove the many evils of social and domestic life—line upon line, precept upon precept—a little here, and a great deal more there, can alone accomplish the great work o reformation, and restore the wasted, sin-polluted lives of our fellow-beings to a condition of moral purity; but we must admit that Dr. Cowan has done all that any lover of his race can do to check the downward course of the ignorance, thoughtless, and sinful.

8

9

[From the Farmer, Bridgeport, Conn.]

Upon no topics connected with our physical well-being does so much ignorance prevail, and consequent abuse or wrong-doing, as upon those so fully treated of in this book. The poet has told us that "the proper study of mankind is man. He might have put it in stronger terms and truly said that *the most important* study of mankind is man. But a false modesty has forbidden and prevented the discussion of the topics referred to, so intimately connected with the best interests of society, and the result has been an accumulation of moral evil, wickedness and crime, which no amount of effort seems now adequate to remove. The author of this book however has ventured to undertake the work of reform, and make a beginning on the subject with a manly frankness and religious earnestness befitting its great importance. He has no faith in negative virtue, or ignorant obediance, and adopting the motto: "knowledge must precede virtue," he fully discloses the relations of the sexes and plainly lays down the rules upon which physical redemption must be archieved, and the great social and moral evils referred to remedied. The book should have a wide circulation. The author has dedicated it to "all the married, and particularly those who contemplate marriage." He should have dedicated it to "all the world, and the rest of mankind," for its expositions and teachings are important not only to the married and those who contemplate marriage, but to all, both of high degree and low degree, civilized or savage." Its study cannot fail to give such a knowledge of the human system and physiological laws as will promote the health and purity of both body and mind.

[From one of the World's Workers.]

I sincerly believe if "The Science of a New Life" whenever read by an intelligent individual, it will do him or her more good than the getting of Religion in the popular way. My heart is full of thanks for its author. Ever since I was a young man, I have taken much interest in reading books of like contents, but I never found a work that went in such good earnest to the bottom of the subject of Human Reform. I verily believe that any agent who will sell 1000 copies of "The Science of a New Life" will be the means of accomplishing more positive and lasting good than any fashionable preacher will accomplish in forty years of his ministerial service, for the kind of preaching that is now mostly needed, is that which teaches and enlightens people on the subject of generation, securing to posterity a sound virtuous and intelligent generation, and where this is accomplished there will be less need to talk of Re-generation.

[From the Syracuse Courier.]

The Science of a New Life is the title of a new and valuable treatise by Dr. John Cowan, on all that pertains to marriage. The author is masterly and exhaustive in his treatment of topics so vitally connected with the Christian perfection and perpetuity of the race; and while his language is plain, it is never suggestively impure or unchaste. The book will educate in a direction where it is greatly needed.

[From The American Wesleyan.]

There is a growing desire for knowledge in regard to the wonderful phenomenon of human life. Dr. Cowan writes not to gratify an idle or prurient curiosity, but to give knowledge, which will lead to obedience, virtue and happiness. The book is for the thoughtful and earnest reader, and no such reader will rise from its perusal without a conscious elevation of thought, and a stronger desire to live a pure and worthy life.